Praise for Bor

'*Borderland* deftly combines thorough re   with the author's intimate first-hand knowledge of place, as he revisits sites on foot in an extended field trip. Hubbard's unflinchingly questioning approach to the contested spaces he encounters is written with the ease of an armchair traveller's guide. The result is a peregrination peppered with gems of descriptive detail and astute personal reflections. Ultimately, *Borderland* isn't just about Kent. It's a book that scrutinises how – wherever we live – we perceive, shape, reimagine and reinvent place to suit our own uses and desires.'

Sonia Overall, author of *Heavy Time*

'It's been called the "frayed edge" of England, but our coastline is by no means just wearing out. As emerges from this highly revealing excursion around the coast of Kent, it is also being restitched and fortified as the frontline of an "exclusionary nationalism" thanks to which even insects and oysters are being asked to prove they're not aliens. Although horrifying in places, as the times demand, *Borderland* is full of contrary energy too.'

Patrick Wright, author of
The Sea View Has Me Again:
Uwe Johnson in Sheerness

'A brilliant book. Superficially, a story of part of the Kent coast. However, under its surface, *Borderland* is a search for England's soul – and soullessness.'

Danny Dorling, author of *Rule Britannia:*
Brexit and the End of Empire

'A timely interrogation of the connection between place and identity in the post-Brexit era. Hubbard's Kentish borderland is an ever-shifting space, rife with contradictions, culture clashes, and eco-anxiety.'

Gareth E. Rees, author of
Car Park Life

'With an impressive mix of erudition and accessibility, Phil Hubbard's *Borderland* shines a light on an English South East that is rarely apprehended – let alone comprehended – by Middle England and the London establishment. Venturing into a Kentish coastal terrain transformed into a new debatable land by Brexit and recurrent migrant crises, Hubbard manages to combine sympathy for the plight of refugees with great sensitivity in exploring wider questions of twenty-first century citizenship, national identity, and political representation. This is a book which asks all the right questions with immense eloquence and remarkable understanding of a people and a place.'

Alex Niven, author of
New Model Island

'A powerful, poignant and beautifully written journey through the frontier lands of Brexit Britain. This is travel writing with a purpose, charting an anxious and often hostile landscape with care and passion.'

Alastair Bonnett, author of *The Age of Islands:*
In Search of New and Disappearing Islands

Borderland

MANCHESTER
1824

Manchester University Press

Borderland

Identity and belonging at the edge
of England

Phil Hubbard

Manchester University Press

Copyright © Phil Hubbard 2022

The right of Phil Hubbard to be identified as the author of this work has been asserted by them in accordance with the Copyright, Designs and Patents Act 1988.

Published by Manchester University Press
Oxford Road, Manchester M13 9PL

www.manchesteruniversitypress.co.uk

British Library Cataloguing-in-Publication Data
A catalogue record for this book is available from the British Library

ISBN   978 1 5261 5386 9   hardback

ISBN   978 1 5261 5387 6   paperback

First published 2022

The publisher has no responsibility for the persistence or accuracy of URLs for any external or third-party internet websites referred to in this book, and does not guarantee that any content on such websites is, or will remain, accurate or appropriate.

Typeset
by New Best-set Typesetters Ltd
Printed in Great Britain
by TJ Books Ltd, Padstow

Contents

1 The new edge of Europe?   1
2 Natives   23
3 Albion-on-Sea   50
4 Defending the nation   77
5 The white horse   105
6 Boat people   138
7 The strange coast   168
Afterword: the Kent variant   200

List of figures   209
Acknowledgements   212
Notes   214
Index   246

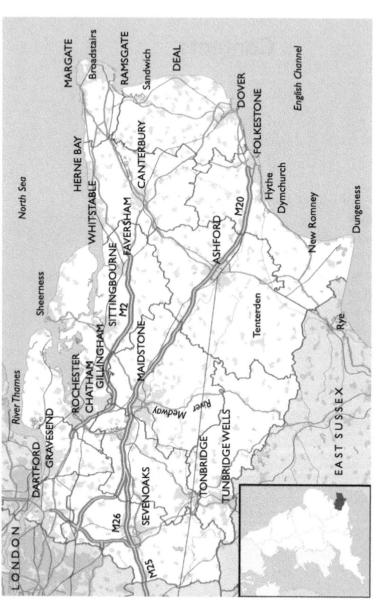

Map of Kent. This map was redrawn and amended by the author using the base map from https://commons. wikimedia.org/wiki/File:Kent_UK_location_map.svg (licensed under the Creative Commons Attribution-Share Alike 3.0 Unported, contains Ordnance Survey data © Crown copyright and database right).

1
The new edge of Europe?

Looking out over the port of Dover, with the endless stream of boats coming in and out, every British citizen is reminded that belonging here has never been about blood or genes. It's simply about being at home on this discrete island and being aware of the privileges and responsibilities that brings.

Julian Baggini, writer-in-residence, the White Cliffs of Dover, 2012[1]

In the south-east corner of England, the cliffs of Dover mark the point where the chalky uplands of the North Downs give way to the sea. Glimmering and vast, these dirty-white cliffs stretch eight miles either side of Dover, rising steeply to 350 feet to the east of the town. Here, the National Trust's White Cliffs Visitor Centre regales day-trippers with facts about the local flora and fauna. Thirty of the fifty orchid species thought to grow in Britain have been found here, the rarest being the early spider orchid. Other plants thriving on this chalk upland include wild thyme, marjoram, broomrape, horseshoe vetch and sea carrots. Blue butterflies are found in abundance, as are meadow brown and marbled white. Skylarks, ravens and herring gulls are also present, and sometimes peregrine falcons or kittiwakes can be spotted. Dexter cattle and two herds of Exmoor ponies have been brought in to graze the area, ensuring that more modern methods of farming and machine-cutting do not disturb this fecund biodiversity.

The white cliffs attract their fair share of twitchers and nature enthusiasts. But visiting in the summer of 2019, I noted that most visitors were content to park up and shuffle a few yards to the National Trust café, where they sat to enjoy coffee and cake while looking out over a spectacular view. Beyond the horses chewing grass in the foreground, the cliffs drop away precipitously, giving way to the vast Eastern Docks below. Lorries, cars and coaches line up to wait for incoming vehicles to disembark from ferries via linkspan bridges, having cleared passport control and customs on their entrance to the docks. Children run around excitedly, anticipating family holidays; lorry drivers pace anxiously during the checks of their vehicles; documents are inspected, itineraries confirmed. The whole spectacle of embarkation is choreographed by the hi-vis-clad port authority officials who usher vehicles into regimented lines, gesturing busily.

But most visitors to the White Cliffs café are staring well beyond the harbour walls, across what the French call *La Manche*, and towards the horizon. Even on a cloudy day it is possible to glimpse a blue-grey smudge of land twenty-one miles distant. When the

1.1 The view from the white cliffs

visibility is good, and the haze lifts, the cliffs at Cap Gris-Nez and Cap Blanc-Nez on the Pays de Calais headland are visible, with the village of Wissant nestled in the cleft between them. To the north of Wissant is Sangatte, a commune whose dubious fame is that, for nearly a decade, it hosted an informal camp for refugees attempting to enter the UK. Shut down by Nicolas Sarkozy in 2002, the refugees were displaced up the coast towards Calais. Located to the east of the port, the 'Calais Jungle' emerged to become the notorious home for an estimated 10,000 refugees, including large numbers from Afghanistan, Eritrea, Iraq, Somalia and Syria. Following rising anxieties about the numbers attempting to hitch a ride on departing lorries, in 2016 this squatter settlement was separated from the N116 highway by 'the Great Wall of Calais'. At over a thousand metres long and four metres high, the wall reportedly cost over two million pounds, paid for by the British government.[2]

From the cliffs of Dover, it is only possible to see the tops of the taller buildings in Calais, and none of the draconian security infrastructure that surrounds the port is visible. The 'Calais Jungle' is in any case long-since bulldozed, its refugees evicted in autumn 2016 and bussed to centres in undisclosed parts of France. But media headlines continue to circulate in the British press about the formation of new settlements along the French seaboard. In 2019 Help Refugees estimated that 600 refugees were still camping in Calais, and 1,000 in Dunkirk, twenty miles up the coast. In the same year, some 1,900 displaced people were thought to have attempted the journey across the English Channel, most in inflatable dinghies, ribs and kayaks.[3] Despite the COVID-19 lockdown, the numbers increased dramatically in 2020, with more than 8,400 reaching the UK by boat, most landing on the beaches of Kent. In 2021 the numbers rose again, exceeding the 2020 total by the end of July, with more than 1,000 crossing on one November day alone.

Recent academic work in international relations and geography insists that every international border produces its own spectacle, constructed out of myriad representations of border crossing.[4] If this is the case, the cliffs of Dover have borne witness to the dramaturgy that constitutes the UK's contemporary 'border crisis'. In the last decade, the UK media have fixated on images of refugees seeking to cross the English Channel here at its narrowest point. Images of bodies squeezed into the back of lorries, or cowering from the waves in rubber dinghies, are routinely deployed as evidence of the 'threat' posed by a rising number of refugees.[5] Except that these people are rarely referred to as refugees: more usually they are described as economic migrants, a dehumanising category that ignores the factors that have pushed them from their homes. In the right-wing corners of the press, the term 'illegal' is added for good measure. The fact there are few legal routes for asylum seekers to use to gain access to the UK becomes the basis for assuming that many – or even all – of those crossing the English Channel in small boats or stowing away in lorries are 'bogus' asylum seekers.

The often scaremongering representation of a 'border crisis' unfolding in the English Channel was arguably influential in many people's decision to vote for Brexit in 2016, being prominent in the media leading up to the Brexit referendum.[6] That vote ushered in a political agenda based on a tighter control of national borders, one based on exclusionary visions of nationalism that have sometimes taken racialised form. In his book *Brexit Unfolded*, Chris Grey argues that those voting for Brexit often mistakenly conflated free movement *within* the single market with migration *into* the EU from outside, with the rise in asylum seeking taken as *prima facie* evidence of this.[7] So while the Leave campaign's arguments were often directed towards the financial costs of EU membership, most commentators have concluded that the decision of the UK to leave the EU was strongly shaped by voters' concerns about cross-border mobility and migration. For many Leave voters, images of refugee crossings seemingly fuelled anxieties about the permeability of the British border, galvanising the desire to leave the EU. These concerns appeared particularly pronounced among older, white voters in

those regions sometimes described as 'left behind': areas still struggling with the legacies of deindustrialisation and manufacturing
decline.[8] In this sense, the mantra of 'taking back control' was as
much about the eclipse of the British Empire and the decline of
the UK as an economic force as it was about the imagined interference of European legislation in national affairs.[9]

The coincidence of Brexit and the rise in asylum seekers arriving
by boat has led to the Dover cliffs taking on charged symbolism in
debates about national identity. This symbolism builds on established
tropes of belonging, with historian Paul Readman suggesting that
the white cliffs have been used to bolster British identities since at
least the nineteenth century.[10] Famously, Matthew Arnold's 1867
lyrical poem 'On Dover Beach' employed the cliffs as a metaphor
for the national values that he felt were under threat, invoking both
patriotism and faith via reference to the 'cliffs of England' protecting
from the 'grating roar' below.[11] By the twentieth century they were
firmly woven into the national psyche as the gateway to England:
writing in 1920, travel journalist Walter Jarrold memorably termed
them 'the white walls of Albion' (England's original Roman name
of Albion being derived from the Latin *albus*, meaning white).[12]
The two World Wars consolidated this mythology: for soldiers on
continental battlefields, the idea that they would once again view
the white cliffs was pivotal in rituals of military departure and
homecoming. Acknowledging this, in November 2019, 101 years
on from the end of World War I, a Dakota aeroplane dropped
750,000 biodegradable poppies over the cliffs, honouring those who
had made the ultimate sacrifice for their country.[13]

Given the persistence of these myths of military endeavour and
national sacrifice, it is not surprising that patriotic representations
of the white cliffs of Dover have been invoked by those arguing
that severing ties with the EU is the best thing Britain has ever
done. For some they have become iconic of Britain's elemental
insularity, propping up myths of the 'island-nation'. Here, it is
telling that they have also featured in some overtly racist discourses

1.2 Jason deCaires Taylor, *Pride of Brexit*

that equate the whiteness of the cliffs with ideas of purity and patriotism.[14] But in recent years they have also been the backdrop to more critical commentaries on the departure of Britain from the EU. In April 2019, for example, the activist group Led by Donkeys projected a 50 by 75 metre SOS message on to the cliffs, sending photographs of this to Emmanuel Macron and Angela Merkel via Twitter, imploring them to allow time for a 'people's referendum'.[15]

Another artwork, *Pride of Brexit* by Kent-based environmental artist Jason deCaires Taylor, was also ephemeral, but arguably more powerful in its imagery. Known for underwater statuary drawing attention to coral bleaching and sea level inundation, Taylor sculpted three lions that he left in the surf at the bottom of Dover's cliffs. Invoking the symbolism present on the Royal Arms of England, as well as the English football and cricket shirts, these three lions are not the proud beasts that surround Nelson's Column in Trafalgar Square, but emaciated and exhausted.[16] In many ways, they evoke the border spectacle by appearing to be refugees, washed up on the beach. The suggestion here is that the nation is turning its back on Others, its pride washed up on a 'Brexit tide'.[17] This was underlined when Taylor reinstalled these lions on the Thames embankment opposite the Houses of Parliament, this time daubing them in graffiti and slogans invoking the language of toxicity surrounding the Brexit debate. Take Back Control. Get It Done. Brexit means Brexit. Taylor's artwork hence connected two iconic sites – the Houses of Parliament and the cliffs of Dover – to pose important questions about British identity at a time of political turmoil.

The borderscape of Kent

Standing proud over the English Channel, the cliffs of Dover figured prominently in media coverage as the UK withdrew, sometimes painfully, from the EU. More than a mere icon of Englishness, the cliffs became a symbol of 'islandness' and the rupture with mainland Europe. In this book I extend this line of argument, showing that many other sites along the Kentish coast also speak to questions of national belonging and identity, albeit not always in such obvious ways. This book takes the form of a journey, in which I travel from Whitstable on the north Kent coast, via Margate on the Isle of Thanet, past the Cinque Ports of Sandwich, Dover and Hythe down to Britain's most south-easterly point at Dungeness. Along the way, I alight on sites that seem to emphasise Britain's physical, political and cultural separation from continental Europe. I focus on the hostile architecture that symbolises Britain's ambivalent relationship with its European neighbours: this is a militarised landscape of castles, Napoleonic-era sea forts, World War II tank traps, hidden bunkers, abandoned airfields, Martello Towers, repurposed barracks, radar stations, the remnants of gun emplacements and border lookouts. These are sites designed to repel, to exclude and to distance. A landscape of defence and defiance.

But my argument is not simply that the traces of the border in the Kent landscape affirm senses of separation from continental Europe: this very same coast has, after all, been shaped by its maritime trade and commercial connections with Europe. As well as its ferry terminals at Dover and Ramsgate, and the now-defunct, weed-enveloped hoverport at Pegwell Bay, the Kent coast is pock-marked by the infrastructures that brought a *transmanche* region into being during the period of EU membership. Most notable – and the source of repeated moral panics about its permeability by refugees and terrorists alike – is the Eurotunnel. Emerging from beneath the Channel at Shakespeare's Cliff (between Folkestone and Dover), *Le Shuttle* disgorges its payload at the vast 350-acre terminal for passengers and vehicles located just inland at Cheriton, with the Eurostar passenger train stopping, intermittently, at the international terminals at Ashford and Ebbsfleet *en route* to the London terminus at St Pancras. But there are many other connections that bind Kent to the continent. There are no less than three high-voltage direct electricity current connections, constructed in 1961, 1986 and 2020 respectively, with associated converter stations at Lydd, Sellindge and Cheriton. The landfall facilities associated with multiple subsea communication cables – Rembrandt 2, Hermes South and Rioja 2 – can also be found along the Kentish coast, with American firm Equinix currently constructing an optical submarine cable running 200 miles between London and Paris, heralded as the 'data equivalent of the Channel Tunnel'.[18] And while Manston, Lympne and London Ashford airport (the latter formerly known as 'Ferryfields') no longer have regular passenger services to France, all three have at various times connected Kent to the continent through a mix of budget and private flights.

Kent is, then, in many ways the most European part of England. Over recent decades, there have been several high-profile cross-border projects involving Kentish local authorities and partners from France, the Netherlands and Flanders, and in 2004 the Chief Constable of Kent drew up a formal initiative for cross-border cooperation with the prefect of Pays de Calais. *Électricité de France* runs Dungeness power station and has owned the 468-acre Dungeness Estate on which it is sited since 2015. Many European businesses have located to Kent, especially in proximity to the international station at Ashford, and there are large numbers of transnational commuters who use the county as a base for working between London and Paris.[19] The streets of Canterbury and Charles Dickens's Rochester are often thronged with European tourists and school exchange visitors, who flock to these cities in the Easter and summer vacations. The University of Kent claims to be the UK's 'European University' and has campuses in Paris, Athens, Rome and Brussels as well as Canterbury and Chatham, with up to 40% of its staff and one in ten of its students estimated to be EU nationals. Along the county's coastbound motorways, adverts highlighting the bargains to be had in the wine warehouses of Calais are a banal reminder of proximity to the continent, and nearer the coast French radio begins to interfere with British FM and AM signals. French food markets are common, and the town of Sandwich hosts an annual 'Le Weekend' festival with a Normandy food fair accompanied by accordion players. The *Tour de France* came to Kent in 1994, to celebrate the opening of the Channel Tunnel, and again in 2007.

Kent has been indelibly shaped by the real and imagined relationship between Britain and Europe, a relationship that has oscillated between outright antagonism and reconciliation and *entente cordiale*. My argument in this book is that Kent's borderscape reveals the layers of successive episodes when continental Europe has been drawn closer to Britain and times when it has been pushed further away. This figures the border not simply as an increasingly securitised boundary line between the wanted and the unwanted, but a mechanism of connection and encounter, somewhere where ideas of national identity are constantly worked through. Indeed, while territorial borders are currently being hardened and securitised in much of the world, this very act of hardening seems to be increasing anxieties about their permeability, spreading confusion and

Borderland

insecurity.[20] There are, then, important connections between processes of bordering and the rise of exclusionary nationalisms. By scrutinising the material and aesthetic form of the border, I hope to contribute to our understanding of these connections, exploring how contemporary senses of national belonging and identity are mapped on to, and out of, the borderscape.

Here, my focus on the visual and aesthetic rather than the political and legal is deliberate, with the notion of borderscape emphasising the *visible* impress of the border on the landscape.[21] Bringing the idea of landscape into dialogue with the notion of borders is conceptually useful, as it helps us appreciate the work that the border landscape does in constructing ideas of what the nation is and the values it embodies. Cultural geographers have long argued that we can 'read' the landscape to reveal how society has organised space and time according to specific belief systems and cultural values.[22] A key idea here is that landscapes become normalised in such a way that the political work they do is effaced. As Don Mitchell explains, landscape 'represents an attempt to naturalize and harmonize the appropriation of labour and to impose a system of domination, consent, control, and order'.[23] Part of this work is the construction of a national identity: Michael Billig famously claimed that the nation is a mundane and unquestioned presence in everyday life, saturating currency, language and custom.[24] In this sense, landscapes also do active work in reproducing ideas of national belonging, with particular landscapes regarded as a synecdoche for the nation itself. In Britain, for example, it is the pastoral, rural landscape that often stands for the nation, as encapsulated in the work of Gainsborough, Turner and Constable, and serially mediated via innumerable postcards, tea towels and biscuit tins depicting *Flatford Mill* or *Mr and Mrs Andrews*. As geographer Peter Taylor argues, these celebrated landscapes of rurality and tradition bring together 'an actual (or aspired) sovereignty, the history of a territory, as well as a selection of routinized habits, events, memories, narratives and iconographies related to the purported national identity'.[25]

The myth of England as a 'green and pleasant land' is, of course, one that does not encompass all parts of Britain, or for that matter England. Rather it is a myth mapped out of, and on to, a more limited repertoire of southern, rural landscapes.[26] It also relies upon racialised and classed exclusions: as sociologist Sarah Neal writes, 'the connections between the countryside, nation and racialisation have had particular longevity'.[27] Geographer Divya Tolia-Kelly likewise suggests that the association of whiteness and rurality is hard to displace, despite numerous attempts to decentre elite discourses of the English landscape. As she describes, post-colonial engagements with landscape are needed to 'unravel the layerings of narratives of "strangers", "others", and "blackness"' that are often subsumed in dominant representations of rurality and tradition.[28] But despite the obvious mismatch between images of a rural idyll and the multicultural realities of modern Britain, idealised rural landscapes are still recurrently deployed by politicians in their attempts to manufacture consensus about what it means to live in an 'island-nation'. Indeed, Alex Niven concludes that this selective imagining of Englishness has become more, rather than less, prominent in the twenty-first century, invoked in a variety of reactionary cultural and political projects (not least the pro-Brexit campaign). It has become, concludes Niven, 'a cultural daydream of the neoliberal classes'.[29]

With its hop fields, church spires, village greens and quaint orchards, the representation of Kent as the 'Garden of England' conforms to this construction of English nationhood.[30] This is an imagery mapped out of a landscape of sinuous villages cleared from the ancient woodlands, and the small and irregularly shaped farms and hamlets that still characterise the areas between the rolling chalklands of the North Downs and the Weald lowlands on the Sussex border. The 'high', or central, Weald itself boasts picturesque villages full of white, weatherboarded and tile-hung houses, while the peripheries of the 'low' Weald are more pastoral, with a mix of arable farming and fruit growing. S. W. Wooldridge, first Professor of

Geography at King's College London, described the Weald as 'the place where London ends and England can begin'.[31] The Kentish Weald also featured as the setting for H. E. Bates's 1958 novel *The Darling Buds of May*, adapted for TV in the 1990s. This introduced Catherine Zeta-Jones to the world, and cemented David Jason's status as national icon through his representation of the loveable rogue 'Pop' Larkin, a 1950s Kent smallholder constantly resorting to shady deals to supplement his household's income. Launched in the post-Gulf War 1990s recession, the series went immediately to the top of the UK TV ratings, with 18.5 million tuning in for one episode. *The Darling Buds of May*'s warm and hazy rural imagery, coupled with gentle innuendo and storylines about the idiosyncratic ways of country folk, appealed immensely to Sunday night viewers who wallowed in its representation of a timeless post-war England where the world moved resolutely to the rhythms of nature.[32] A 2021 remake – *The Larkins* – was described by Sean O'Grady in *The Independent* as 'a sort of Brexit Television, set in a post-war green and pleasant England that never was and never will be, but for which so many feel an overwhelming nostalgia'.[33]

Fruit growing, hop farming and wine production are still important in Kent's economy, but 85% of Kent's orchards have been removed in the last fifty years, often to allow farmers to gain EU subsidies for grazing and arable crops at a time when English apple varieties such as Coxes and Spartans were falling out of favour with domestic consumers.[34] At the same time, market towns such as Ashford and Maidstone have been ringed by endless new estates of commuter housing. It is predicted that up to 150 square kilometres of new housing will have been constructed between 2003 and 2031, with 158,000 new homes being completed in this time, the majority on greenfield sites.[35] Occasionally, campaigners bemoan the reduction of ecological diversity that this entails, as well as the loss of productive farmland at a time when concerns are being raised about food shortages in the UK. Yet the new homes are generally snapped up quickly, often by Londoners seeking to release equity by escaping the hyper-inflated housing market of the capital, attracted by the highspeed rail links connecting Kent to London. Elsewhere, rural outhouses have been converted to tech-barns and farms replaced by business parks. Mobile phone masts jut out of hillsides. Ancient woodlands have been turned into paintballing arenas. Neither town nor country, much of Kent conforms to environmental campaigner Marion Shoard's description of the contemporary edgeland – a dismal landscape of 'rubbish tips and warehouses, superstores and derelict industrial plants, office parks and gypsy encampments, golf courses, allotments and fragmented, frequently scruffy, farmland'.[36]

But even if Kent is no longer a predominantly rural county, a hazy, romantic notion of Kentish life endures, reinforced through the blending of countryside heritage traditions and consumer culture in the many farm parks and living museums that celebrate Kent's rural traditions. But in this book, I am less interested in how Kent's countryside perpetuates English rural imaginaries, and more in Kent's relationship with continental Europe as it is manifest in the landscape, particularly at the coast. This is a landscape that has had national resonance in recent debates about identity and belonging, particularly those emphasising the idea of Britain as an 'island-nation'.[37] In arguing this, I am not suggesting that the coastal landscape of Kent is as visually pleasing as some of the more idyllic or manicured rural landscapes that are iconic of Englishness. However, following geographer Matthew Gandy, I propose that when we talk of iconic landscapes we should not only focus on the aesthetically pleasing or the monumental.[38] Much of the Kentish coast, for example, is not especially beautiful. The white cliffs of Dover are a case in point: constantly undermined by the sea, tunnelled under, farmed over, and distinctly off-white, they have nonetheless taken on deeply symbolic qualities. As historian Paul Readman writes, the cliffs' 'associations with national defence, homecoming and homeland, national culture and history matter more than their physical characteristics taken in isolation'.[39]

This book offers a series of reflections on the Kentish coast – and adjoining landscapes – to explore how this borderscape resonates with broader understandings of identity and nationhood at a time of Brexit, COVID-19 and the European 'migrant crisis'.[40] In doing so I approach the Kent borderscape not as a place, space or region, but rather as a distinct, often bleak and scruffy, landscape. This is an occasionally inhospitable landscape of windswept marshlands, arid shingle headlands and muddy coastal flats. At various times, the book will explore the symbolism of a carbuncular sea wall at Dymchurch, the sheer weirdness of the Dungeness headland, and the iconography of Margate's brutalist 1960s tower block, Arlington House. Elsewhere it will step gingerly on to the Kentish mudflats where 'non-native' oysters are controversially cultivated, and crunch along shingle beaches that are receding in the face of climate-induced sea level change. On the way, it will stop for refreshment in the waterfront hostels and restaurants of gentrifying coastal towns including Folkestone and Margate, towns where 'Down from Londons' (DFLs) are displacing working-class communities. These towns are now home to a mixed population of displaced peoples, eccentric artists, tourists, fisherfolk, bohemian writers, sexual dissidents, racists and refugees. They are also sometimes uneasily poised between past and future, home to crumbling port facilities, abandoned amusement arcades and disused army barracks, but also celebrated eateries, trendy boutiques and impressively ambitious programmes of public art. Located between land and sea, these seaside towns are characterised by what Daniel Burdsey terms 'coastal liquidity', a concept that 'encourages us to acknowledge the contested pasts, the messy and unfinished presents, and the uncertain futures of seaside and coastal places'.[41]

A deep topography of the border

This book moves around the Kent coast, chapter by chapter, exploring a landscape that is full of contradiction: important in shaping myths of nationhood, and abutting a rural landscape of apparent abundance, but also somehow on the margins. It does this at a time when writing about the marginal has become oddly fashionable. The 'new nature writing', for example, is full of this stuff. Following in the wake of Richard Mabey, the shelves of the average bookshop groan under the weight of books about 'unofficial' Britain.[12] Though written with due deference to traditional modes of writing about the natural world, many key works in this tradition eschew pristine or unspoilt nature to focus on more prosaic landscapes: the frayed boundary between urban and rural, liminal spaces, and places of abandonment.[13] Much of this writing disrupts any neat binary between nature and culture.[14] Indeed, the work that has been placed in the genre of 'new nature writing' often focuses on the intimate relationship between landscape, place and people.[15] It tells a story that is personal *and* political, often using autobiography as a tool for environmental critique.[16]

Blending elements of autobiography, travelogue and natural history in its attempt to explore forgotten, and often threatened, British landscapes, the 'new nature writing' is inherently, although often implicitly, concerned with questions of nationhood and identity.[17] Traditionally, English nature has been depicted as vulnerable to 'foreign' influences of various kinds: urban encroachment, predatory invasive species, climate change and so on. Specific spaces and species have hence been celebrated for their national significance, and others neglected or expunged. Nature conservation is, as Maano Ramutsindela argues, essentially a bordering process.[18] Sociologist Ben Pitcher emphasises this when he proposes that 'distinctions between "native" and "non-native" species are not only a means of deciding on which nonhumans "belong" to the nation but are also a struggle over the qualities of the nation itself'.[19] This noted, a key characteristic of 'new nature writing' is that it is less preoccupied with differentiating native from foreign. Instead, by revealing the diverse forms of life emerging in liminal and forgotten space, it revels in 'the biological communities assembled through the dense comings-and-goings of human life, rather than the discrete and undisturbed relations between particular species and habitats that are the staple of conservation biology'.[50] The surge of writing on edgelands, and their figuration as ecologically recombinant landscapes, is of particular relevance for my exploration of the Kent borderscape, given that it rejects 'official' visions of the English countryside.[51] As Hannah Lilley argues, the 'senses of place, nature, and humanity familiar to the cultural and ecological landscapes of Britain' are becoming less certain thanks to the new nature writing, something that is particularly welcome in an era of unprecedented global environmental change.[52]

At this point much of this 'new nature writing' merges into recent writing on British landscapes in history and geography. Examples include David Matless's evocation of the Norfolk Broads at a time of climate change, Shelley Trower's exploration of Cornwall's identities as written out of its distinctive geology, and Sophia Davis's remarkable investigation of Suffolk as an 'island county'.[53] While all are regional in focus, their ambition is often more expansive, showing how narratives of national identity are constructed with reference to valued 'natural' landscapes.[54] While archival methods are to the fore, this literature also displays a willingness to register the landscape as something that is felt and experienced. As Matless explains, 'landscape is worked through all senses, though with attention to the ways in which hierarchies of sense operate; the truths of sight, stories overheard, sounds and textures of objects'.[55] This desire to describe landscape as it is sensed suggests a particular mode of engagement with the landscape: a *journeying through* that searches for 'sequences of emergences, affinities and distanciations'.[56] This is not a scientific endeavour grounded in objectivity: it leads us instead to particular sites, especially those where the tensions of landscape are felt most acutely. Spectral inhabitations, ruins and abandoned sites feature prominently, suggesting that the landscape is haunted by that which has been as well as that yet to come. These are the places where we can sense how the land has been shaped by those who have passed through before us.

This interest in hauntology and the way the past prefigures the present takes us close to the terrain occupied by psychogeography.[57] Sometimes dismissed as a distinctly middle-aged male pursuit, psychogeography has its origins in the work of the Situationist Internationale in the 1960s, and their attempt to understand the impacts of the capitalist city on emotions and behaviour. Methodologically, psychogeography divines the psychic contours of place via the *dérive* – a driftwork that transcends productive and leisure time and encourages a critical engagement with one's surroundings.[58] In the contemporary era, much psychogeographical writing aims to strip back the urban spectacle to reveal a sinister geography of surveillance and social control.[59] Some practitioners also use these methods to explore ideas of 'deeper' time, uncovering the 'bones beneath the street' which speak to debates on climate change and species extinction.[60] Escaping its traditional urban confines, psychogeography has also engaged with the rural landscape, linking local natures to more expansive topics. Exemplary is Patrick Keiller's film *Robinson in Ruins* (2010), in which the mythical Robinson keeps rubbing up against a landscape shaped by wider forces, experienced as absent presences: 'big systems, huge infrastructural networks, the military, the financial crisis' and so on.[61] Unconstrained by conventions of style or genre, writers including Will Ashon, Justin Hopper, Sonia Overall and Luke Turner have also blurred psychogeography, autobiography and nature writing in their perambulations of the English countryside.[62] Anita Sethi's exploration of the Pennines, which links geography and geology to questions of race and nation, is especially significant in this regard, using an uncompromising first-person narrative to displace the implicit whiteness of much landscape writing.[63]

However, when writing of the Kent landscape it is impossible to ignore David Seabrook's *All the Devils are Here* (2002), an idiosyncratic exploration of the coastal towns of North Kent and the Isle of Thanet. Somewhat ignored on first publication, the book has grown in stature thanks in part to its frequent citation by Iain Sinclair and other psychogeographers as worthy of special attention. Sinclair termed Seabrook the 'dole queue de Quincey', and, unquestionably, his description of the coastal resorts of Margate, Broadstairs and Deal helped establish the idea that these are grubby seaside towns, seething with malcontents.[64] Seabrook emerges from his book as an unreliable narrator whose motives for exploring the lives of some of the more questionable characters who have lived on the Kent coast are never quite clear. Moreover, his death in 2009, alone in his flat near Canterbury West station aged just 48, shortly after the publication of his second book (on the 'Jack the Stripper' murders in 1960s London), created a mythology around him suggesting that he might have dug too deep when researching the underworld. But his account certainly demolishes the idea that Kent has a benign, soft coastline, and offers a somewhat paranoid reading of the borderland that finds it haunted by memories of what it once was, and what it might have become.

Following in Seabrook's footsteps – as well as those of innumerable cultural geographers, new nature writers and psychogeographers – this book adopts a technique of reading and writing landscape that could, perhaps grandiosely, be termed *deep topography*. As distinct from, but related to, psychogeographical methods that explore the subconscious impact of environment on behaviour, deep topography involves what Will Self describes as 'minutely detailed, multi-level examinations of select locales that impact upon the writer's own microscopic inner-eye'.[65] Walking remains central here as a mode of becoming knowledgeable about the landscape, with accompanying practices of note taking and photography important for disclosing traces of defunct temporalities and technologies.[66] Walking can hence reveal present absences: certain things that could be there but are not.[67] For Divya Tolia-Kelly, this involves consideration of the archaeologies of race and the excavation of the 'other' narratives subsumed within landscape histories that glibly celebrate colonialism and imperialism.[68] This awareness of the interlacing of past and present is also present in geographer James Sidaway's solitary walking on the South West coastal path, in which he finds geopolitical traces of the past folded into the textures of the everyday. Sidaway concludes that walking constitutes a mode of encounter that reveals the 'personal, public, and global through the processes that (over time) produce and bind them'.[69] Following Sidaway, my deep topography is one where past and present coexist, a personal reading of the landscape which explores how past iterations of the border shape the contemporary.

Borderland is, then, a coastal driftwork, an exploration of exclusionary nationalism and bordering via a coastal perambulation that draws on emergent traditions of psychogeographically inflected nature writing as well as more established cultural geographical traditions of reading, and writing, the landscape. While it is grounded in my own encounter with landscape, it also recognises the importance of innumerable cultural representations in shaping that encounter, particularly poetry, painting, music, film and statuary. Indeed, this book makes frequent reference to such cultural representations, especially when these explicitly flag issues of identity and belonging. This includes a rich tradition of travelogue and literature which, as Len Platt demonstrates, has sometimes depicted the coastal fringes of Kent as a weird, remote and unworldly realm populated by smugglers, grotesque figures and criminals.[70]

What follows is a loose series of journeys along and across the border, reflecting on the way that the histories and geographies of the Kentish coast inform contemporary constructions of national identity. This reflection is also part-autobiographical, with my reading of the contemporary landscape informed by my own pasts. I was born and raised in Kent and spent a good deal of my youth cycling on Romney Marsh, fishing in the Royal Military Canal, pumping pocket money into the dismal arcade machines at Folkestone's amusement park and swimming off the beach at Hythe. But my engagement with the borderscape took new forms from 2009 onwards, when I returned to Kent after years living in the English Midlands and began to regularly walk stretches of the coast that were still unknown to me. Then, in 2016, just as the Brexit vote happened, I moved to a new job in London and my relationship with the Kent coast changed again. Suddenly, I became aware of the ways in which the Kent coast provided a focus for media commentators and academics trying to understand quite why Brexit was happening. It was not so much that Kent's coastal communities were being figured as 'Leave' hotbeds (though all but one of the county's authorities voted to leave, and only 41% of the county's population voted to remain): rather it was that Kent was being depicted as the 'frontline'. Given predictions that the impacts of Brexit would be keenly felt near the ports of Folkestone and Dover, journalists descended on the Kent coast, asking residents if they feared gridlocked roads, rubbish-strewn streets and the prospect of food shortages if a deal with Europe was not thrashed out. Even though I had by then left the county to live elsewhere, I wanted to return, to see this – to feel it – for myself. I embarked on a series of coastal walks, timed to coincide with Brexit, albeit its constant deferral turned this into a commemoration of a non-event. From Whitstable to Dungeness on the English Coastal Path; back to Hythe along the Royal Military Canal; from Canterbury to Dover on the Pilgrim's Way; around Romney Marsh. Blistering walks that sometimes brought the borderscape into focus, but at other times involved a more futile search for meaning.

But on 31 January 2020 – 'Brexit Day' – the idea of the Kent coast as the new 'edge of Europe' certainly came into sharper focus. That morning, the white cliffs of Dover appeared on the front of the *Daily Mail*'s Brexit 'souvenir edition' which hailed 'A New Dawn for Britain'. Later that day, Dover's Tory MP Natalie Elphicke shared Twitter footage of a celebratory fireworks party on the cliffs that she claimed would be visible from Calais, held partly in response to the cliffs being used as the backdrop for anti-Brexit messages. The first of these was organised by Anthony

Hook, a Kent-based Member of the European Parliament, paid
for via crowdfunding. This projected the message 'We still love
EU' on the cliffs in multiple languages. Later in the day, the protest
group Led by Donkeys followed up on its previous pro-refugee and
pro-Remain messages by projecting plaintive video footage of World
War II veterans speaking of their sadness at leaving the EU. One,
97-year-old Stephen Goodall, said, 'at my age I shan't be living
much longer but I hope that, for the sake of my children and my
grandchildren and my great-grandchildren, that England, Britain
will move back to be much closer to Europe than what we have
done now'.[71] At the video's end, the EU flag appeared, its stars
disappearing one by one until just one remained, commanding:
This is our star, look after it.

This book does not speculate about the longer-term impact of
Brexit or the way it will transform the lives of those living on and
near the border. Some of those on the Kent coast, and the citizens
of the nation in general, are clearly regretful or fearful for the

1.3 Projection on Dover cliffs

21

future after Brexit, others defiant and hopeful. But irrespective of whether Brexit proceeds in an orderly manner over the coming years, it too will leave traces on the landscape. It might be memorialised, or produce landscapes of mourning, but equally it might be forgotten, relegated to a footnote in a complex history that stretches back centuries and even millennia. *Borderland* is an archaeology that aims to strip away the layers of this borderscape to explore this ambivalent history. In doing so, it poses important questions about the future of our 'island-nation' at a time of unprecedented global change, ultimately arguing that the contemporary crises of global displacement, climate change and ecological disaster require us to work across international borders, not harden them.

2

Natives

What is the difference between a Whitstable oyster and a bad one?
One is a native, the other a settler!
　　　　　　　　　　Charles Harper, *The Kentish Coast*, 1914[1]

Long before Eurotunnel, High Speed One and the skein of motorways that now connect London to the ports, Kent was defined by
its position in the south-east corner of England. The Celtic name
for Kent – *Canto* – is often explained as meaning a rim or border.
Another explanation is that it means the 'coastal district', an epithet
that fits with geographer Halford Mackinder's judgement that 'the
Kentish promontory, of such vital significance for the inhabitants
of the islands, has a unique physical history, distinguishing it from
the feature-system of all the remainder of Britain'.[2] Irrespective of
this etymology, Kent's identity is defined by the coast as much as
the countryside: Visit Kent's website boasts that there are 350 miles
of coastline, an unlikely figure given that the long-distance coastal
pathway from Camber to Dartford amounts to only 207 miles,
including a loop of the Isle of Sheppey. But how much of this can
be defined as coast in a conventional sense is also debatable. Much
of the north Kent coast is not seaside but the low-lying estuarine
fringe of the Thames, Medway and Swale rivers.

　　This estuarine landscape has been much written about in recent
times. Rachel Lichtenstein's *Estuary* is a key reference point, a

psychogeographical trawl of the Thames from Tower Bridge to the sea that taps into the liminality of the north Kent coast and those who live on its muddy shores.[3] Also noteworthy is Patrick Wright's *The Sea View Has Me Again* – an extraordinary cultural geography of the Isle of Sheppey told through the story of exiled German author Uwe Johnson.[4] These works, and others besides, draw attention to the culturally problematic status of the communities along this part of the English coast, a 'half-land' of absence and presence defined by the tide, and still scarred by the devastating flood of 1953.[5] The slippery, elusive nature of a landscape moulded by water has also attracted many writers working in the tradition of the 'new nature writing', keen to celebrate the distinctive ecological value of this often-maligned part of England. Carol Donaldson's *On the Marshes*, for example, blends observations from an 80-mile solo walk around this coast with her past memories of living and working in this marginal landscape (initially as part of a loose collective of wardens on an RSPB reserve before moving into a bungalow on the fringes of the Medway towns following a traumatic break-up with her fiancée).[6]

Designated an Environmentally Sensitive Area in 1993, the North Kent Marshes consist of around 14,000 hectares of lightly grazed pasture sitting behind mudflats and saltings. The intertidal zone is rich with samphire, purslane, saltmarsh vetch and brackish plants such as strawberry plover and hairy buttercup, while on the drier areas to the rear there are rare flora including the bird's foot trefoil and hog's fennel. Collectively, the marshes, ditches and dykes host a wide range of aquatic fauna, including water voles, grebes, avocets, dunlins, plovers and whimbrels. European eels are also present, though tidal defence works have reduced their ability to migrate naturally, with sluice gates often blocked by debris that inhibits their movement. While much of the marsh is designated as RSPB Reserves, ongoing development remains a threat. While the Lower Thames Crossing, confirmed in 2017, will be a bored tunnel designed to avoid significant impact on wetland habitats, the wider Crossing scheme will involve fourteen miles of new road that will impact significantly on the breeding bird community. The on-off London Resort theme park on the Swanscombe peninsula will also have potentially deleterious impacts on local wildlife, with nearly 2,000 species of invertebrate thought to be inhabiting the development site, including the sea aster mining bee and the distinguished jumping spider. Redshanks are present through much of the winter, and nightingales and ring ouzels are common in spring. A pair of peregrine falcons are also frequent visitors, having set up nest in the chalk cliffs of a former quarry nearby.

In February 2021 the Kent Wildlife Trust, together with the RSPB and Buglife, lobbied Natural England to designate Swanscombe Marshes as a Site of Special Scientific Interest, arguing that it is of national importance, being home to more threatened species than any other brownfield site in the country. Despite the best efforts of environmental campaigners, much of this unique biodiversity is likely to be lost in the coming decades, with the promise of post-COVID-19 job creation outweighing consideration of the less tangible ecosystems services provided by the marsh and mud: the theme park has been deemed a Nationally Important Infrastructure Project, allowing it to sidestep much of the usual planning regulation. Were the low-lying North Kent Marshes a more fashionable landscape this might, of course, be different, but it is hard to argue that it is beautiful. It certainly does not conform with the myth of the Garden of England, or the type of pastoral landscapes that have come to symbolise English national values. It is full of derelict industrial sites, such as the old Richardson's cement works at Conyer Creek, or the brickfields of Lower Halstow, which abut a coastline encrusted with the ashen, broken remains of the brickmaking process. Offshore, there are abandoned World War II defences and Napoleonic forts, such as the hulking Grain Tower and, five miles off Sheppey, the spidery crab-like forms of the rusting Red Sands Maunsell Forts, anchored to the seabed. At Motney Island, and in the sludge of Faversham Creek, the outlines of rotted barges emerge from the mud at low tide alongside long-abandoned wharves and dry docks. Elsewhere there are traces of long-dismantled railway lines serving once-booming businesses such as the Uralite asbestos factory on the Hoo peninsula, Greenhithe's Imperial Paper Mill and Blue Circle cement at Northfleet.

These relict sites stand fly-tipped and unloved, and the marshes often feel desolate and abandoned, the bleak flatness of the landscape only interrupted by pylons marching across it.[7] It was this sinister atmosphere that famously inspired the opening scene of Dickens's *Great Expectations*, when Pip encounters Abel Magwitch, escaped from a local prison hulk – 'a man who had been soaked in water, and smothered in mud'. In thrall to Dickens, a host of writers and artists have been drawn to this landscape, summoning forth its ghosts.[8] One of the most remarkable recent attempts, Brian Dillon's *Great Explosion* from 2015, reveals the now-somnambulant landscape of Oare Marshes as the scene of one of the most tragic and forgotten episodes of World War I. It was here in 1916 that sparks from a boiler fire at the Cotton Powder gunpowder works ignited a pile of empty TNT bags, starting a fire in Building 833 that spread to two subsequent gunpowder-processing sheds, causing three substantial explosions. One left a crater 150 feet in diameter and up to fifteen feet deep. Dillon suggests that the blast caused windows to crack along the seafront in Essex and was even heard in France. Over one hundred died that day, with 73 buried in a mass grave in nearby Faversham, their bodies unidentified. One ambulance driver was so traumatised by what he saw that he hanged himself the day following the explosion.[9]

For Dillon, an awareness of what happened at the site – not reported in the press for fear of demoralising the nation – points to the fragility of human existence on the marshes. Little remains of the massive gunpowder works now except for rotted jetties, some chunks of concrete and a few bumps in a field near Uplees, next to the Swale channel that separates the Isle of Sheppey from the mainland. Wildlife has reclaimed the site:

If you walk this summer through the nature reserve surrounding the place where building 833 stood – nothing there but a shallow declivity of the ground – you will find the dykes are filled with weed, so they look almost solid. And if you crouch towards the water, clouds of pond skaters teem on the surface, which remains unmoved till you stand and cast a shadow on the ditch, causing the insects to panic, sending countless ripples through the water, speeding across the flat green plain.[10]

In his book, Dillon talks of his own melancholia, having moved to Kent from Dublin in his twenties and finding himself lost. His account of the Great Explosion becomes mired in detailed discussion of the capacity of sound to travel across the marshes, and an ultimately futile search for the remains of Building 833. In many ways, the book is about the traces we leave, and the way that the landscape absorbs these. Often compared to Sebald's *Rings of Saturn*, *The Great Explosion* transforms landscape into biography.[11]

When Dillon's book was published I was living in Faversham, and could readily relate to his search for meaning as I walked in

2.1 Faversham Creek

the surrounding Dickensian landscape of 'mudbank, mist, swamp
and work'.¹² Long before the gunpowder, brickmaking and brewing
industries that marked it out as one of the most industrious Kent
towns of the nineteenth century, Faversham was an important
medieval market town and important centre of shipbuilding, with
easy access to the sea via the Swale channel. From the eighteenth
century onwards, Thames barges (the HGVs of their day) were
constructed and repaired in Faversham, taking its hops, bricks,
beer and gunpowder to London and the East Anglian ports beyond.
Subsequent silting up of the channel, the decline of the Pollock
shipyard that operated on the Creek between 1916 and 1970, and
the closure of the Fremlin (Whitbread) brewery in 1990 undermined
its manufacturing industries, with only the Shepherd Neame brewery
– the oldest in Britain – remaining.¹³ This deindustrialisation, coupled
with reduced demand for agricultural labour in the local countryside,
led to rising unemployment and a well-known drug problem in
the town: a series of heroin deaths in the early years of the twenty-
first century led to Faversham somewhat unfairly being nicknamed
'brown town' by the media.

I liked Faversham very much. It boasted a picturesque medieval
town centre, a bustling weekly market, and cheap, regular train
services to London. Yet because of its reputation, it largely resisted
gentrification and retained an unpretentious atmosphere. I moved
into a Victorian terrace built from characteristic yellow Faversham
brick on the edge of the town centre in 2009, my neighbours a
mixture of retired teachers and lecturers in one direction, and
builders and plumbers in the other. Beyond my road was one of
the town's large council estates, whose population took to the streets
in large numbers during the Hop Festival to take part in the beery
boisterousness that accompanied this annual celebration of local
brewing: I once witnessed a Ford Fiesta taking a wrong turn on to
the main street during the Festival, only for it to be lifted up,
head-high, and turned around by a cheering crowd, much to the
bemusement of its occupants. Despite this undertow of alcoholic

excess, most of the pubs in the town were welcoming enough, and
it was here over a pint of Shepherd Neame that I encountered
any number of local 'characters', many of whom seemed to have
connections to the remnants of the boat-building industries, who
waxed lyrical about the town's former music scene and disappeared
at the end of the night in the direction of the motley caravans,
sheds and houseboats around the muddy Creek. Iron Wharf, which
offered moorings for boats in a terminal state, seemed to be the
destination for many, a quirky DIY community wedged between
rusting Thames barges and dry docks.

When film-maker Tony Grissoni chose Faversham as the setting
for his 2011 drama series about a provincial English town torn
apart by a spate of killings, I completely understood. The idea
of a disgruntled male shooter prowling the misty marshes while
hunting down all those who had wronged his family had an eerie
verisimilitude.[14] When aired on Channel 4 in 2013, *Southcliffe* was
not greeted with much local enthusiasm, although a half-hearted
'tourism trail' was published for those who might want to visit the
Creek-side settings featured in the series. But it did prompt imitation.
A year after its airing, a 27-year-old local man in a vodka- and
amphetamine-induced state decided to visit one of the filming
locations, the isolated and allegedly haunted Shipwright's Arms
on Faversham's Hollowshore, threatening the landlord with his
air rifle in scenes eerily reminiscent of the TV series. In 2017 the
75-year-old BAFTA-nominated Shakespearean actor John McEnery
likewise walked into the local Wetherspoons pub brandishing an
imitation handgun, flamboyantly demanding after-hours service
from startled bar staff. A star in Franco Zeffirelli's *Romeo and Juliet*
in the 1960s, McEnery was acquitted of possessing an imitation
firearm, but died the following year, being described in obituaries
as a 'troubled' actor who struggled with alcoholism and lived on a
converted trawler. Faversham certainly had its fair share of people
like McEnery – men who had washed up in the town having lost
their job, home, or both.

Despite being located on the Creek, and defined by its relationship with the sea, Faversham never felt like a coastal town. Indeed, Faversham tends to define itself in relation to its near-neighbour Whitstable, which stands at the point where the mudflats of Estuary England give way to an altogether different landscape of sunny shingle beaches and jaunty seafront eateries. Many drinkers I encountered in Faversham pubs derided Whitstable as everything that Faversham was not. Inauthentic. Twee. Gentrified. They had a point. Faversham had a patina of Dickensian grime staining its yellow-brick terraces, with the brewery at the heart of the town giving it a workaday feel. Running parallel to the beach, Whitstable's Harbour Street was, in contrast, a riot of pastel shades, trendy boutiques and art galleries full of maritime-themed paintings. And although Faversham's market was good for heavily discounted but out-of-date biscuits and crisps, Whitstable was a veritable foodie paradise. Independent bakers, gentrified Scandi coffee shops and gourmet delis aimed at a discerning middle-class clientele proliferate. Two of its restaurants – Samphire and Harbour Street Tapas – were listed among Britain's best 50 restaurants in Waitrose's *2018 Good Food* guide, while the quirky Wheeler's oyster bar, founded in 1856, regularly attracts rave reviews in the national press. Two miles from Whitstable harbour is The Sportsman pub, an icon of the same culinary landscape, which, along with JoJo's in neighbouring Tankerton, has been repeatedly lauded by arch-foodie Jay Rayner in *The Guardian*. In 2010 the New Economics Foundation named Whitstable Britain's most 'home-town' – as defined by its proportion of independent shops as opposed to retail multiples – suggesting that it had developed a foodie culture in which environmental, social and economic sustainability were co-dependent.

Whitstable's reputation as a culinary hotspot has consolidated its position as a must-visit destination. It is now a regular chart-topper on the list of Britain's best seaside towns, its Instagrammable beachside eateries and coastal accommodation attracting swooning reviews. This was not always the case. In 1914 the town was described as 'a singularly unattractive place; the more you see of it, the less you like it … the streets are narrow and mean, without the saving grace of picturesqueness, and the sea-front adds to the squalor by being occupied by the railway-station and a very coaly dock'.[15] One of its most famous sons, William Somerset Maugham, spoke of it unfavourably, christening it 'Blackstable' in his 1930 novel *Cakes and Ale,* and writing that 'in winter the natives … walked down the empty street with a hurried gait, screwing themselves up in order to expose as little surface as possible to the bitterness of the east wind'. As recently as the 1980s Whitstable was described in *The Times* as 'a very lived-in town, unprecious and unprecocious … there's little enough in the way of hotels, Guide Michelin recommended restaurants and all the rest that make life supportable'.[16] At that time Whitstable was not yet incorporated into circuits of gentrification, with apparently little existing to attract the yuppie London set. But in 2000 the same newspaper offered a rather different perspective in an article tellingly entitled 'A Stone's Throw from Islington':

> In Harbour Street and High Street I found the town working hard at being an offshoot of the London 'village'. The holidaying Chiswick or Clerkenwell shopper would feel at ease browsing in *Naturally Harbour Stree*t, *Marco Polos, Sea Gulls* and *Flamingos,* and *Artwork Blue* (all fashion and design shops) … I took a frothy cappuccino in Tea and Times ('Established 1990' – that's longevity worth boasting about) sitting on a bottom-contoured high stool and planned my day.[17]

The notion of DFLs (Down from Londons) was certainly widely established at this time, with author and Whitstable resident C. J. Stone lamenting in *The Independent* in 1999 that the town was becoming the 'new Chelsea' and that trendy media figures were jostling with TV producers and City analysts for a seat in the 'overpriced' Royal Oyster Stores restaurant, and discussing their latest projects in over-loud voices at the boutique Hotel Continental on the far side of the harbour.[18]

By the mid-2010s Whitstable appeared thoroughly gentrified, no longer subject to piecemeal improvement by outsiders but apparently dominated by DFLs who were pushing house prices ever upward:

> Whitstable has reached stage four of gentrification. We've had the Shabby Artists stage, the Cute Vintage Shop stage, the Actually Quite Posh Delis Have Opened stage. Now some serious money has arrived: The Building Of Fancy New Houses That Look As If Their Owners Have Watched Too Many Episodes Of Grand Designs stage. This lot aren't content with discreet renovations of weatherboarded fishermen's cottages. They want swagger. They want bling. I hope it's not the town's downfall.[19]

Preston Parade, at the Seasalter end of town, has become a focus for these Grand Designs – ultra-modern rebuilds in the new seaside vernacular of minimalist glass and steel, accented with Farrow & Ball's Ultramarine Blue. Once an unremarkable development of interwar dormer bungalows, but with access to its own private stretch of beach, in 2020 this was pronounced the most expensive street in East Kent, with average properties costing £1.37 million, most having trebled in value in under twenty years. Residents include musicians and TV stars, including Gregg Wallace, Harry Hill, Faye Ripley, Suggs and David Essex.

Various factors can be speculated to have caused the change in Whitstable's fortunes. Like much of Kent, Whitstable has always been shaped by its connections to London. The coming of High Speed One in 2003, providing a fast, efficient rail service between St Pancras International and the Kent coast, was a pivotal moment. Travelling by train along the north Kent coast, leaving Faversham through the orchards of Graveney and the soggy pastures of Seasalter Marsh, Whitstable Bay opens dramatically in front of the passenger, offering a first tantalising glimpse of the sea after an hour's journey from London. In winter, it can be as bleak a vista as can be imagined, an unkempt weedy beach of mud and shingle lapped by a blank, brown sea, with the massive grey turbines

2.2 Whitstable beach

of Vattenfall's Kentish Flats offshore wind farm receding into the distance. But in summer, the beach comes alive with red and white valerian, mallow and clumps of pale blue sea holly, the sun illuminating brightly painted beach huts that change hands for up to £150,000 each. Behind the sea wall, shabby-chic seafront houses look out on quirky gardens decorated with driftwood, pebbles and shells. Healthy-looking residents sit out on their decking or in front of beach huts with bottles of wine and Sunday supplements, the very embodiment of the gentrified coast. On a sunny day, this vista offers the day-tripper from London the opportunity to engage with a distinctive imagination of the English seaside. This is not one emphasising frivolity or the working-class vulgarity of the kiss-me-quick hat but a more middle-class vision of leisured consumption which celebrates the *authenticity* of coastal living. This is a vision that has transformed a peeling, neglected Kentish seaside town into a location for second homes, curated boutiques and fashion shoots, as well as the well-attended Biennial art festival and a lively music scene.[20]

Oysterfication

Arguably, Whitstable has gentrified because it appeals to those who have one foot in the world of bourgeois capitalist success and one in the bohemian world of creativity, media and art.[21] Traces of its productivist past remain in its salty, weather-beaten streets, clap-boarded homes and functional harbour, complete with asphalt works and aggregate storage, and it is not so gentrified that all its rough edges have been smoothed. Crucially, the continuing presence of a small fleet in the town's harbour sustains the idea that this is a fishing community, allowing connections to be made between contemporary forms of foodism and traditions of aquaculture that have been reworked in a tourist-friendly landscape of harbour-side stalls and *ersatz* fishermen's huts. At weekends the harbour is regularly packed with visitors who wander through its market, perusing goods handcrafted from driftwood while consuming seafood from well-established businesses such as West's Whelks and the Crab & Winkle. Here, there are obvious synergies between the consumption of seafood, tourist investment and place imagery in which fishing and aquaculture are valued for preserving 'traditional' ways of life, albeit the gentrification of the town simultaneously threatens these ways of life.[22]

But it is the oyster that appears central to the town's revival. Arguably, without the presence of oyster cultivation in the town, it is entirely possible that Whitstable would not have gentrified at all: in many ways, the celebration of local distinctiveness and authenticity appears to rest on the town's singular association with oyster cultivation.[23] Aquaculture here dates at least to Roman times, when the oysters found off the coast of Whitstable were reportedly exported to Rome because of their unparalleled quality. When the town was linked to Canterbury by one of Britain's first commercial railways in 1830, this was quickly dubbed the 'Crab & Winkle' line because of the town's seafood industry. By the 1860s as many as one hundred boats and five hundred fishermen were employed in dredging and shucking local oysters, which, in pickled form, had become a staple of the diet of London's working poor. Whitstable's oyster companies sent some fifty million oysters per year to Billingsgate at this time. But in the twentieth century, domestic demand waned following national food poisoning scares linked to oyster consumption.[24] Harsh winters did further damage to oyster stocks, with the sea freezing off the north Kent coast in 1963, trapping boats in the harbour for days. By the 1970s the main local producer, the Whitstable Oyster Fishery Company, was operating a single dredger and selling just a few dozen oysters to harbour visitors every day.

Despite this, the waters between Whitstable beach and the Kentish flats some five miles offshore remain ideal breeding grounds for oysters, filter-feeders that depend upon the fresh waters washing down the Swale and Thames, as well the local Gorrell stream. As oysters suck in and filter out this nutrient-rich water, they digest suspended phytoplankton and zooplankton. What they cannot digest, they eject as pseudo-faeces, which, coated in mucous, falls to the seabed to be processed by anoxic bacteria. The cleaner, de-acidified water that oysters leave behind is what just about everything else needs to live. Fish and invertebrate life are hence abundant in the warm, shallow waters of Whitstable Bay. This unique marine confluence encourages Whitstable oysters to grow fleshy bodies that subtly reflect the specific biophysical conditions of their residence. Whitstable, alongside Falmouth (Cornwall) and Maldon (Essex), is one of the few places where native oysters (*Ostrea edulis*) continue to be harvested from traditional beds. In 1997 they were given EU Protected Geographical Indication (PGI) status to recognise their place-specific qualities: these 'native' oysters are renowned as more meaty, metallic and clean-tasting than other, imported oysters. Whitstable natives are, then, much sought after by seafood connoisseurs, and celebrated as 'authentic' British produce, not least by the 40,000 or so gastronauts who descend annually on Whitstable for its exuberant Oyster Festival.

Held every July, the festival is kicked off by the symbolic landing of the first catch of oysters, and the blessing of the catch on Reeves Beach. Over the subsequent weekend of events, children construct 'grotters' from oyster shells on the beach and competitors attempt to eat six oysters in the fastest time. There is a colourful parade down Harbour Street, a tug of war on the mudflats, a samba band, and fireworks in the evening. There is also drinking. A lot of drinking. Though crowds take their time meandering through the food fair around the harbour, and bumbling through Harbour Street's boutiques, most end up sitting on the beachfront with pints of oyster stout or glasses of prosecco carried out from beachside pubs, consuming them alongside their oysters or fish and chips from a local takeaway. There's barely an inch of beach left to sit on, and the beer cans and wine bottles accumulate rapidly, plastic pint glasses crunching underfoot. Despite regular patrols during the weekend, and the installation of larger rubbish bins, chip wrappers and discarded beer cans litter the seafront, picked over and scattered by the local seagull population. The festival was forced to downscale in 2017 following complaints about problems of littering and anti-social behaviour among the estimated 60,000 festivalgoers.

Though it proclaims ancient origins, the Oyster Festival is an invented tradition, begun by volunteers in 1985 at the precise moment when oyster cultivation threatened to become a thing of the past. By that time, the Whitstable Oyster Fishery Company had been legally reconstituted as a property company under the auspices of Barrie Green and his business partner, who bought the company in 1976. The festival was an overt attempt to imbue the town with an identity that was to become highly marketable, as Britain's foodie revolution began to encourage domestic culinary tourism. Whitstable oysters were easily incorporated into emergent ideas of 'traditional' food production because of their embedding in a regional food culture, with the idea that native British oysters form part of a sustainable aquatic ecosystem consolidating connections between foodism, environmental preservation and a heritage of aquaculture that stretches back centuries.

Images of British oysters being washed down with champagne in seafront bars have reinvigorated demand for Whitstable oysters, and, at the same time, revitalised the reputation of Whitstable. Riding on this success, the Whitstable Oyster Fishery Company has expanded to employ over 150 staff in its various businesses, including a brewery, a hotel, a quayside bar, a beachfront oyster shack and fishermen's cottages and holiday accommodation, all decked out in a marine-heritage aesthetic. Alongside this, it has expanded oyster cultivation, and in 2009–10 started to farm imported Pacific oysters in mesh bags attached to metal trestle tables on the foreshore, with the presence of these making the (renewed) production of oysters highly obvious to any visitor to the town.[25] In 2018 it put out around six million juvenile oysters on these trestles, harvesting around a hundred tons the following year, equivalent to around one million oysters.[26]

There is, then, some irony that the contemporary Oyster Festival claims to celebrate time-honoured customs – marking St James Day, when oyster fishermen traditionally received their annual dividend – but now involves the mass consumption of imported, non-native oysters. But the robust, flatter, Pacific oyster *Magallana gigas* has several advantages over the native: it has a faster growth rate, typically reaching edible size in two years (as opposed to 4–5 for the native). Moreover, it is a triploid oyster with an extra set of reproduction-inhibiting chromosomes, whereas the diploid native tends to be inedible in the summer when spawning, initially as a male, then in following years as a female. This harvesting of non-native oysters has ensured that the Whitstable Oyster Fishery Company has been able to meet demand in the busy summer months and cater to the festival crowds.

2.3 Trestles on foreshore, Whitstable

This oysterfication of the town is now so pervasive that for many visitors the oyster will be the one thing they associate with Whitstable (irrespective of the fact that whelks, cockles, Dover sole, skate and lobsters are also landed here). While Whitstable once sent oysters to London, it is Londoners who now come to Whitstable to experience a particular mode of authentic coastal consumption. It is this that feeds gentrification: short-stay visitors down from London buy properties as well as oysters, turning residential housing into second homes and weekend lets. In Harbour ward (which covers central Whitstable) the proportion of higher managerial, administrative and professional workers nearly doubled between 2001 and 2011. In the same period the number of properties with no usual resident, a figure that includes holiday lets and second homes, rose from 172 to 415. Though average house prices topped £400,000 in 2019, the town's combination of outside living and leisure, when coupled with a thriving food and arts scene, have retained strong appeal for DFLs: in 2020 Whitstable topped a

2.4 Beach hut for sale, Whitstable

league table of the 152 Best Coastal Towns to move to in the UK, further boosting its attractiveness to Londoners looking to escape the capital during the COVID-19 lockdown.[27]

Contesting the coast

Whitstable has changed markedly from the quiet coastal town that actor Peter Cushing first moved to in 1958. Cushing referred to his home there on Island Wall as his 'village' residence, making regular visits to the Tudor Tea Rooms, buying his cravats at local tailors Hatchard's and spending hours by the beach painting sea scenes until his death in 1994. Cushing might not have approved of Whitstable's recent transformation. Hatchard's is now Costa Coffee, and the Oxford Picture Hall, which closed in 1984, reopened in 2011 as a Wetherspoons pub named in Cushing's honour. Cushing's View, a wooden memorial bench in the car park behind the sea wall, is on the busiest part of the seafront, often heaving with tourists loaded up with takeways and drinks, the car park itself invariably full of tourists circling in vain pursuit of a space. Compared with the town that Cushing knew, and the town I first visited in my youth, Whitstable is often now simply too much – too busy, too braying, too parked up.

There is, then, a degree of local resentment at the way that DFLs have pushed up house prices, changed the High Street into a boutique-heavy tourist trail and turned the town into a foodie paradise. The closure of some long-established businesses, house prices that are no longer affordable for many locals, and increasing pressures on parking are among the chief complaints. The town has become a victim of its own success, with new development accused of eroding its character. Much of the disquiet has been targeted at the Whitstable Oyster Fishery Company, as although its entrepreneurial activities have boosted local trade, some feel that it has pursued its business to the ultimate detriment of the town. Particularly sensitive here has been its ownership of the beach, with local campaigners (the Whitstable Beach Campaign) alleging that the placement of trestle tables on the foreshore has displaced recreational swimmers and sailors. Local campaigners have fought for a 'right to roam' over the beach and unsuccessfully lobbied to have the trestle tables removed from the intertidal zone.[28] The company also faced criticism when it converted a boat storage facility that it bought from Canterbury City Council for £165,000 into a seafront housing development, ultimately valued at a combined £10 million: a 2017 High Court judgement ruled that the council had indeed disposed of the land at 'less than the best consideration', but declined to quash the sale.[29]

These legal struggles are nothing new for the Whitstable Oyster Fishery Company, which had its origin in the 1792 sale of the maritime part of the manor of Whitstable to the company of dredgers who had worked the oyster beds 'since time immemorial'.[30] The company bought the beach from the Crown in 1856. Subsequent case law suggests that the company cannot charge tolls for those navigating over the beach at high tide, but it does have exclusive rights to fish on the beach under a 'public trust doctrine'. A key legal case, *Gann v Free Fishers of Whitstable* (1865), established

2.5 Beach signage, Whitstable

these property rights, ruling that this land had been transferred not for the Crown but in the interest of the public defended by the Crown, namely the maintenance of oyster stocks at a time of overfishing. As early as 1865 the House of Lords defined the concept of public trust in a case brought against the 'free fishers of Whitstable', with the assumption that the seabed had been granted to the Crown by the Lord of the Manor confirming that the company retained exclusive rights to fish there. This legal right was reiterated when the company was reconstituted by Parliament in 1896, with its statutory duties defined as 'regulating, carrying on and managing the oyster fisheries within the limits of the manor and royalty of Whitstable'.[31] Subsequently, this has allowed the company to resist attempts to bring its estate into common ownership, claiming that untrammelled recreational use of the beach and foreshore would interfere with its duty to maintain local oyster stocks. Thus, while the public has a right to swim and sail in the tidal waters off Whitstable, or dig bait when the tide is out, legally they have no general right to go on to the beach or foreshore for these purposes.

It is here that issues of locality, history and identity begin to get complicated. The Oyster Festival, and the heritage industry that goes with it, celebrates a particular idea of traditional aquaculture, of fishermen in smocks and jumpers bringing their catch ashore in their red-sailed yawls. The children building shell grottos on the beach put a candle inside to guide the fishermen safely ashore. But the modern-day oyster worker is not the fisherman of yesteryear. Wearing waders and dayglo jackets, contemporary oyster fishery workers quad bike across the mudflats to monitor black-plastic mesh bags of lab-hatched oysters. These are attached to trestle tables by black banding, an amount of which inevitably washes up on nearby beaches. Local artist Rachael Louise Bailey spent three years collecting 7 km of this banding, creating vast sculptural forms designed to draw attention to marine pollution. A seven-foot-wide black, rubber-band ball entitled *Global* – part of her prize-winning *Black Stuff* installation – was an implicit critique of modern aquaculture. Left in the intertidal zone during the Whitstable Biennale in 2018, it drew interested crowds who waded out to touch and prod it. Making the point that marine pollution is a global issue and knows no boundaries, Bailey's artwork challenged the assumption that modern oyster cultivation is necessarily sustainable and environmentally friendly.

She is not alone. Others have raised questions about the environmental impact of modern-day oyster production. The Whitstable Beach Campaign has not only opposed the positioning of trestles on the foreshore because of their impact on recreational sea-users but has also questioned the wisdom of cultivating 'non-native' Pacific oysters. Here, it is notable that among the many public comments on the Whitstable Oyster Fishery Company's 2018 application for a retrospective certificate of lawful development for the trestles above the mean low water mark was the frequent objection that the company was using them to farm an 'invasive' species. One

2.6 Rachael Louise Bailey, *The Black Stuff*, Whitstable

complainant went so far as to argue that the Pacific oysters 'pose a problem to the delicate eco-system of which the whole town and tourist industry relies on', suggesting that the 'Pacific Oysters will grow exponentially across the whole beach, not just within the oyster racks, and will ruin the balance of the sea-life in this area'.[32] This type of reasoning draws on the observation that oyster larvae can drift on currents from spawning stocks, and these can colonise artificial substrata including groynes and sea walls, as well as offshore wind farms and mussel beds. Indeed, further along the Kent coast, some of the unique rocky chalk reefs off the coast of Thanet have been overwhelmed by invasive oysters, which are accused of displacing existing chalk invertebrates and rare algal surf communities. They are also razor sharp, a hazard for beach users and swimmers. Natural England has undertaken major operations to reduce their density on Thanet's shores, removing an estimated 300,000 since 2011.[33] Its 'coastbusters' team disposes of non-natives with brutal alacrity, using hammer blows to crack open the oyster shells and leaving local gull populations to do the rest.

Despite the Shellfish Association of Great Britain and Fishmongers' Company pointing to the ecological and economic benefits of cultivating Pacific oysters in the UK, their production has been vilified in some quarters. Here, familiar tropes of invasion biology are invoked, with the Pacific oyster positioned as a 'foreign' species threatening to overwhelm native species: C. J. Stone has likened the cultivation of Pacific oysters in trestles to 'growing Japanese knotweed in polytunnels'.[34] But the idea that non-natives might ultimately out-compete natives remains conjectural given that the ecosystem-wide impacts of invasive oyster introduction on flow patterns, sedimentation and nutrient dynamics are not well understood. Indeed, some scientific evidence opposes ideas of out-competition and suggests that non-native introductions can greatly enhance overall oyster populations by creating a more favourable environment for reproduction.[35] And even if non-natives were to become dominant, the Whitstable Oyster Fishery Company's trestles will not necessarily be to blame, given that they contain cultivated triploid oysters that are effectively incapable of spawning.[36] Nonetheless, there are clearly forms of thinking present here that conflate the dangers posed by hazardous, sharp oyster trestles to sea-users, the industrialisation of the Whitstable foreshore and the threat to indigenous fauna and flora.

Eco-nationalism at the border

The figuring of Pacific oysters as a non-native 'threat' implies that questions of bordering extend to encompass environmental matters and are not always about human migration. Confirming this, geographer Juliet Fall suggests that debates about where to draw boundaries around 'natural areas' often collapse into exclusionary nationalist discourses about what belongs where.[37] From this perspective, it could be argued that those arguing for the protection of

British native species are following, perhaps unwittingly, in a tradition of 'eco-anxiety' in which general fears about the permeability of the border are expressed through the figure of invasive animals. In this sense, Pacific oysters fall into the same category as the 'European super fleas', stink bugs, 'Euromoths' and giant continental dormice depicted by the media as threats to UK nature. Cultural theorist Jonathan Davies argues that alarmist coverage of these invasive threats to national ecosystems was especially pronounced in the run-up to the Brexit vote in 2016, with stories 'linking ecological decline, migration, Brexit, austerity, myths of empire, war and landscape' suggesting that environmental anxieties contributed to public concern about the porosity of the British border.[38]

So while oysters are generally regarded as a beneficial presence at the coast, implicated in ecosystem processes including the biological control of pathogens, water purification, formation of species habitat and even coastal defence, the visible, industrial harvesting of 'foreign' oysters at Whitstable seems to have generated particular anxieties about the changing nature of the coast at the precise moment when questions of international mobility were under the microscope.[39] This provides an example of what Ben Pitcher terms *eco-nationalism* – a discourse that conflates distinctions between 'native' and 'non-native' in nature with questions of national identity.[40] Here it is worth noting that aquaculture, and fishing more generally, was a particularly potent motif in Brexit debates, with the symbolism of 'Great British' traditions such as fish and chips mobilised in debates focused on the sovereignty of UK waters. In such debates, the idea that Britain had lost control of its destiny and needed redress was signalled through repeated reference to fishing quotas, with the cultural rather than economic significance of fish emphasised in the rhetoric of Leave campaigners such as Nigel Farage. As such, talk of fish as a necessary part of a good and authentic British diet was one of many dubious 'alimentary discourses' that Muzna Rahman suggests entered the political language of Brexit.[41] Irrespective, organisations such as Fishing for Leave, launched in

2016, suggested that taking back control of 'our' seas was vital for the future of the British fishing industry, arguing that EU Total Allowable Catch quotas were preventing British fishermen from catching 'British fish' (largely ignoring the fact that fish in British waters are no more British than they are French, Belgian or Norwegian).[42] Those arguing for British 'rights to catch' noted the potential for the doubling of the British trawler fleet if EU quotas were rescinded.

I am not suggesting that the Whitstable residents opposing the expansion of non-native oyster production were necessarily sympathetic to such Leave arguments or connected the cultivation of oysters to wider debates on fishing. Whitstable in fact voted 55% to Remain, making it and Tunbridge Wells the only Remain constituencies in Kent. But as a coastal community with strong fishing traditions, Whitstable has been unquestionably caught up in an anti-EU politics that positioned seafood as totemic in debates about British national identity and sovereignty.[43] Indeed, disputes over fishing grounds sometimes figured as prominently in Brexit debates as the 'migration crisis'. Fishing remained near the top of the agenda throughout the drawn-out Brexit negotiations, with Fishing for Leave accusing Theresa May, and then Boris Johnson, of 'selling out' British fishermen. Animosity rumbled on. In April 2018 Nigel Farage returned to Whitstable, joined by Folkestone-based ex-UKIP leader Henry Bolton, to witness the symbolic burning of the fishing boat 'Thereason May' in the harbour, accompanied by forty fishing vessels from around the Kent coast showing their approval by lighting flares whose smoke drifted across the beach.

One of the most memorable scenes of the Brexit referendum campaign was Farage departing from Ramsgate with a flotilla of thirty fishing boats, arriving outside the Houses of Parliament only to be greeted by Bob Geldof in a 'Remain' pleasure cruiser blaring out 'The In-Crowd' over its PA and brandishing signs proclaiming 'You're no fisherman's friend!' I was in London that day, incredulously watching the spectacle unfold on the Thames from the vantage point of King's College River Room, press helicopters hovering overhead. The following day, 16 June 2016, Geldof travelled to the University of York to participate in the BBC's *Question Time* alongside MPs Nicky Morgan and Alan Johnson. By complete coincidence, I had also travelled to York for an urban sociology conference, held in the same building that *Question Time* was to be filmed in. Given that Geldof lived only a few hundred metres away from my home in Faversham, this all seemed rather providential. But in the early afternoon news began to trickle through of the shooting of Batley and Spen Labour MP Jo Cox by a far-right sympathiser who described her as betraying 'white people', shouting 'Britain First' as he attacked her. By the time the conference ended, she had been pronounced dead and *Question Time* was cancelled. We left the conference in numbed silence. The following day's EU referendum campaigning was suspended as a mark of respect. Mass gatherings in London and Batley followed, and a 'More in Common' campaign was begun in her memory (based on her maiden speech as an MP in which she stressed that 'we have more in common than that which divides us').[44]

It is clearly absurd to suggest that those opposing the cultivation of non-native oysters at the coast, or arguing for the end of EU fishing quotas, were driven by the same rabid xenophobia that led Thomas Mair to take the life of Jo Cox in an awful, frenzied attack. But as sociologist Hannah Jones argues, Cox's murder took place at a moment of enormous political and cultural cleavage, with the Brexit campaign encouraging a backlash against the presence of women and ethnic minorities in public life, especially those who espoused pro-EU views.[45] This cleavage was one in which different views of British life were asserted, with a key Leave argument being that the white working class were suffering under the burden of mass immigration, and that 'our shared history and culture' was being undermined by foreign influence. Yet far from framing this as being about race or white privilege, many pro-Brexit sup-porters explained their concerns about immigration in relation to questions of environmental management or the best use of resources. For example, Leader of the House of Commons and Brexit campaigner Chris Grayling suggested that there were simply too many people in Britain, with the countryside being 'ruined by migrant homes'.[46] Organisations such as Population Matters also constantly argued that the UK is the most nature-depleted country in the world, using this to campaign for bans on refugee arrivals. Such 'post-racial' contextualisations suggest that, in the minds of some at least, the control of immigration can be justified in relation to apolitical ideas about the nation's 'carrying capacity'.[47] In this sense, the control of non-human animals – and the boundaries drawn between native and non-native – became conjoined with human migration in Brexit discourse, with ecological as well as economic arguments mustered to position Brexit as a rational reaction to 'globalism'. Significantly, while campaigners were alleging that non-native oysters could damage native stocks, lurid headlines were talking of foreign gangs 'raping' Kent's coastline by illegally removing cockles and shellfish, with the police's Wildlife Crime Unit deploying drones to discourage such activity.[48]

The conflation of ecological security, national prosperity and border control in the rhetoric of Leave campaigners was no doubt persuasive for some voters, but Brexit has so far failed to deliver the anticipated benefits promised for the British fishing industry. At the time of writing, 1,600 boats from EU nations have been licensed to fish in UK waters while British trawlers have been seized and fined by the French authorities for straying into their waters. Paris has stated that British trawlers could be banned from unloading in French ports, and continues to demand more permits for smaller, artisanal fishermen in British waters. More pressing for Whitstable is that the 2021 EU ban on the importation of live, unprocessed seafood from the UK has threatened the oyster industry: clearly, Boris Johnson's 'oven-ready' Brexit did not take shellfish into account. This ban has posed a particular problem for the Whitstable Oyster Fishery Company, given that around half of its stock has traditionally been exported to Europe. With Whitstable oysters harvested from Class B waters, not the cleanest Class A, they cannot currently be exported without pre-processing to remove all traces of *E. coli*.[49] Government plans to help fund new purifying facilities were dismissed by the Whitstable Oyster Fishery Company as inadequate given that the facilities needed to purify the volumes of oysters it exports to Europe would need to be the size of a small swimming pool.[50] In the face of the EU ban, the company has begun to export to the discerning Hong Kong market instead.

Given its long history, there is little question that oyster production in Whitstable will continue to define the town's identity. But legal battles over the designation of the beach as a Village Green continue, and oyster cultivation on trestle tables remains controversial locally. There are clearly many in Whitstable who are anxious about the industrialisation of oyster cultivation in the town, and some worried that the town's foodie reputation is fuelling rampant touristification.[51] Beneath its quirky and touristic facade, Whitstable is, then, a fractured community, one where gentrification is exposing different ideas about the way the town connects to London and the rest of England, as well as mainland Europe and beyond. Unlikely as it seems, the non-native oyster is at the heart of these debates. It is a liminal presence in contemporary Whitstable, regarded as out of place in English fishing traditions, but central to the economies that sustain the town's foodscapes: for some it constitutes an alien presence and a threat to the marine environment, while others regard it as vitally important to the local economy, recognising that it is exported to Europe in large numbers as well as consumed locally. As we will see, debates like this – about what, or who, belongs – are played out in different ways all along the Kentish coast, taking particularly pronounced forms where questions of national belonging and identity intersect more obviously with questions of human migration and mobility. In such instances, discourses of eco-nationalism are replaced by the language of race and racism, with exclusionary nationalism expressed in often violent forms.

3

Albion-on-Sea

The Arcadian dream has fallen through
But the Albion sails on course
　　　　　　The Libertines, 'The Good Old Days', 2002[1]

The Isle of Thanet stands at the north-eastern tip of Kent. This
was formerly separated from the mainland by the Wantsum channel,
once over two miles wide but now little more than a piddling
drainage ditch, scarcely registered by drivers on the A299. The
extent of the channel is more obvious when crossed on foot, as I
did when my walk along the coast continued. I approached Thanet
from Herne Bay, passing the former site of Regulbium (Reculver)
Roman fort, whose perimeter wall remains only in fragmented
form. From here, the English Coastal Path continues along the sea
wall constructed after the 1953 North Sea floods, but the Saxon
Shore Way veers south to acknowledge the western bank of the
former Wantsum channel. Walking straight on, it is three long
miles before the exhausting emptiness of the Wade Marsh (to the
rear of the sea wall), and the narrow shingle beach (to its fore),
gives way to the graceful sweep of Minnis Bay, the first of a series
of fifteen sandy beaches and bays on the Isle of Thanet, all
characteristically backed by chalk cliffs. One of these – Botany
Bay – is probably the most photographed beach in Kent, with its
impressive chalk sea stacks, caves and coastal rock pools attracting
thousands on sunny summer days. Nearby Broadstairs remains the

quintessence of the traditional British seaside resort, reputedly Dickens's favourite holiday spot, replete with colourful ice cream parlours, quaint cafés and nods to the fishing heritage of the town.

For many years the largest town in Thanet, Margate, eclipsed Broadstairs in popularity as a tourist destination, becoming one of the most fashionable resorts in Britain in the early 1800s at a time when Broadstairs was still a small fishing village. Easily reached by single-sailed ships, it was the first coastal town to provide a purpose-built seawater bath, completed in 1736, and it innovated the use of horse-drawn bathing machines, complete with modesty hoods, designed by Quaker Benjamin Beale, which allowed bathers of both sexes to enjoy a modicum of privacy. As the popularity of the resort grew, at least seven bath waiting rooms were built to the rear of the sands, providing swimmers with a sheltered social space in which they could read newspapers, drink restorative seawater and even enjoy piano recitals before their dip into the brine.[2] John Lettsom's elegant 1796 Sea Bathing Infirmary, extended in the nineteenth century, stood as testimony to the therapeutic value of sea air, its tubercular wards opening up on to impressive seafront colonnades. Grand Georgian squares were also completed in the 1770s and 1780s, with a domed town library and the Theatre Royal providing visitors with amenities rarely found in smaller coastal towns. The subterranean shell grotto, lined with local whelks, mussels and cockles, provided a further visitor attraction, albeit one of mysterious provenance.[3]

Margate changed rapidly in the nineteenth century as paddle steamers brought visitors to the town in greater numbers and at lower cost than ever before. The 1846 arrival of the railway station at Margate Sands allowed the town to draw in an even broader constituency, with a pier, pleasure gardens, bandstands, souvenir shops and restaurants widening the range of attractions. By the time mass entertainment arrived in the form of cinemas, the Winter Gardens (1911) and the US-style amusement park Dreamland (modelled on Coney Island, and opened in 1919), the town was developing a reputation as a more working-class resort, as noted by Charles Harper in his 1914 perambulation of the Kent coast:

> Margate the Merry is the oldest and most popular of English seaside resorts and in some opinions, the most vulgar. However that may be, and dismissing the claims of Rollicking Ramsgate and Southend (to say nothing of Blackpool and Yarmouth) to pre-eminence in vulgarity, Merry Margate is certainly a very crowded and unselect place in August and on occasions of popular holiday. Not only the seafaring and the coastwise populations indulge in strong language: conversation in general along the roads is decidedly over-proof.[4]

Throughout the twentieth-century era of mass domestic tourism, this reputation was embellished through an association with the carnivalesque, with the Bakhtinian pleasures of sexual excess, alcoholic exuberance and a release from the routines of the factory floor having particular appeal for the thousands of working-class Londoners who descended on Margate on Bank Holiday weekends. And even when the era of package holidays was ushered in by cheap passenger flights in the 1960s, the refuge of 'seaside nostalgia' kept the tourists coming, preserving many of the traditions of the cockney charabanc.[5] One of the most celebrated episodes of the sitcom *Only Fools and Horses* – 'The Jolly Boys' Outing' – aired in 1989, provides a sense of the enduring appeal of the town by depicting a boozy London lads' 'beano' which delights in the clichés of end-of-the-pier innuendo, kiss-me-quick hats, and frolics between the whelk stalls and amusement arcades, all set to a Chas & Dave soundtrack (their song 'Down to Margate', recorded for a Courage 'Best Bitter' advert, made it into the Top 40 in 1982).

In the twenty-first century Chas & Dave still performed regularly at the Winter Gardens, but, rather than appearing timeless, by then Margate felt ravaged by time. For some, a trip to the town allowed them to revisit holidays from days gone by and connect to the hopes and anxieties of their youth, embodied pleasures such as walking on the sands or eating fish and chips, recapturing long-forgotten sensations and memories.[6] But while Margate's smaller,

3.1 Margate sands

more charming neighbour Broadstairs cashed in on its seaside
heritage and associations with Charles Dickens to retain its reputation
as a family-oriented resort, constant images of deprivation and
decline, layered on top of Margate's reputation as a cockneyfied
resort, rendered it deeply unfashionable, a place to be avoided by
the respectable middle classes.

The result was that, by the turn of the century, Margate had
some of the most affordable housing in the South-East. Following
the house price crash of 2008, the average Margate house cost
£160,000, a full £100,000 cheaper than the South-East average,
making it the most affordable seaside town anywhere on the south
coast bar Plymouth. With large parts of central Margate and
Cliftonville characterised by dilapidated former seaside guest houses
and bed and breakfast accommodation converted to homes in
multiple occupation (HMOs), it is perhaps unsurprising that this
affordable accommodation caught the eye of those London boroughs

53

struggling to house their own homeless populations. Though moving away from friends and family in London was not necessarily something those in housing need wanted to do, for some it was the best – or only – option the local authority could offer them, with the alternative of being shunted from one temporary bedsit to another in the capital a singularly unattractive proposition.[7]

With London boroughs able to use London-weighted Temporary Accommodation Management Fees to support the acquisition of properties in Margate, and able to pay rents at a level that much of the local population simply could not afford, Thanet District Council began to identify a serious risk that Margate's own homeless population would be squeezed out, with a shortage of privately rented dwellings available at the local housing allowance rates that Kent residents could afford. By September 2013 around one-third of those applying for social housing in Thanet came from London, with only 329 council-owned units available for the 5,123 households on its housing register (by far the highest total in the county).[8] Moreover, given that many families moving from London to Kent required support from health and social services, concern was raised that out-migration from London was placing unprecedented pressure on local services, especially those for children.[9]

For many ex-Londoners in housing need, Margate offered a chance of a new start on the Kent coast. But given the economic and social marginality of many of the incomers, it was not surprising that the media began to depict Margate as a 'dumping ground'. A 2012 article in the *New Statesman* pulled no punches in its description of a faded seaside town:

> A games arcade's neon lights bleed into the cold mist … Beside it there's a foul-looking chippy and a few desultory tourist shops, all closed. A hill leads away from the seafront. Up here, past rows of huge Victorian houses, most of them with peeling plaster and rotting doors, there's a small row of shops. A group of children smokes outside an off license. The tattered pub is closed. And just off this street, a huge hotel, bigger than the others. It costs £40 a week to

stay here, and 200 people do … they have one communal kitchen, which is open for just an hour. A family walks in: mother, father, two small children. They have come from abroad and are seeking asylum. They prepare their food for the evening, then leave. Next, an ex-convict, released after eight years. And after him, a street drinker, a paedophile, a heroin addict, and many more come and go.[10]

The article described the 'wrecked wraiths' of drug addicts wandering the seafront, high levels of anti-social behaviour and streets where foster children lived alongside registered sex offenders. Though prone to exaggeration, media stories of dispossession and despair began to stack up. A Congolese asylum seeker fell to his death from the fifth floor of the Nayland Rock hotel, reputed to be hosting asylum seekers at a cost of £350 per week, in the summer of 2006. In 2008 an afternoon clash between two gangs on the seafront escalated in the evening, with two 18-year-olds dying in a house set ablaze by a 17-year-old. In the same year, the scenic railway in the Dreamland amusement park was subject to an arson attack, and only days later the Tivoli amusement arcade was also torched, causing £500,000 of damage. The media headlines came thick and fast as Margate became a metonym for failure – lowest life expectancy in Kent, the South Coast's Worst Beach, Benefits-on-Sea, the Chav St Tropez.

Pawel Pawlikowski's 2000 film *Last Resort* inadvertently cemented this reputation. Made in the immediate wake of the Balkans war that witnessed increasing numbers of Bosnian refugees seeking asylum in the UK, *Last Resort* centres on an Eastern European illustrator, Tanya, accompanied by her 10-year-old son, attempting to meet up with her sometime-lover in London. Interrogated at the border when entering via Gatwick, she is packed off to 'Stonehaven' (Margate). She is housed in a tower block occupied by other asylum seekers (actually Arlington House, the brutalist eighteen-floor apartment building on Margate's seafront sold as luxury flats on its completion in 1964). Shot in various shades of grey, Margate is depicted as a bleak holding tank for asylum

3.2 Arlington House, Margate

seekers, who resort to selling blood to supplement the meagre food vouchers they exchange at the local greasy spoon café. It is in this café that Tanya finds herself talked into trying her luck as a webcam sex worker, much to the anger of the local amusement arcade manager, Alfie (Paddy Considine), who has taken a shine to her. Armed with a baseball bat, Alfie runs amok in the webcam studio, destroying the video equipment and injuring its slimy, smooth-talking proprietor Les (a role played with some conviction by Kent-born porn actor 'Ben Dover'). In the aftermath, Alfie decides that they must get away, with the final scenes seeing Tanya and son jumping into a lorry on the A2, hoping to hitch to London before making the flight home. Alfie waves them off, clutching a single memento of their visit – a children's book illustration that Tanya was hoping to show to potential employers as an example of her work.

Though *Last Resort* does not name Margate, the images of Dreamland in its last faded years, the grubby amusement arcades and graffiti-ridden alleyways at the back of the railway station are all clearly recognisable, as is the concrete slab of Arlington House, the only high-rise block for miles around. The sky is perpetually slate grey, the seaweed-strewn flat beach deserted and uninviting. On its release, local Tory councillors slammed the tourism chief for allowing it to be filmed: perhaps aware of the possibility that local populations would take affront at the title *Last Resort*, former asylum seeker Pawlikowski filmed it under the alias *Russian Lover*. But it is also a surprisingly tender film that aims to humanise the refugee populations often objectified in the media, drawing attention to the plight faced by those having to live their lives in an effective state of suspension.[11] Pawlikowski recounts his first visit to Margate thus:

> My first contact was with the Roma, the Gypsies, who were the only refugees really who interacted with the locals. Even with them, what struck me was how little their world extended beyond what they called Margatta. They would make epic journeys to a strange place at the far end of their known world called Greyva's End [Gravesend]. They are Kurds and Afghans mostly. Some have not even lived in cities before. They are all stunned, many don't move because they don't know what to do. When the local Margate kids go round spitting at them, you can see their shock because they come from cultures where people have manners, where strangers receive hospitality. To me, they looked like they were living inside a Kafka story.[12]

Pawlikowski's film plays on this theme of inertia, with the depiction of Margate as the 'end of the line' reinforcing this. But despite its representation of the town as a 'limbo zone devoid of opportunities',[13] the film is not without humour, such as the contrast between the garish palm tree wallpaper that adorns Tanya's flat and the cold, wet Margate sands below. Although it does not shy away from themes of violence and exploitation, the film celebrates the types of solidarity that can emerge between people thrown together in a space not necessarily of their own choosing. The amusement arcade becomes a *de facto* community centre and crèche, a space that encourages, rather than tolerates, difference.[14] In one of the film's pivotal scenes, we learn amusement arcade manager Alfie's reason for being in the town. He admits that he is an ex-convict who did something he regrets – 'I came here because I fucked up – it's a town full of fuck-ups.' In *Last Resort*, the sea is used to emphasise a sense of insularity, and repeated images of dark, gathering clouds create an imprisoning effect. Although the town is not on a *de facto* island, it might as well be.[15]

These images of an insular town mirror the many academic analyses that have figured deprived coastal communities as the twenty-first-century equivalent of the inner-city areas that were the focus of urban policy intervention in the 1980s and 1990s. In 2007 the Communities and Local Government Committee identified coastal communities as the 'least understood' of Britain's problem areas, naming Margate as a prime example of a community that needed urgent policy intervention because of its physical isolation, high levels of deprivation, transient population, poor housing quality and seasonal unemployment.[16] Likewise, a 2013 report by the Centre for Social Justice profiled Margate as one of five case studies of failing coastal communities, bracketing it with Clacton, Blackpool, Great Yarmouth and Rhyl, all depicted as lagging behind coastal 'success stories' such as Brighton and Bournemouth. The report described a spiral of decline – property prices falling, housing being turned into HMOs, absentee landlords, families moving out, poorly maintained properties and overcrowding. The report paraded damning statistics, such as the fact that 85% of HMOs in Cliftonville West, just to the east of Margate town centre, were hazardous in at least one respect, and that one in twenty homes lacked central heating.[17] Repeating accusations of 'social dumping' by London boroughs, the report suggested that most newcomers were 'dependent' on benefits, noting that between 2000 and 2013 the number claiming jobseeker's allowance increased by 76%.[18]

Walking through the town today, there remain many signs of this deprivation. One of Margate's less envied claims to fame was that in the wake of the 2008 recession, it briefly topped the chart of Britain's most derelict high streets. Multiple chains in particular read the runes and departed with haste, many relocating to Westwood Cross, the soulless but popular retail park in the middle of the Isle of Thanet described by Marion Shoard as the epitome of the 'non-place realm'.[19] Despite enterprising efforts designed to bring former shop units back into active use (the Woolworths that closed down in 2009 briefly became an indoor marketplace for local creatives and craftivists), it remains a gap-toothed high street, with numerous boarded-up and whitewashed shopfronts. Some have newspapers up in the window to prevent the curious from peering in, albeit through cracks I could see that a couple were being slept in, with sleeping bags on the floor and empty food packets and beer cans strewn around. It was unclear if these belonged to 'property guardians' paid to keep watch over the premises and prevent vandalism, or if the premises had been broken into by homeless people seeking shelter over the winter. Many deserted shops were simply frozen in time, one plastered with peeling posters for a circus that had left the town years previously.

Ignoring the hydrogen sulphide reek emanating from the seaweed on the beach, I left the High Street to head down to the sea. Here I witnessed other sites that seethed with memories, haunted by intimations of the past.[20] There were none of the seafront whelk stalls I recalled from my visits as a teenager in the 1980s, the joke shop has closed and some of the amusement arcades I remembered were boarded up. Surprisingly, the Wimpy I used to eat in was still there, but its façade was splattered with what I hoped was red paint, not blood. Wandering the seafront, I found it hard to reconcile it with the busy resort I recalled from my summer visits decades before, when my teenage friends and I would cruise the arcades hoping to win enough money to afford the rides at Bembom Brothers amusement park, the last incarnation of Dreamland before it was dismantled in 2003.

Struggling to orientate myself, I paused at the lido complex at Cliftonville, recalling its bold yellow and red sign from years before. In many parts of the country, outdoor swimming facilities have been revived and restored in recent times in recognition of the therapeutic and well-being benefits of cold-water swimming. In contrast, Margate's lido, opened as the Cliftonville Bathing Pool in 1929, stands abandoned and forlorn. Much of the complex is crumbling away, worn away by neglect and battered by the 1978 storm that also did for Margate pier, the elegant Victorian jetty designed by Eugenius Birch that used to welcome paddle steamers of day-trippers. Many of the bars, stylish 'French' restaurants and changing rooms that cascaded down to the sea-bathing pool are also long gone, though the iron-framed main building remains, boarded up and covered in graffiti. Beneath are older tunnels and heating ducts, including a tunnel that once allowed sea-bathing machines to glide unnoticed out of the changing room and into the sea. These date to the nineteenth century, constructed at a time when sea bathing was regarded as a cure for 'unfashionable ailments' (such as jaundice, shingles and diarrhoea) as well as a fashionable leisure activity that gave the elite a chance to parade their health and status.[21]

But only the bare traces of this complex history remain: the tunnels below the lido are sealed up, accessible only to those intrepid urban explorers who share images of their clandestine place-hacking online.[22] And though the tunnels below the ground have listed status, the buildings above do not, allowing the contemporary visitor little purchase on the layered narratives of place and history that are sedimented here.[23] I stood and watched the North Sea waves crash over the promenade into the sea-bathing pool, which is now silted up with dirty sand, and tried to imagine what the pool looked like when my grandparents visited Margate in the 1930s, when up to a thousand bathers frolicked there at a time. But on a drab day

3.3 Cliftonville Lido, Margate

in March, no one looked much interested in the lido, nor the High Street I had been photographing as part of my continuing interest in so-called 'failing' town centres.[24] Instead, many exiting the town's station were, like me, making a beeline for the Turner Contemporary gallery, designed to house a rotating collection of art centred around a changing exhibition of the works of J. M. W. Turner.

The Turner effect

Turner's association with Margate was long and varied. As a teenager, he went to the non-conformist Thomas Coleman's school in Love Lane, while his mother was incarcerated in the Bethlem psychiatric hospital in Moorfields, London. It was in Margate that his earliest known drawings were completed, later displayed in his father's barber's shop in London and attracting the attention of his wealthy clientele. Though Turner moved back to the family home in Brentford after a few years, he returned to Margate often as a young man, apparently still besotted with Elizabeth White, the sister of a Margate schoolfriend. While abroad in the 1790s he regularly sent letters to her, only to find later that they had been intercepted by her mother, who evidently regarded him as an ineligible suitor because of his limited financial means and abrasive personality. Later finding she was engaged to a local publican, Turner apparently became morose and vowed never to get married himself.

As his career took off after his 1796 Royal Academy exhibition, Turner travelled widely, but he visited Kent frequently, particularly his aunt and cousins at Tonbridge. Reputedly, Turner used to regularly introduce himself as 'a Kentish man'.[25] Prone to eccentricity, and lacking close friends, in his later years he began to visit Margate again, boarding anonymously at a seafront guest house owned by John Booth, who succumbed to cholera in 1833. Turner then began a relationship with Booth's widow Sophia, moving back to London with her in 1846, five years before his death at the age of 76. Mike Leigh's acclaimed 2014 film *Mr Turner* tells their story, albeit most of the scenes set in Margate were filmed in Kingsand, Cornwall.

Turner's pocketbook sketches and images of Margate undeniably contributed to the fashionability of the resort in the early 1800s. By the same token, his time in Margate undoubtedly propelled his career forward by encouraging him to explore new techniques to capture the dynamism of sea and sky. His early oil paintings explored familiar Romantic themes of maritime disaster, but the dozens of sketches and watercolour studies he completed in Margate in the 1830s captured the elemental drama of sea and sky as never before. As an undergraduate geography student at Birmingham in the 1980s I listened to John Thornes, lecturer in meteorology, waxing lyrical about Turner's acute sensitivity to atmospheric changes. He told us that Constable was well versed in meteorological science but opined that Turner better succeeded in communicating the powerful forces of nature, revelling in the chaotic and changeable nature of weather.[26] Indeed, Turner described the swirling skies of the Isle of Thanet as the loveliest in all Europe, suggesting that Margate had a strong attraction that exceeded the charms of Sophia Booth.

The idea of a Margate gallery to celebrate Turner's legacy emerged in the 1990s when local resident and former chair of the Civic Society John Crofts approached the Tate to see if it might loan some of its collection to the town. Out of these discussions, the idea of a Turner Centre slowly took shape, with the local council commissioning the former director of Birmingham's IKON Gallery to explore development options. A major architectural competition was launched in 2001, part-funded by Kent County Council. The winning scheme, submitted by Norwegian architects Snøhetta and London-based Spence Associates, was heralded as Margate's attempt to invoke the 'Bilbao effect', using a bold architectural design to mark out a cultural renaissance in the same way that Frank Gehry's Guggenheim had done for the Spanish town. This design, chosen from more than 150 entries, envisaged an iconic fin-shaped gallery situated on the harbour arm itself, exposing it to the full force of the seas that Turner so often captured. Locals were sceptical whether the gallery could survive at this location, where the North Sea meets the English Channel and the seas are often at their roughest. Estimates began to come in suggesting that the gallery would cost millions to repaint every ten years or so, with a six-metre high test 'obelisk' (unflatteringly referred to as 'Turner's Prick' by some locals) blowing over on the first day of testing, prompting national headlines ('Gallery 0, North Sea 1').[27] As the projected budgets soared, Kent County Council and Thanet District Council decided on a costly but necessary legal action to recoup design fees as estimates of the build cost nearly doubled from £30 to £50 million. The replacement scheme was the eminently more sensible David Chipperfield-designed gallery, located not on the harbour arm but closer to the seafront location of Booth's lodging house, and less exposed to the elements. In effect, this was a smaller version of the gallery that Chipperfield was developing at the same time in Wakefield to house the Hepworth collection, albeit his Margate gallery was designed with wider expanses of glass and roof skylights to make it more open to the sea and sky that were so much the focus of Turner's art. Much of the national media was dubious about the value of an art gallery in a town with high levels of deprivation. Jonathan Glancey, then architectural critic for *The Guardian*, spoke of it as a '£7m gamble' to transform a town 'poorer than it should be' and 'too druggy for anyone's good' into a cultural mecca.[28] Many locals were equally unconvinced that the attempt to reinvent the town as the Bilbao of the Kent coast could ever succeed, especially given that the opening date moved ever backwards. Unofficial polls of residents suggested that the money could be better spent on a new hospital wing, an ice rink or, with no small amount of irony, an industrial-scale cannabis farm. But the local council, emboldened by Arts Council subsidies and the support of Kent County Council, stuck to its guns, believing that the project would stimulate investment and job creation across Thanet and have a 'major effect on Margate's potential as a destination'.[29] This put considerable faith in the creative industries to deliver seaside renaissance, buying into the New Labour rhetoric that proclaimed creativity as *the* symbol of a modern Britain: the *Mapping Creative Industries* report, published by the Department for Culture, Media and Sport in 1998, had established the idea that cultural regeneration was not just about providing outlets for creativity but about fashioning meaningful jobs.

The 2008 document commissioned by the Margate Renewal Partnership – *A Cultural Vision for Margate: The Next Ten Years* – underscored the commitment to producing a 'creative Margate'. This document spoke of embedding the Turner Contemporary in a creative milieu, contributing to a distinctive Margate 'brand' combining seaside heritage with a 'cultural narrative', but also insisting that Margate should be a town where 'culture is for everyone'. Putting art on the High Street was a key part of this, with the acquisition of the former Marks & Spencer store by Thanet District Council (at a cost of some £4.5 million) providing the

Turner Contemporary with a temporary home before the gallery proper opened to the public. Other vacant shops were also enlivened, with the 2009 *Window of Opportunity* project overseen by Emily Firmin – famously the original owner of *Bagpuss* – filling empty shopfronts with papier-mâché art suggesting how the premises might be used in the future. Counting down to the opening of the Turner Contemporary proper, the council put further money into tackling 'eyesore' buildings between the railway station and the gallery by working with artists to bring empty shops back into use. Heather Sawney, Arts Development Officer for Thanet District Council, led this, initially as part of the 'Margate Rocks' art festival. In her view, artists began to find that they were no longer simply begging for short, low-cost 'meanwhile' rentals, and began to be embraced as cultural pioneers.[30]

But when I visited the Turner a few weeks after its opening in 2011 I was underwhelmed. Compared to the initial design, Chipperfield's sheds on the seafront felt half-hearted. The art displayed inside was also a little lacklustre. The centrepiece was a little-known Turner oil painting – *The Eruption of the Souffrier Mountains in the Island of St Vincent* – which, despite its elemental and apocalyptic force, seemed to have little to do with Margate. The remaining small rooms were filled with installation art of a mainly abstract kind, including US-based but Kent-born artist Ellen Harvey's *Arcade/Arcadia* installation in the form of a shed designed to the proportion of Turner's studio, filled with images of contemporary, faded Margate, making a not-too-subtle connection between Turner's Margate and the present. Daniel Buren's *Borrowing and Multiplying the Landscape*, hung in front of the windows to frame the view out to the sea, was the most prominent work. With mirrors to each side, the yellow and grey columns of Buren's circular installation drew the gaze to what Chipperfield's design sought to play up – the relation between the building, the sea and the sky. Turning its back on Margate's sands, the gallery forced the visitor to engage with the vista ahead, with Buren's installation also helpfully obscuring

3.4 The Turner Contemporary, Margate

the car park between the gallery and the sea. But visited on a dull winter's day, the vista was less than appealing, and the outside spaces grey and uninviting.

However, even in 2011 it was clear that the buzz associated with the cultural activities led by the Turner Contemporary (as well as smaller, local arts organisations including The Pie Factory, Limbo and Crate) were having a transformational effect on the town's reputation, with many encouraged to visit Margate for the first time. Subsequent exhibitions, particularly the conjoined Turner–Tracey Emin show based around her infamous £2.5 million 'My bed' installation, were more crowd-pleasing and kept the visitors coming. A 2016 report conducted by Canterbury Christ Church University estimated that for every £1 invested in the Turner, £2.88 of 'social value' was created.[31] By 2018 nearly three million people had visited, generating an estimated £68 million for the local economy, and securing an estimated 155 jobs in the locality.[32] Given these figures, it was unsurprising that the House of Lords Select Committee on Seaside Regeneration proclaimed the Turner a success, concluding in 2018 that 'the creative industries have a clear role in supporting seaside towns to diversify their economies and enhance their local cultural assets'.[33]

It is easy to be cynical about reports that bestow on creative work the magical ability to regenerate place, and reports based on dubious estimates of the 'value added' by art. But there is little question that there has been a 'Turner effect' in Margate, most palpable in the fact that some previously boarded-up and down-at-heel businesses have gone upmarket, with parts of the Old Town, the seafront and Cliftonville experiencing rapid retail gentrification as a new breed of entrepreneurs and creatives have moved in. In 2015 men's style magazine *Esquire* ran a 'city guide' to Margate, profiling the Breur & Dawson vintage shop, the conversion of a former Superdrug chemist into The Sands boutique hotel, and Haeckels, a business which makes cosmetics and beard oil products out of local seaweeds. Other new hipster businesses have emerged – a record shop specialising in mondo horror soundtracks, a coffee shop integrating a yoga studio, and a 'curated' vintage store selling prints and curios. Margate has begun to feel less like the Kent coast and more like Zone 10 London, a seaside Hackney Wick to Whitstable's Islington:

> Margate [once] felt like a brutish, irredeemable place but last summer I'd heard enough positive mentions of it to make me wonder whether this seaside town that had been in freefall for as long as anyone could remember had finally found its bounce: conversations turned on its new 'arty' vibe, people moving there, people even calling it 'Shoreditch-on-Sea' … Men in sharp black Harrington jackets with tartan lining, side-burned and mod-cropped, were drinking pints that glowed amber in the sun outside a bar proudly displaying a Northern Soul fist and a Trojan Records logo on its front … They looked fucking cool, too: an alternative style cult … up-cycling that old spirit of south coast youth culture that Margate was a midwife to. A side street into the Old Town showed a … decidedly more

bourgeois side to this retro-modernist current bubbling away in
Margate: a mid-century Danish furniture shop, a craft beer pub, a
'Delivery to London' sign in a yard with vintage bathtubs and
Seventies reclining chairs.[34]

The idea that Margate is a 'sandy hipster paradise' has clearly caught
on, with the 2015 *Rough Guide* improbably proclaiming Margate
one of the world's top 10 must-see locations. Journalists who once
described Margate through narratives of despair and deprivation
now returned to extol the virtues of the town's arts-based regeneration, depicting it as a cultural renaissance for the English seaside.

Jellyfish, directed by James Gardner (2018), offers a more sanguine
account. A somewhat grimy drama in the 'kitchen sink' tradition,
the story focuses on 15-year-old schoolgirl Sarah (Liv Hill) whose
'speedbump' of a mother suffers from bipolar depression and spends
most of the days in bed while expecting her daughter to look after
and feed her younger sister. Working in a local amusement arcade,
Sarah resorts to supporting her mother by offering hand-jobs to
punters in a back alley behind the bins, with the discovery of this
by her manager leading to a devastating scene in which she is
raped (the camera literally fleeing the scene in disgust, retreating
into the amusement arcade packed with 'Tom and Jerry' slot
machines and soft toys that remind us of Sarah's age). But *Jellyfish*
is not just a poverty safari and makes a series of trenchant observations about the big money coming to town. Gardner has stated
that *Jellyfish* is set in Margate because it is 'a place that's been
caught up in the gentrification process, and what is interesting to
me is that a family like Sarah's, on the fringes of society, were
caught up in it', continuing to explain that 'although the film is
not explicitly about the Margate gentrification process, it does put
it in a very specific social context'.[35] In one scene Sarah is chatted
up in a nightclub by a developer who boasts of selling ex-council
flats and 'former crack dens' for enormous profits. As he puts it,
'It's a fucking gold mine and I'm buying the ground floor'. He
boasts about his modus operandi: 'Strip. Renovate. Repeat.' In a

scene that speaks of local refusal to be caught up in the obscene processes of accumulation through dispossession, Sarah reveals that she is underage, and extracts some of his profits from him by threatening to tell his wife that he flirts with 15-year-old girls in nightclubs.

In the film's climax, Sarah hijacks the school's end-of-year drama show to deliver a foul-mouthed comedy routine in which she decries the hypocrisy of those who welcome the 'Down from Londons' ('the ones with their own teeth', she quips) while ignoring the families reliant on the local food bank. Her rant about the arts-led regeneration of the town ('They say it's going to be the new Brighton!') ends with a painful joke about the Turner Gallery: 'It's hard to believe Tina Turner had time to do all those paintings.' In that simple moment, the film questions the valorisation of a particular notion of culture. Indeed, much of the talk around the 'creative renaissance' of Margate unwittingly divides the town's inhabitants into the so-called 'creative class', deemed to have the capacity to engage with designated creative spaces, and the 'uncreative' classes who populate the more 'ordinary' parts of the town. This of course ignores the multiple ways in which communities are produced through all manner of improvisation, creativity and everyday cultures of resistance.

This noted, it seems that culture-led regeneration has had many positive effects in the town. Margate today seems a much more vibrant place compared with the, admittedly rather grey, day in 2011 when I visited the Turner Contemporary for the first time. In the interim, I had many conversations with lecturer friends from Canterbury and Whitstable who told me about a great new pizza place in Margate (of all places!) or enthused about a great reclamation yard where the owner would deliver pieces of 1950s furniture to anywhere in Kent for free. Clearly, the changing retail offer of the Old Town has proved a significant draw, giving middle-class visitors from across Kent, as well as the DFLs, something to do after they have spent their obligatory thirty minutes or so in the

3.5 Dreamland, Margate

Turner. The publicity surrounding the Wayne Hemingway-revamped Dreamland has been another important fillip for the town, with this retro amusement park having reopened in 2015 to provide a playful counterbalance to the high culture on offer at the Turner.[36]

Bohemia-on-Sea

In the wake of the Turner Contemporary and the reawakened Dreamland, Margate seems to have carved out a new identity, no longer known as a faded seaside town but one that combines retro chic, cheeky seaside fun, designer cool and edgy bohemianism. Nothing perhaps signifies this better than the 2020 opening of the Albion Rooms hotel by indie band The Libertines. Emerging from the arse-end of 1990s Britpop, The Libertines developed a reputation for ramshackle indie guitar pop combining The Clash's ear for working-class sloganry with The Smiths' emaciated aestheticism. Described as equal parts Dickensian street urchins and Wildean

dandies, the band built up a loyal audience in the London East
End club scene at the turn of the century, renting a former brothel
studio-cum-flat in Bethnal Green christened 'The Albion Rooms',
before they broke through with Top 40 hits including 'Up the
Bracket' and 'Can't Stand Me Now'. The combustible relationship between the Kate Moss-dating, heroin-using lead singer Pete
Doherty and guitarist Carl Barat led to multiple break-ups and
reunions, including a celebratory 2004 gig at the Tap and Tin
pub in Chatham, Kent, following Doherty's release from prison
following his conviction for theft.

As part of their co-option of English literary traditions, especially
the visionary poetry of William Blake, The Libertines developed
an originary myth that suggested they were steering the 'good ship
Albion' to the promised land of Arcadia. This imagery was threaded
through their music via lyrical references to England's Anglo-Saxon
pasts, to Boudicca and Queen Victoria, suggesting that they were
inheritors of a particular English spirit.[37] One song even referred to
Napoleon as the 'first anti-Christ' ('Revelations', 2002). In various
interviews, the band explained some of their preoccupation with
the England of yesteryear as about wanting to live in a community
of 'dignity and respect', their songs also referencing kitchen sink
dramas of the 1960s, the comedy of Galton and Simpson, and
The Likely Lads. Tellingly, Doherty and bandmates jammed Chas &
Dave songs in soundchecks and in 2018 put them on the bill during
their takeover of the *Wheels and Fins* music festival in Broadstairs.
All of this suggests a rejection of contemporary cosmopolitanism
and 'soft' foreign cultures, and a celebration of a more rumbustious
and ultimately gendered version of white Englishness in which the
figure of the loveable Cockney rogue looms large.[38]

Given this preoccupation with a faded and even discredited
version of the past, The Libertines' decision to open a hotel in
Margate is readily explicable. In many ways it fits their image of
frayed Englishness: Margate is a resort that still feels slightly seedy
and depressed, but which has a rich social and cultural history ripe

for rediscovery (coincidentally, T. S. Eliot wrote his epic poem *The Waste Land* while convalescing in the Abermarle Hotel just two doors' down from the Albion Rooms). The hotel itself, complete with a William Blake-themed bedroom, recording studio and coffee house, has been variously described as a 'rock and roll hotel', a gentrified flophouse and an Arcadian seaside escape. Rooms are swathed in Gothic velvet, feature Nimbus brass bedsteads and are decorated with skulls, stuffed animals and leopard prints. The restaurant, run by ex-Soho House chef Joe Hill, offers a five-course menu complete with local offerings including Whitstable oysters and Romney Marsh lamb. Residents are provided with an Apple Beats sound system and the bathroom soap is made of Margate seaweed. This suggests that the hotel is aimed at a particular type of Londoner looking for a luxurious weekend escape with a difference – a thirty-something couple, perhaps, hoping to recapture the pre-gentrification atmosphere they experienced in millennial Hackney and Dalston, neighbourhoods where they constructed their own urban pastoral fantasies among the 'ruins' of the inner city.[39] It panders to the bourgeois imagination that feeds off the slightly illicit excitement that comes from being exposed to a little bit of the 'other'. In that sense, the Albion Rooms umbilically links Margate to bohemian London, encouraging further hipster gentrification. However, Doherty denies this, suggesting that

> it's never going to be hipster because you've got that smell that the sea gives out twice a day ... that's why Margate will never be gentrified. However, there is art-led regeneration. We're part of that because it was affordable. You know, we're never going to open a hotel in Old Street or anything like that.[40]

Doherty is a divisive figure, and the fact his dogs mauled a local resident's cat to death did little to enhance his reputation with his new neighbours. Clearly a fantasist, he is at least intelligent enough to realise that some of the Albion imagery he has played with was seized by the far right in the run-up to Brexit. One notable example is *Dark Albion: A Requiem for the English*, written by 'cockney pensioner'

David Abbott, who writes under the alias Man of Kent on the British National Party website. Endorsed by sometime BNP leader Nick Griffin as an 'underground classic', the book has chapters on the origins of the English people, linking this to the arrival of Horsa and Hengist in Pegwell Bay in 449 (the cover depicts the white cliffs of Pegwell Bay and Cliffsend to reinforce the point). Elsewhere it connects the 'browning' of London to the rise of a 'woke' political elite including Sadiq Khan, Baroness Warsi and Keith Vaz, and speculates on England in 2066, with the Union Jack replaced by the Union Mohammed. Published out of Ramsgate, the book is an overtly racist attempt to attach myths of decline to anti-migrant discourse, but by no means an isolated one. Indeed, there have been many studies of the British coastline that suggest that the decline of seaside economies has fuelled localised anxiety over both migration and multiculturalism.[41] The fact that Margate has more than its fair share of reactionary nationalists is something it has in common with some of the other coastal communities that have been depicted – unfairly or not – as embodying the essence of Brexitland.[42]

Margate was not the most pro-Leave area of Kent, but it did vote 64% in favour of Brexit.[43] Notably, Nigel Farage stood as a parliamentary candidate in Thanet South in 2015, with the Conservative Party losing control of the council to UKIP in the same year. That Thanet was the first council in the country to be captured by UKIP appeared to speak of the existence of a large pool of dissatisfied voters who felt abandoned by the main political parties. It also hints at the racial tensions simmering in Margate, with Eastern European migrants often scapegoated as the source of local problems. This sometimes manifests in overt racism. Britain First members reportedly took an armoured Land Rover to the streets to 'protect' Farage when he was out canvassing in 2015, and a White Lives Matter protest was organised in 2016. Thanet has serious form in this regard, with David Seabrook writing of the area's connections to Oswald Mosley's Union of Fascists in the 1930s in *All the Devils are Here*. The reputation echoes down the years. When visiting Margate I was often told to avoid a couple of bars known to be hang-outs for the English Defence League. Racially motivated attacks remain common, with Labour councillor Aram Rawf, who came to Thanet as an Iraqi Kurdish refugee, suggesting that rates in this part of Kent are among the highest in the country.[44] And while UKIP lost all its seats on the council in 2019, some councillors continue to endorse anti-migrant policies. In 2019 Conservative councillor Paul Messenger suggested on social media that the benefits payments given to Muslim families were allowing them to produce large families so that they could launch an 'Islamic State type takeover'.[45] In March 2020, as coronavirus reached the UK, a Chinese student from King's College visiting the town was assaulted by young people who coughed and spat in his face, making jokes about him carrying the 'Chinese plague'.[46] 'White Lives Matter' graffiti and swastikas were plastered across properties in Cliftonville in July of the same year as the world reeled in the wake of the murder of George Floyd.[47]

Such incidents suggest that Margate remains a space where exclusionary myths of national belonging continue to circulate, and where class resentment and alienation is sometimes expressed in racism of the nastiest kind. But the town's burgeoning art scene has helped here, opening up conversations about belonging and identity which need to be had. The *Arrivals* project in 2005, for instance, involved artists from the eight Eastern European nations that had just joined the EU, while in 2006 the *Unite* project brought young French artists to Margate at the same time that British artist Bob and Roberta Smith (aka Patrick Brill) oversaw the *Should I Stay or Should I Go?* initiative, which involved the hanging of colourful banners along Margate High Street posing rhetorical questions: 'Britain or Brittany? The Arctic Monkeys or Mantovani? Kent or Cornwall?' Other projects have also explored Margate's attempts to deal with issues of immigration, with London-based arts group Artangel commissioning artists to collaborate in a one-day arts-based festival, *Exodus* (2006). Part of this comprised the hanging of banner portraits around the town of 22 children who had come to Margate from Congo, Iraq, Egypt and Eastern Europe. This *Towards a Promised Land* project also saw Wendy Eward working with these young people to produce their own art, ultimately hung in a local gallery.[48] The centrepiece, however, was an immersive piece of street theatre retelling the Book of Exodus, in which the tale of one man's attempts to banish refugees, drug users and the homeless from his kingdom culminated in the burning of Antony Gormley's 25-metre high *Waste Man* in the grounds of the (then) defunct Dreamland funfair. This sculpture was constructed from the detritus of modern consumer society – planks of wood, tables, paintings, chairs, keyboards, dartboards, a front door, toilet seats, all donated by local people.

These artworks have, however, left little trace on the landscape. One memorial that does persist though is of a lifeboatman looking out to sea, directly opposite Margate railway station – it is one of

3.6 Michael Rakowitz, *April is the Cruellest Month*

the first things a visitor to the town sees, being practically adjacent to the weather-beaten and inauspicious seaside shelter, now Grade II listed, where T. S. Eliot sat writing the third part of *The Waste Land* ('On Margate Sands, I can connect, Nothing with nothing'). Sculpted by Frederick Callcott, it was erected in 1897 following the capsizing of the lifeboat *Friend to All Nations*, with the loss of nine of the thirteen lifeboatmen on board. It is alongside this sculpture that US-Iraqi artist Michael Rakowitz was commissioned to create an artwork for Margate as part of the 2020 English Creative Coast *Waterfront* project (coordinated by the Turner and other regional arts organisations, including Creative Folkestone, the Hasting Contemporary and Gravesend's Cement Fields). Rakowitz's Margate anti-war memorial, *April is the Cruellest Month*, was inspired by a 1989 tribute unveiled on the corniche in Basra, consisting of 80 bronze sculptures of Iraqi soldiers killed in the Iran–Iraq War: each sculpture pointed across the Shatt Al Arab river to Iran, where they died. When the British army invaded Basra in 2003, the statues were dismantled. Some ended up in monument 'graveyards' across Iraq while others were destroyed. Rakowitz stated that 'Instead of simply rebuilding one of the 80 original sculptures, I am introducing an 81st modelled on the likeness of Daniel Taylor, who served with the Royal Artillery in Basra, Iraq, during the 2003 invasion and, through this sculpture, literally stands in solidarity with the Iraqi people.'[49] Echoing the stance of the lifeboatman peering out to sea, the soldier points out towards Iraq. A plaque on the base of the statue includes a quote from the English poet and soldier Siegfried Sassoon: 'I am a soldier, convinced that I am acting on behalf of soldiers. I believe that this war, on which I entered as a war of defence and liberation, has now become a war of aggression and conquest.'[50] In a town where people too often connect nothing with nothing, this at least seems like a worthy attempt to connect something with something.

4

Defending the nation

Vanguard of Liberty, ye men of Kent,
Ye children of a Soil that doth advance
Her haughty brow against the coast of France,
Now is the time to prove your hardiment!
            William Wordsworth, 'To the Men of Kent', 1807[1]

On the Kent coast, the rise and fall of the tide peels away the
layers of history. Beachcombers regularly find treasure from offshore
shipwrecks, some of them dating as far back as the early medieval
period. Pieces of amber, musketballs and clay pipes are ten-a-penny,
but some finds attract national headlines. In 2018 a group of local
history enthusiasts skirting Whitstable's Tankerton Beach, searching
for the remains of World War II pillboxes, spotted the outline of
a boat in the mudflats. Subsequent archaeological work found it
to be a well-preserved Tudor merchant ship, possibly from the
sixteenth century and thought to be carrying copperas (green vitriol)
at the time of its sinking, indicating the importance of the beach-side
extraction of this chemical dye fixative at the time. More recent
shipwrecks have held deadlier cargo. In 1946, the Polish munitions
ship SS *Kielce* sank four miles off the coast of Kent following a
collision with a steamer. When the Folkestone Salvage Company
used explosive charges to open the hull to remove its payload in
July 1967, the ensuing blast measured 4.5 on the Richter scale and
created a six-metre-deep crater on the seabed, breaking windows

and dislodging tiles in Folkestone itself.[2] The tidal wave that struck the seafront in Folkestone that day did thousands of pounds' worth of damage, causing sunbathers to scatter in panic.

Some of these wrecks remain a threat. The most famous is the US 'liberty ship' SS *Richard Montgomery*, which went down a mile off Sheerness in 1944 with more than 6,000 tonnes of live ammunition on board. While most was removed after the war, nearly 2,000 tonnes remain, inaccessible to salvage teams in the slowly deteriorating hull. Although its rusting masts are constantly visible above low water, there have been several near misses when passing ships have come frighteningly close to the wreck, meaning that the threat of an explosion (and an estimated five-metre-high tsunami inundating the low-lying Isle of Sheppey) remains constant.[3] The German writer Uwe Johnson, who spent his final years holed up in Sheerness drinking himself to death, became preoccupied the risk of an explosion, using this as the basis of his 1979 essay 'Ein unergründliches Schiff' ('An unfathomable ship').[4] The SS *Richard Montgomery* and its deadly cargo remain well known to Sheerness residents, woven into a self-deprecating discourse that acknowledges Sheppey as an unfashionable and maligned place: Dan Tweedy's 40-foot mural on the walls of a local park depicts a sulky mermaid poised over a detonator attached to the hulk of the ship, proclaiming 'Come to Sheerness – You'll have a blast.' But it is not only here that wartime munitions pose a risk on the Kent coast. Metal detectorists and mudlarkers regularly unearth munitions, smoke shells and high explosive rounds. In 2020, for example, eleven unexploded munitions were uncovered at Sandwich Bay, and the next month a father and his two sons found a shell on Folkestone Warren Beach which, when picked up, began to emit white smoke. They quickly buried it again before retreating to the safety of their car. The bomb squad subsequently indicated that it was a phosphorus mortar shell from World War II.

Some of the largest bombs found on the Kent coast were, however, never live. Fragments of concrete-filled barrel bombs (or 'bouncing

4.1 Dan Tweedy, *The Sheerness Mermaid*

bombs') are regularly found at Reculver, near Herne Bay. It was here that some of the final tests of Barnes Wallis's 'Highball' prototype were carried out in 1943, the location being relatively remote and the sea shallow enough that the bombs could, theoretically, be retrieved in the event of sinking to the seabed. Designed to target German cruisers stationed in Norwegian fjords, the bombs were adapted for the 'dambusters' raids on the Möhne, Sorpe and Eder dams that targeted the German industrial heartlands. Over 1,600 people died in the raids, including an estimated 1,000 Russian prisoners-of-war, half of them women. Fifty-three airmen also died, with nearly half the Lancaster bombers shot down. Immortalised in Michael Anderson's 1955 film *The Dam Busters*, the attacks have become iconic of British wartime ingenuity and courage. These are celebrated locally through an exhibit in the Herne Bay town museum, while the Bouncing Barrel micropub, opened in 2013, is adorned with images of the RAF raid. In 2018 a statue of Barnes Wallis was unveiled on Herne Bay's seafront, immediately attracting criticism from the right-wing tabloids for referring to the raids as 'infamous' rather than 'famous'. Responding, the person responsible for the inscription reportedly commented that 'You wouldn't describe them as famous if you were German.'[5]

There is surely no more potent reminder of Kent's wartime past than the bombs and munitions washed up on the shore. In many ways they signify the eternal return of war, being an uncanny reminder of the legacies of conflict. Marianna Torovnick refers to the idea of 'wartime consciousness' as something than can persist long after hostilities are over.[6] In this chapter I elaborate on this idea, suggesting that the palpable, material reminders of war on the Kent coast perform particular forms of 'memory work', linking local senses of place to past military endeavours that loop back into the present. This argument is, of course, contestable. Kent is certainly not a heavily militarised county in the same way that the Hampshire/Surrey borderlands of Aldershot, Camberley and Farnborough are, studded as they are with barracks, military museums and training facilities. Similarly, Kent lacks the constant reminders of military activity found on Salisbury Plain, where tanks and armoured cars churn up the chalk downlands, or the 'tactical training areas' of Wales and Scotland where low-flying jets regularly shatter the peace and quiet.[7] But looking more closely, it is apparent that the mundane scenery of the Kent coast does not just conceal unspent munitions, being pockmarked with multiple reminders of a sometimes violent history of aggression and defence.

From the late Middle Ages onwards, much of the north coast of Kent, from Belvedere down to Faversham, constituted a significant chain in a British military-industrial archipelago of shipbuilding, munitions and gunpowder production bound into networks of colonial trade, slavery and warmongering. Chatham Dockyards was in many ways the focus of this activity, and remains a popular tourist attraction that has unsuccessfully lobbied for UNESCO World Heritage status on several occasion. It finally ceased operations in 1984 after having built over 500 ships and submarines for the British Navy. In the Napoleonic era, huge earthworks, gun emplacements and defensive walls were constructed to defend the docks, the 'Great Lines' subsequently refortified by the Royal Engineers, who moved their training college to nearby Brompton in 1855. Brompton Barracks is now the only operational military installation in Kent. Sheerness Barracks, next to the dockyard, closed in 1960, the Royal Marines left Deal for Portsmouth in 1996 and Shorncliffe Barracks near Folkestone closed in 2016. Controversially, Howe Barracks in Canterbury was leased by the Ministry of Defence in 2015 to the London Borough of Redbridge, which now uses it to house tenants for whom there are no homes left in their borough. Lodge Hill Ordnance Depot, near Chatham, remains for sale, saved from the threat of housing development by the discovery of 85 pairs of nightingales. Most recently a bomb disposal training site, in 2020 it was used for the filming of a *Batman* movie.

Away from Chatham Dockyards it is arguably on the coast facing the continent that one becomes most acutely aware of Kent's role in defending the nation. Ever since Julius Caesar made landfall in 55 BC, this coast has been fortified on multiple occasions to defend against foreign invasions. At Richborough archaeologists have excavated parts of a 700-metre-long Roman defensive wall thought to be the original base for the Claudian invasion of AD 43. Two centuries later, the by-then large civilian town of Richborough itself was converted into a five-acre fort to defend against the Saxon invaders, its walls eight metres high in places. Other Saxon Shore forts were built by the Romans at Lympne, Dover and Reculver. Subsequently, the coast was fortified by Henry VIII's castles at Sandgate, Deal and Walmer; a run of 27 stocky Martello Towers arrayed along the shoreline between 1805 and 1809; the 28-mile Royal Military Canal running from Iden to Seabrook as a defence during the Napoleonic Wars; World War I anti-invasion trenches, infantry blockhouses and gun emplacements; World War II sea forts and anti-tank concrete blocks; coastal pillboxes; Cold War radar stations; civil defence observation posts; and nuclear bunkers. Arguably, the security fences and CCTV surveillance that surrounds the Eurotunnel constitutes the latest fortification of the coast. All

4.2 Pillboxes, Warden Point

this defensive architecture marks Kent out not as the Garden of England but as the Guardian of England. Fortress Kent. The Bulwark Shore.

The key to England

In her insightful analysis of the geopolitics of the Channel Tunnel, legal scholar Eve Darian-Smith proposes that Kent's identity as the embodiment of historical rural England is one that has relied on it being imaginatively distanced from the landscapes and cultures located across the narrow strip of the English Channel. She suggests that its inhabitants have invested in a powerful and emotive mythology that establishes the Garden of England as a sacrosanct landscape, a buffer zone between the national seat of governance in London and foreign territories that needs to be maintained at all costs. Darian-Smith proceeds to argue that successive threats from overseas – whether in the form of rabid rats, cheap imports or flows of 'illegal' immigrants – have been depicted by the county's residents as existential threats, described through metaphors of invasion.[8] These metaphors resonate powerfully because of Kent's historical role as the military frontline at many points in British history. It is this history that is embodied in the many memorials, monuments and military structures arrayed around the coastline.

Nowhere is Kent's militarised and defensive coastline more obvious than at Dover itself, where Britain's largest castle looms over the docks. Traditionally described as 'the key to England', its immense earthworks and walls enclose a Roman lighthouse, an impressive Norman keep and a labyrinthine series of defensive Napoleonic tunnels that were repurposed as military hospitals and command centres in both World Wars. Sold as part of the 'White Cliffs Experience', a series of multimedia exhibits describe how these tunnels were used to mastermind the 1940 Dunkirk evacuation when a flotilla of 800 boats rescued 300,000 British troops from the beaches of northern France. Part of the Cold War Civil Defence Corps control room has now been turned into an 'escape room', challenging participants to secure the bunker before enemy missiles strike. Another part of the tunnels has been turned into an interactive exhibition where a nurse guides visitors through a series of rooms documenting the journey of a World War II pilot fighting for his life.

Dover Castle today is a curious site. It is a heritage theme park of sorts, allowing families to dip into different periods of history, with regular re-enactments and tours led by costumed interpreters. But it is also a site that narrates a particular version of English history, not one of ordinary folk and working lives but of great men and great battles. Although there is a strong emphasis on individual sacrifices and the violence of war, many of the attractions clearly pander to the nationalist sentiments of those who still regard World War II as the country's finest hour. A German friend of mine visibly blanched when describing his visit there, recounting that the educational materials given to his children felt grounded in the kind of *Boy's Own* 'Tommy vs Fritz' stereotypes he had not encountered since the 1970s. On one of my many visits I was surprised to see that the castle keep had been given over to a James Bond exhibition, ostensibly playing on Ian Fleming's links to Kent (he lived just outside Canterbury, as legend has it on the 007 bus route to Sandwich). Yet, in many ways, Bond is an icon of a particular type of Britishness, written by Fleming as a quintessentially English action hero defending the nation against the threat of godless communism during the Cold War: tellingly, one of the earliest James Bond novels, *Moonraker*, has the traitorous Hugo Drax attempting to trigger a landslide on Dover's white cliffs as Bond swims below. Exhibits like this, consciously or otherwise, cement the idea that a particular form of patriotic heroism has been needed to ensure that the nation is defended from the evils that emanate from overseas.

This noted, there is little question that the people of Dover made enormous sacrifices in times of war. In World War II Dover was colloquially known as Hellfire Corner. Following the first raids of 1940, local children were evacuated to rural Sussex and the town's population shrank from around 40,000 to a little over 16,000. Despite this, nearly two hundred civilians were killed by bombing in the town, and nine hundred properties wrecked, making it among the most badly bombed British towns. Post-war, much of what survived was beyond repair, necessitating mass demolition and rebuilding. Renowned planner Patrick Abercrombie, who oversaw the rebuilding of Hull, Plymouth and Bath, advised Dover Council to replace the destroyed esplanade and Marine Parade with open gardens, linking town and harbour, to ensure that the town would function as both resort and port. Unfortunately, despite the protestations of the Royal Fine Arts Commission, a nine-storey block of flats was built which still dominates the seafront some sixty years later, cutting off the town from the coast, meaning that the sea is no longer visible to those shopping in and around Dover's town centre. Any pretence Dover might have ever had to be a resort

4.3 Dover Castle

town was lost. The pier, erected in 1893 for tourists wanting to take a steamboat down to Hastings, was damaged in 1925 and demolished shortly afterwards. Other signs of Dover's tourist industry (the ice rink, the Grand Hotel and the elegant sweep of the Georgian Marine Parade) are also long gone.

Dover today is rarely described in glowing terms, even by those who live there. Despite piecemeal efforts to regenerate the 'Old Town', the legacy of bad planning and the economic decline of the ferry business and local paper mills is palpable in boarded-up shops and crumbling pubs. The town also has some of the most affordable housing in Kent, arrayed in parallel streets of nineteenth-century terraces built for port workers and paper mill labourers, with one regularly topping polls of the most dangerous street in the county, reputedly marked by cannabis factories and violent altercations. The juxtaposition of this very ordinary town and its extraordinary defences is one that creates a distinctive sense of place. As well as Dover Castle, perched on the white cliffs, there is Fort Burgoyne, a Napoleonic-era 'Palmerston' fort defending the town from attack from the north; a series of World War II bunkers along the Canterbury Road at Lydden Hill; and, standing proud above the town, the Swingate Chain Home Radar Station, an early warning system built in 1936 to forewarn of potential enemy attacks. Four towers were built, nearly four hundred feet tall. Of these, only two remain, one decked in microwave transmitters which link the Frankfurt stock exchange to the Euronext datacentre in Basildon, enabling high-frequency trading.

To the west of the town, on the elongated hill between the River Dour valley and the Western Docks, there are yet more fortifications. The Western Heights rise vertiginously above the town, built on the site of a former Roman lighthouse in the Napoleonic era. These defences comprise a series of ditches, 50 feet deep and lined with red brick, designed to be swept with artillery fire in the event of invasion. Though not particularly noticeable to the many car-borne travellers passing through the town, the Western Heights fortifications are more extensive than Dover Castle itself, having played an arguably equally significant role in the defence of the town. By 1864 they were home to upwards of 4,000 troops and were defended by one hundred and sixty guns. During World War II the central Drop Redoubt became a lookout post surveying long-range shelling from France, with the tunnels beneath the ground here serving as operations centres. Post-war, it was used as the filming location for Pater Watkin's 1965 controversial *War Game*, which depicted the aftermath of a nuclear strike on RAF Manston. Following that, it fell gradually into disuse, and became an illegal dumping ground, but the impressive Citadel at the heart of the complex was converted to a prison, and latterly, between 2001 and 2016, was used as an Immigration Removal Centre for those seeking asylum on arrival in the UK. Visiting the site in 2015, David Herd, Professor of English and organiser of the Refugee Tales project, noted that the English Heritage information boards that surrounded the site were oddly silent about this function, as if embarrassed by the fact that asylum seekers fleeing conflict were being kept in a grim, prison-like structure.[9] An unannounced inspection of the facilities by the Prison Inspectorate in 2014 concluded that:

> A recurring theme of our inspection was that Dover looked and felt like a prison and was too often run like one, even though it held low-risk detainees who were not serving sentences for criminal offences. Some aspects of physical security were excessive, and Dover is probably the last custodial facility in Britain that is still surrounded by a moat. Procedural security sometimes lacked proportionality. The reward scheme was inappropriate and worse, its application punitive.[10]

Clearly not fit for purpose, the centre nonetheless became the subject of lurid media headlines. In 2015 *The Sun* ran a story describing the construction of a '£4m dental suite' at the centre, arguing that 'illegals' were leaving with gleaming teeth while 'locals' faced six-week waits for treatment. A worker at the centre was quoted: 'When these people go home they've got better teeth than my family', continuing 'the way we cater to their needs is out of control'.[11]

In an editorial written on the day after Brexit, journalist Patrick Cockburn suggested that the view from the Western Heights takes in many of the key features shaping British life in the age of Brexit and COVID-19. Here he shifts focus from France, just across the Channel, to the town below, suggesting that Dover residents felt that the EU had done nothing good for the town, with forty-eight years of membership coinciding with the decline of maritime services, the closure of the town's paper mills and rising unemployment. Describing the town as 'moribund', Cockburn concludes that the EU became the scapegoat for this decline, with Brexit the convenient vehicle that expressed local grievances:

> Dover provides a telling parable about modern England because it not only contains side-by-side examples of the success and failure of globalisation, but it is filled with reminders of a more glorious past. Henry II's magnificent 12th century fortress, the greatest medieval castle in the country, is close to the headquarters of the Dunkirk evacuation, dug deep into the White Cliffs. Both sustain

the nationalist conviction that Britain is better off on its own. But an undiluted diet of ancient victories and achievements, with all the defeats and humiliations left out, fosters an over-confidence based on wishful thinking about the real world and a dangerously misleading belief that 'we did it before and we can do it again'.[12]

Here, Cockburn is not conflating provincialism with parochialism, but insisting that the world has changed in ways that have sometimes been hard to grasp for those at the sharp end of deindustrialisation. As has been more widely noted, the Leave mantra of 'Take Back Control' had obvious appeal for those feeling 'left behind', with the exclusionary nationalism peddled by Farage and others painting a seductive vision of an island retreating from a world that was no longer playing by 'English' rules.[13]

Listening to the landscape

Leaving the Western Heights, the North Downs Way dips down before rising precipitously again up to Round Down Cliff. Here there are dramatic views of the Channel and, behind the cliff, Farthingloe Valley, mythologised as the home of Sir Gawain and Lady Farthingloe at the time when King Arthur was defending the nation against Saxon invaders. More prosaically, it was here that, between 1988 and 1993, a thousand Eurotunnel workers were housed in temporary accommodation blocks that sprawled up the hillside. Nothing remains of those, and the chalk downland here appears somewhat windswept and inhospitable, the only obvious signs of human occupation an assortment of concrete remnants littering the hillsides. On closer investigation, it becomes clear that some of these are venting chimneys for the railway tunnels completed in 1844 for the Folkestone to Dover stretch of the Southeastern mainline. But the purpose and origins of some of the other obtruding concrete platforms and lookouts perched precariously atop the cliffs are less obvious, many vandalised or crumbling into the sea. Hougham Gun Battery, built in 1941 to house the 520 Coastal

4.4 Sound mirror, Abbot's Cliff

Regiment Royal Artillery, for example, has largely vanished, but miscellaneous lichen-encrusted pillboxes, platforms for anti-aircraft guns and several Nissen hut entrances remain as remnants of what was once an important fortress. More adventurous bunkerologists have been known to clamber down 20 feet of cliff face to access the timber-lined entrance that is the only way into the deep shelter situated beneath the battery observation point.

But perhaps the most striking military remnant on this stretch of coastline is the large concrete sound mirror at the top of Abbot's Cliff. This forerunner of radar resembles a 'listening ear', designed to concentrate into audibility those forms of distant noise (approaching aircraft engines, for instance) that would otherwise exist beyond the range of human hearing. Built in 1928, this appeared in Eric Ravilious' *Bombing the Channel Ports*, painted in 1941 during the period when he was a war artist based in Dover. A masterful composition of green and grey, it apes the pastoral tradition of English water-colourists such as J. M. W. Turner or Samuel Palmer by emphasising

89

the sinuous chalk ridges of the North Downs, but then subverts this through an emphasis on the alien and modern in the landscape. The sound mirror is at the centre of the picture, with the flat, lifeless Channel behind illuminated by searchlights and fire. A large, circular glow on the horizon suggests that a bomb has hit its target in Dover or Ramsgate.

Once part of the London Air Defence warning system, the mirror remains an unsettling presence in the landscape. Like many of the other derelict military sites and ruins along this stretch of the coast, it has been enthused over by bunkerologists and brutalists alike and has become oddly iconic in recent years. In Daisy Haggard's 2019 *Back to Life*, a BBC2 black comedy concerning a woman returning to her parents' home after eighteen years in prison, the sound mirror is the backdrop to a murder, with a young girl having her head smashed against it in a fit of rage. The sound mirror becomes a recurring motif in a story that often focuses on the lack of compassion and forgiveness shown towards outsiders in English society, and the failure to look for the good in people. In *Back to Life* the function and history of the sound mirror is never spoken of, but its obsolescence speaks to questions of modernity and Englishness, being woven into a wider narrative of national conservatism and denial (tellingly, Haggard's character is ostracised by her white neighbours, but embraced by her neighbour Billy, played by Adeel Akhtar, the first non-white actor to win the best actor award at the TV BAFTAs). The sound mirror is also used to explore related questions of identity and belonging in photographer Joe Pettet Smith's project *In Defence of Lost Causes* (named after a book by Slavoj Žižek) in which he reflects on an unproven family myth that his grandfather was the designer of these flawed technological innovations.[14]

For essayist and historian Brian Dillon, the fact that the sound mirrors never functioned effectively because of ambient noise, being abandoned long before World War II, makes their meaning even more undecipherable. He writes of the mirrors as persistent reminders of the failure of modernism, as objects that have simply lived too long.[15] Are these monuments to a failed modernity, perhaps? Or is our obvious fascination with their anachronistic forms related to continuing anxieties about threats that lie beyond our field of vision and that we cannot predict? Significantly, in 2019 performance artist Selina Bonelli used the sound mirror as the location for her 'recollecting fears' project, asking participants to reflect on the role of listening devices at a time when too many fail to listen and responsibility is offloaded on to Others: 'the migrant, the asylum seeker, the working-class'.[16] Such questions about Otherness arguably take on more weight in the wake of COVID-19, not least given the attempts by some politicians to frame coronavirus as a foreign threat, something that might be effectively countered not through improved public health and social care but through processes of re-bordering.[17] Here it is important to stress that COVID-19 not only contributed to racist stereotypes of minority groups, but happened in a context of 'already-pronounced xenophobia' and populist nationalism.[18] Sociologists Malcolm James and Sivamohan Valluvan draw out the irony here: nationalism intensified at the moment when the problems it was contending with were becoming inescapably immanent. As they write, 'just like the challenges of climate breakdown and capital's fleet-footed ability to escape govern-ance, the threat of pandemics requires a radically global and radically post-imperial scale of accountability and action'.[19] In some ways, then, the sound mirrors stand as a monument to the follies of exclusionary nationalisms in a post-imperial age.

Landscapes of remembrance

From Abbot's Cliff it is a twenty-minute walk along often crumbling clifftop paths to the Battle of Britain memorial at Capel-le-Ferne. Remarkably, this is one of three Battle of Britain museums in Kent (alongside one at Manston Airport focused on Spitfire and Hurricane aircraft, and a larger collection at Hawkinge which boasts artefacts from over 700 crashed aircraft). At Capel, the national Battle of Britain memorial sits on the site of a former airship-launching platform and gun battery, again commanding spectacular views over the Channel. Opened by the Queen Mother in 1993, the memorial is formed of a large propeller-shaped chalk insignia sunk into a circular grass amphitheatre. The proportions are not dissimilar to a Neolithic henge, suggesting a continuity of occupation here, with its creator Harry Gray suggesting that the chalk propeller alludes to earlier traditions of chalk art in the landscape, most notably the Uffington horse.[20] To the centre of the propeller there is a sculpture of a pilot, seated cross-legged, looking out to sea, with the badges of the 63 squadrons that participated in the Battle of Britain carved into the pedestal at the base. To the rear of the site is the Foxley-Norris memorial wall, its sombre black panels listing all those allied airmen who took part in the Battle, around 1,500 of whom died. It is a contemplative and moving memorial – the pilot gazes out to sea waiting for comrades who never returned as visitors move along the memorial wall looking for names of fathers, grandfathers, uncles and relatives who also made 'the ultimate sacrifice'.

There is nothing about this pilot that indicates his nationality or rank. Many descriptions on social media nonetheless assume that this is one of the 'few' – the RAF pilots who fought in the Battle of Britain. This is understandable – the Spitfire pilot has become a powerful personification of the English character, depicted as defiant, plucky and brave; the Spitfire itself has become a design icon, regarded as elegant and agile, a triumph of flowing, British organicism over the modern rationality of German engineering.[21] Manufactured initially by Supermarine in Woolston, Southampton, Kent has nonetheless claimed the Spitfire as its own. Kent was certainly the only county to have its own Spitfire squadron during the war, paid for by subscription and flying out of Biggin Hill. Many of the other Spitfires that fought in the Battle of Britain took off from Kent's wartime airfields, Hawkinge, Manston, Detling,

Dover, Headcorn and Brenzett among them. The memorial museum itself is shaped like a Spitfire wing and there is a full-size replica Spitfire alongside a Hurricane there. On the Isle of Thanet, Manston's Spitfire and Hurricane collection has a Spitfire simulator and one of the few remaining Spitfires to have seen wartime action. The Kent cricket team became the Kent Spitfires in 1999, sponsored by Shepherd Neame's Spitfire Ale ('the Bottle of Britain', launched in 1990). All of this helps consolidate the idea that World War II was fought over Kent, and that the few were fighting to defend the ways of life associated with the bucolic rurality of the Garden of England.

From the Battle of Britain memorial it is a steep descent to Folkestone through The Warren, the large country park created by successive collapses of the town's East Cliff, particularly the 'Great Fall' of 1915. Left ungrazed and given over to recreation, The Warren is a Site of Special Scientific Interest, a pleasant mix of dense wooded glades and scrubby chalk meadows, zig-zagged

4.5 Battle of Britain memorial, Capel-le-Ferne

by paths and bisected by the Folkestone–Dover railway. Passing the remains of a Roman villa on the cliff above East Bay, and three Napoleonic Martello Towers, the England Coastal Path descends from here past Sunny Sands into the town's harbour. During World War I, thousands upon thousands passed through this harbour. Some were on their way to the Western Front, others arriving to seek a new life away from the turmoil of the continent. From autumn 1914 onwards, the sight of crowds of hungry and emaciated Belgian refugees alighting on the harbour arm was a near-daily occurrence, and over the course of the war nearly 100,000 European refugees passed through the town before moving on to purpose-built settlements in other parts of the country. In just one day in October 1914 an estimated 16,000 Belgian refugees arrived in the town. They were provided with hot meals by local inhabitants who set up a Refugee War Committee and circulated a 'Franco-Belge' newsletter for the new visitors. Frederick Bobby, who had just purchased a series of houses on the Sandgate Road for the development of Bobby's department store (later Debenhams), postponed demolition of the properties to allow them to be occupied by the newcomers. King Albert of Belgium visited on several occasions, being generous with his praise for the townsfolk, stating that 'Folkestone had earned the admiration not only of the Belgians, but also of the whole world … the whole civilised world knew how the town of Folkestone had received them with such cordiality which would never be forgotten.'[22]

Save for a re-enactment of the landing of Belgian refugees in 2019 as part of the Folkestone Fringe festival, such acts of hospitality are seldom remembered. The fact that Folkestone once willingly harboured terrified and starving refugees fleeing the horrors of war is not commemorated. Instead, the local townscape is littered with memorials to the hundreds of thousands of British, American and Canadian soldiers who disembarked from Folkestone for the trenches via its now twin-town, Boulogne. One of these was the celebrated poet Wilfred Owen, whose last act before his fateful final journey to the Western Front in August 1918 was to swim off Folkestone's Sunny Sands:

> My last hours in England were brightened by a bathe in the fair green Channel, in company of the best piece of Nation left in England—a Harrow boy, of superb intellect & refinement, intellect because he detests war more than Germans, and refinement because of the way he spoke of my going away; and the way he Spoke of the Sun; and of the Sea, and the Air; and everything. In fact the way he spoke. And now I go among cattle to be a cattle-driver ...[23]

This allusion to cattle encapsulated the conditions faced by the rank-and-file soldiers who were being grimly herded into trains in military camps around the country, destined for Folkestone and the other channel ports. In Owen's poem 'The Send-Off', written in 1916, he asked: 'Shall they return to beating of great bells, in wild trainloads? A few, a few, too few for drums and yells may creep back.'[24] His 1917 poem 'Anthem for Doomed Youth' put it more simply: 'What passing bells for these that die as cattle?'[25] Owen himself died in action barely a week before the end of the war, with the news reaching his mother via a telegram that arrived on Armistice Day.

Owen's brief but significant stay in Folkestone made Sunny Sands the obvious site for a 2018 project, overseen by film-maker Danny Boyle, commemorating the centenary of the end of the war. Boyle had previously directed the London Olympics 2012 opening ceremony, an affective manipulation of nationalism that was well received in most quarters.[26] As well as centring the importance of the NHS, Boyle's opening ceremony was a noisy celebration of British industrialisation and cultural innovation, albeit punctuated by a moment of quiet reflection in which the performers stood, hats off, in silence as the cameras focused on scenes of poppies while the commentator quoted from Rupert Brooke's 1915 'The Soldier', noting the 'corners of so many foreign fields remaining forever England'. Boyle's *Pages of the Sea* project was likewise conceived to unite the nation in remembrance. Part-funded by the Imperial War

Museum, and featuring the efforts of many community groups, the project involved making portraits of individuals in the sand on beaches around the country, with the winter tide rising to remove these as onlookers gave thanks. At Swansea, it was the face of Dorothy Watson, a munitions worker killed in an industrial accident; at Lyme Regis, rifleman Kulbir Thapa, the first Gurkha to win the Victoria Cross; at Roker in Sunderland, Hugh Carr, who died in the trenches at Poperinge in 1917. At Folkestone, it was Wilfred Owen's face that was carved in the sands, approximately sixty feet across, before Poet Laureate Carol Ann Duffy's 'The Wound in Time' was read to a large and respectful crowd: 'History might as well be water, / Chastising this shore, / For we learn nothing from your endless sacrifice, / Your faces drowning in the pages of the sea.'[27]

Duffy's poetry is also inscribed on a series of plaques, paid for by the Roger de Haan Charitable Trust, half-way up the road that leads from the harbour to the top of Folkestone's Leas Cliff. Here, the poem is 'An Unseen', her response to Owen's 'Send-Off', referring to soldiers walking down the road towards the 'dying time'.[28] The placement of these lines half-way up the road acknowledges it as the route trodden by many who went to war. The local Shorncliffe Barracks in Cheriton, first established in the eighteenth century, was an important staging post and training camp during World War I, and many soldiers were said to have eaten their breakfast there in the morning only to arrive at the trenches of the Somme in time for tea. Seen off by military luminaries including Field Marshal Montgomery, it is often recounted that these soldiers walked the three miles from the barracks to Folkestone Harbour down Sandy Lane, along the clifftops of Folkestone Leas and finally down Slope Road to the waiting boats via a final cup of tea at the Harbour Canteen (reopened by volunteers in 2018). This was the same route many took when returning, shell-shocked and broken, from the frontline. Shorncliffe Barracks had its own hospital, run by the Canadian Army Medical Corps, while on the Leas several hotels and convalescent homes were converted to military hospitals to cope with the constant flow of invalids. In 1921 Slope Road was renamed the Road of Remembrance and lined with rosemary. A small memorial cairn was placed at the top of the road. The inscription on the cairn quotes from Shakespeare's *Hamlet* – 'rosemary for remembrance' – and below that there is a quotation from Tennyson's 'Ode on the Death of the Duke of Wellington': 'Not once or twice in our rough island story, the path of duty was the way to glory.'

However, the events of World War I are most obviously signified today not through the shaggy rosemary planted along Remembrance Road or lines of poetry, but the hundreds upon thousands of crocheted red poppies yarn-bombed to the iron railings at the side of the road. These first appeared in 2013, the brainchild of local textile designer Di Burns whose great-grandfather had been stationed at Shorncliffe Barracks during World War I. Initially 165 poppies were installed, one for each section of railings. In 2017 Soroptimist International members crocheted another 3,000, all to an identical pattern, swelling the numbers, and both they and the 'Purl Queens' have added to the number over time, replacing those that have become faded and bedraggled. In 2019 local beach artists Ben Braudy and Angus Cameron also assembled seven large poppies from painted red pebbles on the beach below Remembrance Road, signifying the seven months between the Armistice and the eventual signing of the Treaty of Versailles. Meanwhile, at the top of Remembrance Road, a new memorial arch has been built, a slender construction of marine-grade stainless steel looping gently over a stone compass indicating the directions of the commonwealth nations. Opened by Prince Harry in 2014, the memorial arch was not uncontroversial, and its location near to the McDonald's restaurant on West Terrace led many wags to dub it the 'McDonald's arch'. Initially, the arch was supposed to project holograms of soldiers, but rising costs and technical problems put paid to this. Despite being made of stainless steel, the arch began to rust just a year after being finished, with the bolts holding it together staining

4.6 Poppies on beach, Folkestone

it and requiring extensive cleaning. Initially paid for by donations, it is now owned by the local council, which spends an estimated £6,000 a year cleaning and renovating it.

Visiting Folkestone as a child in the 1970s and 1980s I do not recall such an obvious concentration of war memorials. I do remember poppies being placed annually on the 1920s war memorial and I have a vague memory of marching with the cub scouts in a Remembrance Sunday parade around the town. But the material infrastructures of memorialisation have brought the war more obviously to the surface and placed it front and centre in the history of Folkestone. These are no longer sites of remembering, but of *commemoration*. The distinction here is important.[29] Edward Casey argues that places retain the past in a way that can be reanimated through our remembering of them, pointing to the significance of a collective memory that is sparked off through encounters with material artefacts and traces in the landscape. For Casey, commemoration combines this form of memory work with a profoundly embodied notion of co-remembering, with personal recollection, place memory and social ritual entwining to reshape and even reinvent the past. Sites of commemoration are, then, important in creating shared senses of culture and identity, constructing ideas of nationhood through a manipulation of affect that generally emphasises continuity rather than change.[30]

The collective desire to experience a sense of historical continuity at a time of flux and political uncertainty is understandable. Yet it threatens to paper over diverse interpretations of the past and ignore the ambivalence of history. The commemoration of some people and events inevitably means that others are overlooked or underplayed. Moreover, Folkestone's spaces of commemoration prop up place myths whose historical accuracy is somewhat dubious. For example, the local Conservative MP Damian Collins proudly proclaimed the memorial arch as a tribute to the 'ten million' troops who marched down Remembrance Road – a figure greater than all the Allied soldiers who served in World War I. Others point out that soldiers did not walk from Shorncliffe Barracks until relatively late in the war, with most arriving by train direct to the harbour station. Southampton was probably a much busier port during the war, with up to three million troop movements in each direction.

Even so, Folkestone's proximity to the continent, and the fact that it suffered direct bombing in both World Wars, seems to have cemented the mythology of sacrifice and service as a foundational story of the town. Local pride and patriotism blur into one, and war itself is abstracted. Sometimes it takes relatively unsubtle gestures to remind the visitor of the horrors of conflict. Mark Wallinger's 2008 installation *Folk Stones* consists simply of 19,240 numbered pebbles cemented into a concrete base on the Leas Cliff promenade. Each represents a British soldier who lost his life on the first day of the Battle of the Somme. Christian Boltanski's sound installation *The Whispers*, also from 2008, invites people to sit on benches facing towards France and listen to recordings sent from servicemen to their loved ones. Boltanski was an artist whose work explored ideas of collective memory and transience, and the repeated hearing of these words drifting on the wind is haunting and elegiac.[31]

Along the eight-mile stretch of coast from Dover to Folkestone there is, then, a rich archaeology of militarised endeavour that seethes just below the surface of the visible, rising into view at points where it has become imbued with competing meanings. Different sites summon forth different emotions and affects: pride, gratitude and adoration, but also guilt, sorrow and remorse.[32] In the last quarter century or so, the former appears to have gained the upper hand, with Patrick Wright arguing that it was Thatcherism that first established remembrance as a *de facto* test of loyalty to the nation. Writing in 1994, Wright argued for 'reducing the militaristic emphasis, which tends to make remembrance a glorification of war rather than an occasion of reconciliation'.[33] But in the years leading up to, and immediately after, the decisive Brexit vote of 2016, such arguments were nowhere to be seen: the nation seemed to be in the grip of a bellicose nationalism drawing sustenance from myths of wartime heroism. Social media buzzed with indignation if a newsreader or TV presenter did not wear their poppy with pride. In 2016 the FA railed against FIFA's £18,000 fine when the poppy was incorporated into the England football shirt, supported by an outraged media and government. St George flags festooned cars and houses during major football competitions, 'Jerusalem' is played before every day of a cricket Test Match. And far from receding into the distance, icons of World War II have now become marshalling points in a new discourse of post-Brexit national resilience. During the COVID-19 lockdown, Boris Johnson implored the nation to show the 'Dunkirk spirit'. World War II veteran Captain Tom Moore became a national hero; Vera Lynn re-recorded 'We'll Meet Again'. Signs appeared thanking the NHS and the army. Some Victory in Europe parties became 'Victory over Europe' parties.

But of course, not everyone who wears a poppy, visits sites of memorialisation or attends the annual 'War & Peace Show' at

Folkestone's former racecourse is a rabid nationalist or even a Leave voter. People invest in these symbols for different reasons. Indeed, the commemoration and memory of war is something that has been pursued by those on both left and right. For the latter, World War II was our finest hour, a display of British resolve and ingenuity in the face of adversity. At various times, Brexiteers including Boris Johnson, Jacob Rees-Mogg and Andrea Leadsom referred to Churchill's 1940 'Finest Hour' speech as they tried to garner support for the Leave vote. For them, Brexit offered a pathway to the 'broad, sunlit uplands' that Churchill once promised rather than the abyss of a new dark age. Such rhetoric appeared particularly attractive to the 'left behind', white working-class voters impacted by years of austerity, unaffordable housing and reliance on zero-hours contracts. Yet those on the left have also not been afraid to invoke the mythical spirit of what Clement Attlee termed the 'people's war'. Veteran film-maker Ken Loach, for example, produced an unapologetically nostalgic 2017 election broadcast for Jeremy Corbyn in which the Labour leader emphasised his desire to bring the NHS 'back to us' and lead a government that worked for all. Loach's earlier 2013 documentary *Spirit of 45* was widely interpreted as an unofficial propaganda film on behalf of the Labour Party, one that described how 'wartime spirit' resulted in an unprecedented expansion of the welfare state.

The 1940s, however, were a period of extreme poverty and food shortages. The king and queen were booed as they toured bombsites. In blitzed British cities, residents looted and stole from the dead in desperation. The authorities threatened to introduce martial law. Far from showing heroic resolve, many Londoners simply fled. A classified Ministry of Information document from the height of the Blitz, dated 10 September 1940, gives a sense of the plight of the nation:

> Morale remains unchanged today. Voluntary and unplanned evacuation of East End families continues, and although it is largely confined to women and children, some men are also going. Families

in the Deptford area are making for the hop-fields in Kent, taking with them such of their belongings as they can carry ... There is, however, little evidence that these efforts to escape are due to defeatist feelings, but are simply because the people are thoroughly frightened ... People also angry at inadequacy of compensation of wrecked and burnt-out houses; grumbling and dissatisfaction openly voiced ... Class feeling growing because of worse destruction in working-class areas; anti-Semitism growing in districts where large proportion of Jews reside owing to their taking places in public shelters early in the day.[34]

The sense here is of a society falling apart rather than pulling together. Much of this is now widely understood, but it has not stopped a rosier discourse circulating that mythologises this as a unified age. Even the design aesthetics of wartime have crept back into the mainstream through the mass reproduction of the 'Keep Calm and Carry On' poster, designed to boost British morale. Except now the message has been twisted in new directions, encouraging new forms of 'authentic' consumption. We are implored to keep calm and consume real ale, hand-crafted gin and sourdough bread. Programmes such as *The Great British Bake-Off* and *The Great British Sewing Bee* perpetuate the myth of a 'waste-not, want-not' society steeped in the Blitz spirit, while Cath Kidston cashes in on the seemingly endless appetite for the Union flag by making it a centre-piece of its range of shabby-chic, overpriced floral fashions. Owen Hatherley describes this as symptomatic of 'austerity nostalgia' – a warm and fuzzy politics of affect and identity that mythologises and reimagines the 1945 post-war consensus, the NHS, the Blitz spirit.[35]

Even for someone of my age, a Generation X child born of baby boomers, there is something oddly comforting about the design aesthetics of the immediate post-war years. Many of my colleagues and friends seem to buy into the shabby retro-futurism that combines a penchant for Festival of Britain colours, civic modernity and post-war utility ware. In that sense, there is little difference between their homes and the themed tearoom at Dover's South Foreland lighthouse which has been decked out in 1950s décor. Here, the

National Trust invites us to 'gaze upon the wonders of china tea pots in a vast variety of sizes and colours … a mix matched assortment of china cups and plates, all decorated in floral, chintz, gold trimmed spouts, pearlescent nacreous coatings, countless shades of blues. An endless supply of beauty embellished into china.'[36] On stopping here to rest weary, blistered feet and enjoy tiffin and tea mid-morning, I find it akin to stepping into a heritage theme park, yet it is also oddly of the moment, and not so different from any number of hipster-run shabby-chic cafés found elsewhere on the coast. The constantly piped Vera Lynn music, embellished with vinyl crackle for verisimilitude, begins to take on hauntological qualities of the type enthused about by cultural commentators such as Mark Fisher and Simon Reynolds. There is a strange metaphysics of presence here, as notions of past and present collapse. The recording is from another era, but the white cliffs remain and Vera Lynn, at that time, was also still with us. Is this a simulacrum of the past or is this our present reality? The ambience makes me slightly woozy. I exit into the cold morning air to clear my head.

James Meek's wonderful analysis of Brexit, *Dreams of Leaving and Remaining*, argues that World War II and its aftermath still loom large in the nation's psyche because 'it was both the ultimate St George event, the slaying of the Nazi dragon, and the ultimate Robin Hood event, the spur to the creation of the welfare state'.[37] Both left and right invoke the wartime spirit, and hark back to a time of supposed national unity. The corollary of this is a coercive culture of remembrance which imbues militarised landscapes with patriotism and pride. Given that Kent has been on the frontline of England's defence for centuries, it is perhaps unsurprising that its coastline has become the focus for so many acts of memorialisation. Walking the Kent coast, war haunts every footstep, with the relics of the World Wars arrayed along the coastline to remind residents of the twentieth-century conflicts that caused so much privation, death and destruction. For some of these residents, those long-finished wars remain a very real threat, embodied in the unexploded munitions regularly found on Kent beaches and the 1,400 tonnes of explosive on board the *Richard Montgomery*. But the real problem for many on the Kent coast is not so much that they are threatened by the past but that they are seduced by it. Unable to generate any new memories of their own, the population continually pays homage to past military endeavours, slipping into a nostalgic nationalism that celebrates British isolation and dismisses the idea that we might ever be truly European.

5

The white horse

The Northmen came about our land
A Christless chivalry
Who knew not of the arch or pen
Great, beautiful half-witted men
From the sunrise and the sea.

G. K. Chesterton, *The Ballad of the White Horse*, 1911[1]

The idea of the landscape as witness to history is one deeply ingrained in the folklore of the Kent coast. This includes three moments often identified as pivotal in the making of the nation: the Roman invasion beginning in 55 BC, the arrival of the Germanic leaders Hengist and Horsa in AD 449 and St Augustine's landing in AD 597, which brought Christianity to Britain. Each of these events is commemorated in the Kentish landscape – via Caesar's plaque on Walmer beach, a cross to St Augustine at Ebbsfleet in Thanet and, most dramatically, the Danish Hugin longboat at Pegwell Bay – but the details remain largely conjectural, with scant archaeological evidence to support them. It was searching for proof of the first of these that led Augustus Pitt Rivers, that great innovator of modern archaeological methods, to undertake one of the first archaeological excavations in Kent at Castle Hill, or what he knew as 'Caesar's Camp'.

For centuries Castle Hill, part of the chalk downland above Folkestone, had been romanticised by painters and poets as offering a vista over a historic slice of English countryside. Edward Hasted, writing in 1799, suggested that

> the prospect over this delightful vale of Folkestone from the hill … is very beautiful indeed for the pastures and various fertility of the vale in the centre, beyond it the church and town of Hythe, Romney Marsh, and the high promontory of Beachy Head, boldly stretching into the sea. It is altogether as pleasing a prospect as any in this country.[2]

Hasted emphasised the strategic importance of the hill, which allowed the invading Romans to look out over the Channel while symbolically subjugating the 'distressed' Britons below. On this basis, *The Handbook for Travellers in Kent and Sussex*, published in 1858, stressed that the pleasures of the eye at Castle Hill entwined with 'memory and imagination', alert to the layering of history: it suggested that the 'Roman watchtower' was later replaced by an encampment built by King Eadblad of Kent – son of Aethelberht and Bertha, and the first Anglo-Saxon king to convert to Christianity – and ultimately superseded by a Norman enclosure built by the Lords of Avranches.[3]

The assumption had long been that the earthworks on top of the hill were the remnants of Caesar's first fortress, built in 55 BC to protect the Roman ships anchored on the beaches below from aggressive forces. However, in an address to the Kentish Archaeological Society in 1876, W. J. Jeaffreson poured scorn on this idea, suggesting that there was no way anyone could reasonably conclude that 'the Romans at all – much less Caesar – were ever brought into actual connection with this particular locality', concluding that 'to set the whole question at rest an inexpensive exploration of the ground is required'.[4] By the time Pitt Rivers began his excavations in 1878, his reputation as an archaeologist had been cemented by his celebrated work at Stonehenge, as well as notable excavations in Essex, Sussex and Oxfordshire. He was surely the man to find evidence of the first Roman invasion.

A military man, trained at Sandhurst, Pitt Rivers was no stranger to Kent. In the 1850s he was charged with establishing the Hythe musketry school, training troops to use the new 'minie' rifles that replaced the increasingly anachronistic Brown Bess flintlock muskets. Hythe was deemed a suitable location for the training given its expansive beaches which allowed a large firing range to be constructed between Hythe and Dymchurch redoubt (it remains Ministry of Defence property, complete with a mocked-up 'Fighting in Built Up Areas' village that includes faux-Arabic street signs such as 'Abdul's café'). Pitt Rivers arrived in Hythe in 1851 with his wife, Alice, daughter of the Whig politician Lord Stanley, and although it is documented that their time in Kent was happy, it was blemished by their first child being stillborn. Alice was left alone in Hythe for months at a time – Pitt Rivers went to fight at the Battle of Alma in the Crimea in 1854 and was then stationed in Malta, where Alice finally joined him in 1856.[5]

Promoted to Major General, Pitt Rivers returned frequently to Kent in the late 1860s at a time when he had begun to expand his interest from collecting guns and weapons into a more encompassing interest in archaeology. Systematic fieldwalking on the Isle of Thanet in 1868 resulted in him collecting a range of flint artefacts including spearheads and scrapers, and a subsequent excavation uncovered Romano-British ceramics alongside animal bones and stone tools.[6] This led him to believe that the earthworks on top of Castle Hill were indeed Romano-British, as per the legend. Assisted by sappers from Folkestone's Shorncliffe Barracks, the excavation of Castle Hill was undertaken between 3 June and 5 July 1878, with eighteen trenches cut through the earthworks revealing hundreds of shards of medieval pottery and ceramics, but nothing from the Romano-British period.[7] What was thought to be a Roman watchtower was, Pitt Rivers concluded, a Norman ringwork castle.

Subsequently, there have been other notable archaeological excavations in the vicinity of Castle Hill. Rather than being driven by scientific curiosity per se, these were expedient 'rescue' excavations associated with the construction of the Channel Tunnel.[8] Announced in 1964 by Ernest Marples, then Minister of Transport, work on the tunnel began in 1967. Progress was slow, and only around 1,400 metres were completed by 1974, at which time the recession and oil crisis forced the abandonment of the project by the cash-strapped UK government.[9] But within a decade, plans to link Britain and the continent via a tunnel were reheated, with Thatcher and Mitterrand agreeing on a privately financed twin-tunnel scheme promoted by the Channel Tunnel Group. The Treaty of Canterbury was signed in 1986 by the French and UK governments, paving the way for the construction and operation of the fixed link. Tunnelling began again in 1988, with the rail terminal at Honeywell Coombe, Cheriton, being opened in 1994, adjacent to the M20 motorway. As such, the Channel Tunnel begins its 50 km route to Coquelles in the Pays de Calais directly under the ditches of the Norman enclosure excavated by Pitt Rivers on Castle Hill.

Thousands pass Castle Hill every day, either as drivers on the M20 or passengers on *Le Shuttle* or Eurostar trains. Few, however, take the route I approached it by in the late summer of 2020: the Pilgrim's Way, the long-distance path that connects Winchester to Canterbury and beyond. Running along the southern escarpment of the North Downs, the Pilgrim's Way is one of Robert Macfarlane's 'old ways', a path whose history is haunted by the footsteps of innumerable walkers who have passed before, not least those making the journey to Canterbury to visit Thomas Becket's memorial. As Macfarlane writes, 'For pilgrims walking … every footfall is doubled, landing at once on the actual road and also on the path of faith'.[10] Former Archbishop of Canterbury Rowan Williams reasoned that pilgrims walking the path are attempting to 'cut through the clutter of institutions, and achieve self-discovery, through an engagement with the imaginative power of history and the spiritual draw of the past'.[11] But my interests were purely secular, and partly nostalgic. I was returning to a hill that I must have driven or cycled past hundreds of times over the years, but which I had not climbed since 1980.

Clambering up the steep chalky sides of the Norman motte atop the hill, I am rewarded with an impressive vista. A modest 500-foot hill, it nonetheless offers dramatic views across the Kent countryside towards the borders of Sussex, with the squat form of Dungeness power station visible in the distance, and the wind farm at Little Cheyne prominent in the drab flatness of Romney Marsh. In the foreground, the town of Folkestone, and its suburb Cheriton, stretches out before me. Looking down, I struggle to reconcile it with the view that I would have had forty years earlier, let alone that which Pitt Rivers would have seen as he excavated busily in the 1870s. Much of what is visible is of recent origin, and the view arguably now says less about English history and imagination and more about the integration of Kent into a European 'space of flows'. Immediately below the hill, Junction 13 of the M20 is surrounded by multiple industrial and business parks. Amid the usual retail sheds, gyms and DIY stores stands Martello House, the three-storey office of the UK Border Agency, the base for the team dealing with clandestine crossings of the Channel. Facing this, on the other side of the M20, is the ElecLink Folkestone Converter Station. Completed in 2020, it is the UK terminus for the 51 km one gigawatt cable that runs through the tunnel to a similar converter station at Peuplingues near Calais.[12] But dominating the view is the 160-hectare Eurotunnel terminal. Looking down on this is to witness a constant and noisy ferrying of cars, lorries and coaches on and off *Le Shuttle*, a complex choreography of tolls, border checks and customs inspections that encapsulates the logistics of cross-border mobility.

There is one other notable twenty-first-century addition to the landscape here: a white horse composed of limestone slabs laid out in trenches on the scarp slope above the terminal, fully 160 feet long. Designed by Charles Newington in 1998, the horse was intended as a welcome to England, the first thing a traveller

5.1 Channel Tunnel terminal, Cheriton

would see when exiting the Channel Tunnel. Promoted by Joanna Lumley and Spike Milligan among others, for many years this millennium project was mired in planning controversy. English Nature objected to the white horse's construction in a Site of Special Scientific Interest renowned for nationally rare plants including bedstraw broomrape and spider orchid. Despite local authority support, the environmental objections mounted up, forcing a planning inquiry. At the inquiry, the local MP Michael Howard suggested that the potential for ecological damage had been 'vastly exaggerated', and stressed the importance of the horse in place promotion, pronouncing that 'the economy of Folkestone could be transformed if only a small proportion of the large numbers of people who leave or enter the country through the Tunnel were to stop to enjoy the area's attractions'.[13] Planning permission was finally granted in 2003, but Friends of the Earth challenged the inquiry's decision, arguing that ignoring English Nature's advice was a clear breach of the EU habitats directive.[14] Supporters of the horse spoke of EU interference and the press made much of the

The white horse

fact that European law might be used to prevent a 'very British' tradition of chalk figures in the landscape.[15] Those arguing for the horse ultimately prevailed, and it was finally completed in May 2004 with the assistance of Gurkhas from Folkestone's Shorncliffe Barracks. Today, the galloping white horse provides a 'first, and last, memorable glimpse of England' for those passing through the Eurotunnel terminal.[16]

Tunnel visions

The Eurotunnel terminal and associated works represent perhaps the most obvious evidence of the re-territorialisation of the UK border during its membership of the EU. This was a period when the UK and Europe entered an unprecedented phase of cross-border cooperation, but when British political discourse perversely began to fixate on the porosity of its borders and the economic threats of migration, not least from those nations who joined the enlarged EU in the twenty-first century.[17] This preoccupation with securing the border is in plain sight at Cheriton in the guise of Martello House, the Traffic Terminal Control Centre, omnipresent CCTV and automatic number plate recognition systems, not to mention large numbers of border police constantly at work. But there are other less obvious forms of spatial and temporal control in play here, including the logistical procedures that coordinate and schedule movement at a distance. In this regard, Chenchen Zhang argues that the border is 'performed into being' not only 'by the everyday policing of the infrastructural and vehicular spaces *there*, but also through institutional and representational practices done *elsewhere*, in UK and EU laws, parliamentary debates, popular press, trans-national solidarity activisms and so forth'.[18] Crucial here is the 1991 Sangatte protocol, which allows for extraterritorial control, meaning that the border between European Schengen space and the UK effectively exists at Cheriton – as well as Ashford, Ebbsfleet and St Pancras. By the same token, UK border police operate at the

Eurostar terminals at Brussels, Paris Nord, Lille International and Calais-Frethun, as well as the Coquelles shuttle terminal.

The presence of French border police in the UK, and, conversely, the British in France, is evidence of a juxtaposed control regime designed to smooth the journey of travellers through the tunnel by removing the need for immigration controls on arrival. It also serves as a tangible and permanent reminder of the linkage between Kent and Nord Pays de Calais, which, from 1990, became collectively defined by the EU as the Transmanche region, with funding available under the EU INTERREG programme for regional development and infrastructure projects. This funding focused on five strategic areas: transport linkage, economic development, education programmes, tourism development and environmental protection.[19] Signs proclaiming EU investment began to proliferate around Kent, ranging from funding for a new a new cross-channel cycleway and a 'green route' through the county to physical improvements at Dover Castle designed to make it more accessible to a wider audience.

Physically, then, the border between the UK and continental France remains as defined by the Treaty of Canterbury in 1986, the breakthrough point mid-Channel where tunnellers Graham Fagg and Philippe Cozette first shook hands and exchanged flags in December 1990. But in other respects, the border is no longer a simple linear boundary between the two nations, but an extraterritorial system of biometric control that exists at different points in a space of flows.[20] Despite the frequent deployment of the idea of 'Fortress Europe', this space of flows actually *encourages* people to cross borders, albeit this is conditional on points-based systems differentiating between those who can crossly legally and those who cannot. Those in the former category include students travelling under the EU Erasmus exchange programme, migrant labourers employed seasonally as fruit pickers in Kent's farms as well as 'higher-skilled' workers (who the sociologist Adrian Favell refers to as cosmopolitan 'eurostars').[21] Before Brexit, these populations moved smoothly through a border that was barely perceptible to them, with checks occurring when travellers accessed the highspeed link rather than when they disembarked in the UK. But this did not mean that there was any less control of the border regime, with the UK government undertaking pre-emptive measures involving sophisticated identity management designed to prevent 'illegal' migration before it even happened.[22] Simultaneously, the government pushed the border *inward* into the social institutions of everyday life by encouraging the citizenry to be constantly vigilant about the presence of racialised Others in their midst, creating the 'hostile environment' famously promoted by Theresa May and the Conservative Party.[23] In many senses, the UK border is now both nowhere and everywhere: as Etienne Balibar argues, 'borders are being both multiplied and reduced in their localization and their function, they are being thinned out and doubled'.[24]

This noted, the completion of the Channel Tunnel meant that England and France could no longer be easily depicted as divided by a maritime border.[25] Instead, from 1994 the UK was increasingly understood as part of a cosmopolitan and networked Europe, a connection that nationalists and Brexiteers repeatedly sought to sever in the next quarter century. This sense of connection to the continent is certainly hard to escape in the vicinity of the Cheriton terminal given the visible presence of French gendarmes and border police. Yet it is also palpable elsewhere in Kent, not least around the M20 motorway corridor that stretches from the shuttle terminal to the M25 via Ashford and Maidstone, much of this running parallel to the High Speed One route to Ebbsfleet International, Stratford International and finally London St Pancras. Along this route there is not just the sight and sound of the Eurostar to remind locals of the links to the continent, but also roadside signage, adverts for wine warehouses near the Cité Europe shopping centre at Calais, and Channel Tunnel FM radio constantly broadcasting updates on shuttle waiting times.

From the age of seven I lived in this corridor, in Mersham, a small village ten miles to the north-east of Folkestone. The village felt close-knit, with the church, pub and sports club the anchors of community life. At the top of the village was the Hatch Estate, a deer park owned by the Knatchbull family, with Lord and Lady Brabourne living in the village in a classical Queen Anne house. To the bottom of the village, Swanton Mill stood on the East Stour, its large waterwheel driving two vast millstones in much the same manner as it had at the time of its construction in the fifteenth century. Though the village was not particularly picturesque in a chocolate-box sense, it felt rooted in traditions of Kent life. But as the preparation for the Channel Tunnel ramped up, my consciousness of being connected to Europe became increasingly strong. The M20, which had been constructed parallel to the A20 at the top of the village in 1981, became increasingly busy when the 'missing link' between Maidstone and Ashford was opened in 1991, with coastbound traffic heading for the ports now seeing this as quicker than the traditional Watling Street (A2) route. Around that time, my father began working on the construction of the CEGB Sellindge Converter Station, just a couple of miles up the road. In essence, this was a vast electrical substation (completed in 1986) designed to import French electricity via the high-voltage *Interconnexion France Angleterre* that originated in Bonningues-les-Calais. Then, with the opening of the Channel Tunnel in 1994, Eurostar trains started passing through our village on the existing Waterloo to Folkestone line used by Southeastern services. Given the age and condition of the track, these trains travelled at a maximum of 100 mph, and while the government had initially assumed that this track would be sufficient for the volume of cross-Channel rail traffic, by the time the Eurotunnel was open it had been decided that a new highspeed link for trains travelling at up to 180 mph would be constructed through our village, parallel to the existing track.[26]

Given that Kent was benefiting from substantial EU investment, it might have been anticipated that local populations would be positively disposed towards this new transport infrastructure, not least because it promised to dramatically reduce travel times to London. But opposition to development in the English countryside – already pronounced in the South-East in the 1980s – was manifested in vociferous NIMBY protests along the length of the highspeed line, many of these protests starting years before the route was confirmed. Orchestrated by the Campaign for the Protection of Rural England and the Kent Trust for Nature Conservation, protest groups formed in towns and villages along the proposed route, with Eve Darian-Smith noting that the 'Garden of England' mythology was often invoked by campaigners.[27] Opponents alleged that the link would destroy valuable agricultural land, create visual and noise pollution, and destroy flora and fauna. At some rallies, the amplified noise of a French TGV was played to the crowds to simulate the disturbance anticipated, with protestors suggesting that this would make their homes unsellable. Few appeared enamoured of the prospect of faster train travel, with some even arguing that the money could be better spent on repairing potholes in local roads.[28]

However, Darian-Smith writes that for many protestors there appeared to be more at stake than the likely economic and environmental impacts, with the tunnel symbolically and ideologically representing the penetration of the 'ancient homeland' by Europe. Here, Darian-Smith notes the frequent use of a 'rape' metaphor positioning Kent as vulnerable to the unwanted advances of its lascivious Other, continental Europe.[29] These types of discourses mirrored the literature of invasion that emerged in the late Victorian and Edwardian era in the wake of the abandoned 1882 tunnel workings, when the 'French threat' generated disproportionate fears of political, cultural and sexual infiltration, expressed in images of 'insidious forces gnawing at the national body'.[30] Remarkably, the anxieties about subterranean invasion that stymied the Channel Tunnel in the nineteenth century persisted in some quarters, albeit the focus shifted somewhat from fears of military assault to concerns about rats bringing rabies through the tunnel. Here, rats represented a potent but problematic metaphor of invasion which

Darian-Smith concludes was related to postcolonial imaginaries of English statehood.[31]

Despite this opposition, the £5.8 billion Channel Tunnel Rail Connection ultimately tore a swathe through the Kent countryside, involving the construction of 152 new viaducts and bridges along its 67 km route, as well as the compulsory purchase of around 300 dwellings. Not all were demolished – in our village the timber-framed and Grade-II listed Bridge Cottage, erected in 1622, was placed on a concrete raft and moved, painstakingly slowly, to its new location eighty metres to the north-west, its progress tracked by national TV as we watched on. Further along the line, a new £250 million 'cut and cover' tunnel was created adjacent to the village primary school, designed to appease those fearful of the impact of noise pollution on local schoolchildren. During its construction, archaeological evidence of Iron Age smelting was found in the field above, before this was dug up and replaced by 'Eurostar Meadow', a two-hectare paddock complete with ceremonial plaque unveiled in 2003 by the short-lived Minister for Transport, John Spellar. Rather than acknowledging the scar that High Speed One created through the village, the plaque proclaims that Eurostar Meadow brought the village 'together again'.[32] Now hidden in a thick tangle of brambles, the plaque appears long forgotten, the one-time vehement opposition to High Speed One also a seemingly distant memory. Villagers have become acclimatised to the regular swish of the highspeed Eurostar through the village, which, like the constant hum of the motorway before it, is now as much part of the rural soundscape as the chirp of the morning chorus or the hourly chiming of the bells of St John the Baptist church.

This story – of once angry NIMBY populations becoming inured to the presence of the highspeed connection – is repeated along its route. In this regard, the novelty of Ashford's station being renamed Ashford International has also long since worn off. Opened in February 1996, the highspeed line obliterated much

5.2 Eurostar Meadow, Mersham

of the previous station structure, as well as the neighbouring art deco Picture House, the only cinema in the town at that time. But this demolition appeared to be quickly forgotten because of the economic benefits promised by the new rail connection, with the improvement to the creaking Southeastern train network ultimately enhancing connectivity to London as well as the continent. Indeed, although much initial talk was about the development of Thames Gateway in North Kent (following geographer-planner Peter Hall's idea for a new linear city), it was Ashford, with its dramatically reduced journey times to London, that was to witness the most striking transformation in the immediate wake of the Channel Tunnel's opening.

Smooth space

Traditionally, Ashford was a market town, fulfilling a similar role for East Kent as the county town Maidstone performed for West

117

Kent. Situated between the Weald and the North Downs, and linked by road to Faversham, Canterbury and Romney, it connected North Kent to South as much as the coast to the capital. Its role as Kent's most important livestock trading centre was enhanced through the construction of a permanent cattle market in 1856, served by a dedicated station stop and sidings. By that time Ashford was also an important railway town, with the Ashford Railway Works and accompanying workers' New Town completed in 1850. However, Ashford was essentially a small, rural town until the post-war era, when it was identified as an 'overspill' town for London council tenants. Many of these moved into the Stanhope estate to the south of the town and worked in the new manufacturing businesses emerging on the town's outskirts. The combination of two of these – Batchelor's foods and Propriety Perfumes Ltd (now Givaudan) – meant that those approaching Ashford could often smell it before they saw it, the heady mix of mushy peas and *eau de toilette* wafting up the Stour valley on a south-westerly breeze. The town's expansion was not, however, matched by imaginative civic planning. The Tufton Centre was the epitome of the drab 1970s shopping precinct, the elegant Victorian Corn Exchange demolished to make way for functional council offices and the town's ring road cut through the historic East Hill with scant regard for the townscape. The town was dubbed 'Trashford' by local residents, described by *Guardian* columnist (and Ashfordian) Stuart Heritage as 'a plain, grey pointless mound of narrow horizons and squandered opportunity'.[33]

The opening of the international station in 1996 and the coming of High Speed One in 2003 thus provided Ashford with an opportunity to change its image from that of a flat, prosaic and rather dreary market town to that of a vibrant town with European connections, less than two hours from Paris and only 38 minutes from London. The ensuing expansion of Ashford has been extraordinary. A town with a population of 28,000 in 1961 expanded to 118,000 by 2018, with new houses being built at a rate of over 600 a year. Despite the obvious problems of building on or near the River Stour floodplain, there has been a massive expansion of housing to the south of the town, manifest in developments whose names remind us that a few years previously these were greenfield, agricultural sites. Following the government's 2004 Regional Planning Guidance (RPG9) for the South-East, 1,000 new homes have been built at Cheeseman's Green, 1,080 at Finberry Village and 5,750 are underway at Chilmington Green. Around 60% of this new housing is sold to Londoners, who continue to work in London, using the town as a dormitory suburb.

In recent years, rates of new business formation and relocation in Ashford have far exceeded the South-East average, with companies including PageSuite, Tarkett and Wilkins Kennedy attracted by relatively affordable office rents in flagship developments including Connect 38 and the revamped International House.[34] Adjacent to the international station, the McArthurGlen designer outlet, with its distinctive tented structure designed by Richard Rogers, was expanded in 2019 at a cost of £90 million. Other recent developments near the international station include Chapel Down's Curious brewery, relocated from Tenterden, a Hilton hotel and a planned high-rise residential block dubbed 'Ashford's Shard'. Tellingly, the town's central cattle market – established in 1856 by the Ashford Cattle Market Company, the longest-running registered company still operating in the UK – vacated its town centre location next to the station in 1993 to make way for the highspeed line, relocating to the southern orbital road. Part of its former site is now occupied by Elwick Place Leisure Park, opened in 2018. One of the major tenants of the (still half-empty) leisure park is Macknade Fine Foods, a farm shop that has its origins in a pick-your-own business started by Frederick Neame in Faversham in the nineteenth century. The only reminders of the former cattle market are the faint outlines of cows carved into the car park wall by artist Cathy Streeter, apparently unnoticed by the customers loading cheese and charcuterie into their SUVs.

5.3 Former cattle market, Ashford

But the most palpable change to Ashford over recent decades has not been its verticalisation, or the radical overhaul of the station's environs, but its outward expansion, and the endless hooping of new circulatory roads around its now-shrunken medieval core. Ashford ring road opened in 1978, a one-way tourniquet around the town centre which witnessed much boy-racer, furry-dice madness in the 1980s. The M20 linked to the town's northern bypass in 1981, with Junction 10 subsequently linked to the southern orbital road in 1993, creating such gridlock that a new Junction 10a was opened in 2020. The former floodplain and water meadows of the East Stour are now bisected by the A2042 which links the international station to the Park Farm housing development, Eureka Business Park and the southern orbital road; the Great Chart A28 bypass is being widened and turned into dual carriageway, anticipating more traffic from the 'South Ashford Garden Community' (the new homes at Chilmington Green and Kingsnorth). In short, the town has become decentred: much of the life of the town centre has been sucked out by the designer outlet, retail parks and supermarkets that serve the sprawling, inchoate housing that has absorbed, and destroyed, a series of surrounding hamlets.

This obliteration of place, and the transformation of so much rural land surrounding Ashford, is highlighted in *Darkmans*, Nicola Barker's 2007 Booker-prize-nominated novel. The 835-page novel is ostensibly about a father (Daniel) and son (Kane) and their relationship with a wayward neighbour, Kelly, and her new Kurdish friend, undocumented migrant Gaffar, but it is also about the traces of the past that resurface in the present.[35] The book begins, perhaps fittingly, in the French Connection pub on Ashford's southern orbital road with Daniel and Kane discussing the sale of illegal prescription drugs. They are interrupted by the arrival of Dory, the dazed and narcoleptic German husband of a local chiropodist, seemingly possessed by the spirit of the devilish John Scogin, a malevolent jester from the court of Edward IV who has been disturbed by the Eurotunnel construction works.[36] The sprawling and often bewildering plot then takes in a bungled building job, antique forgery, mysterious dead birds, a cigarette-burned carpet and religious conversion. Throughout, Ashford is to the fore, a town depicted as increasingly connected to elsewhere but out of touch with itself. In a passage highlighted by Alissa Karl in her analysis of *Darkmans* as a critique of contemporary neoliberalism, the intriguingly named forger Peta Borough describes the town:

At its centre beats this tiny, medieval heart, but that heart is surrounded – obfuscated – by all these conflicting layers; a chaos of buildings and roads from every conceivable time frame. It's pure, architectural mayhem. A completely non-homogenous town, utterly half-cocked, deliriously ramshackle … And then, clumsily imposed on top – the icing on the cake – this whole crazy mishmash of through-roads and round-roads and intersections and dead-ends – Business Parks, Superstores, train stations, train tracks – which slice blithely through all the other stuff, apparently *aiding* it on the one hand, yet completely *disregarding* it on the other.[37]

Tellingly, the dénouement of the novel finds the protagonists stuck in traffic, a scenario all-too-familiar to those in the queues for Ashford's designer outlet at the weekend. Linear time collapses and the promise of ceaseless mobility is betrayed. This tension between speed and slowness is played up repeatedly in the novel, with Peta Borough also describing Ashford as a town 'which professes to celebrate journeying while being basically almost unnavigable on foot'.[38] Invoking Marxist urbanist Henri Lefebvre, Huw Marsh concludes his reading of *Darkmans* by suggesting that Ashford is a town alienated from itself, its stylish new-build estates the quintessence of boredom, its road system indicative of the ultimate triumph of exchange over use value.

Depicting the town as a proliferation of non-places, *Darkmans* effectively encapsulates twenty-first-century Ashford. But a year after the book's publication, the town undertook what became perhaps the most obvious symbol of its integration into a European space of flows: its infamous experiment in 'shared space'. Originating in the work of Dutch traffic engineer Hans Monderman, the original aim of the shared space initiative was to reduce accidents and congestion, but it also proved attractive to local authorities in Britain because it allowed them to remove kerbs, street signage and road markings, creating a less cluttered, more aestheticised streetscape. The logic is simple: by removing obvious signage and lane markings, and imposing a blanket 20 mph speed limit, it is assumed that drivers and pedestrians will be more accommodating of one another, dispensing with any need for formal pedestrian crossings and creating a more seamless flow of traffic. Ashford was the first local authority to implement the idea, transforming its ring road south of the town centre, and producing some incredulous reactions from petrol-heads. Jeremy Clarkson derided it in his column in *The Sun*, suggesting that 'doing away with lights and pelican crossings is a bit like doing away with bolts in the scaffolding on a building site in the hope the labourers walk around a bit more carefully'.[39] For many locals, the scheme seemed to be more suited to the continent, and distinctly un-British in its inception. Initial news of near misses hit the headlines and generated further cynicism. Subsequent assessments of its impact were more sanguine, highlighting reduced accident rates, but a 2011 study by the University of Western England suggested that it produced anxiety among both drivers and pedestrians, with women in particular preferring the previous road layout.[40] Disability charities also pointed out that shared space was particularly difficult to navigate for those with visual or hearing impairments, and the concept was quietly dropped from national road design guidance in 2018.

Though a full ten miles from the coast, the radical transformation of Ashford's roads illustrates how the Kent borderscape changed as the county became more integrated within a European spatial imaginary. This imaginary rejected the insular exceptionalism of the island-nation in favour of a road and rail network promoting European integration. According to Ole Jensen and Tim Richardson, the idea that spatial integration would achieve European political

5.4 Shared space, Elwick Place, Ashford

123

harmonisation emerged in the 1980s, becoming an EU priority in the 1990s as a *monotopic* vision of Europe as a frictionless society gained policy traction. Central to this was the idea of a Trans-European Transport Network, the network of roads, railways and seaways agreed in principle in 1996. As Jensen and Richardson describe, the TEN-T vision was truly international – 'an integrated network of modern highspeed roads, railways and other infrastructure crossing the European continent, filling the missing links between national transport systems, and applying state of the art information technology to the operation of the network'.[41]

Ultimately, the UK's enthusiasm to link to this network was fatally compromised by the failure of the wider British population to buy into the European project. This became acutely obvious at the time of the Brexit debate, when the Remain campaign failed to successfully articulate the benefits of staying in Europe.[42] Arguably, the seeds of this scepticism about European integration were sown in the 1980s, when Thatcherism's emphasis on individualism fostered opposition to the projects of monetary union and legal harmonisation, with these often portrayed in the right-wing media as representing the surrender of sovereignty to foreign powers.[43] Frequently, this manifested in media articles that were overtly Francophobic. In 1990, a few short years before the opening of the Channel Tunnel, *The Sun* famously ran its 'Up Yours Delors!' headline, encouraging the 'frog-haters' of England to assemble on the white cliffs of Dover to show their displeasure towards the president of the European Commission. In the same front-page article it predicted that the English would soon smell the 'first whiff of garlic' through the tunnel.[44] In Kent, these xenophobic sentiments informed opposition to the Channel Tunnel construction, the routing of High Speed One and initiatives such as Ashford's shared space, all of which were seen as unwelcome additions to the landscape. In time, these incursions were to some extent forgotten, but cynicism towards the European project of spatial integration lingered on, not least because the transport infrastructure built in Kent did little to improve local travel and mobility. Indeed, one predictable outcome of increasing connectivity with Europe was that local roads regularly became gridlocked, not because of problems occurring in Kent, but in and around the tunnel itself.

Road to nowhere

In the years immediately following its opening, the Channel Tunnel failed to achieve its passenger forecasts, losing £925 million in its first full year of operation.[45] A fire in 1996 caused a major interruption to services, with the HGV shuttle route cut for several months after a serious blaze that caused a locomotive to stop twelve miles into the tunnel. Yet despite these setbacks, passenger and freight numbers rose steadily and, by 2016, there were 21 million passenger movements, exceeding the numbers travelling to and from the UK by sea. This created increased volumes of traffic around the tunnel terminal, adding to the existing traffic using the ports of Dover and Ramsgate. While this was usually accommodated by the M20 and improved M2/A2 routes, any problem with the running of the tunnel – fire, derailment, industrial action, bad weather – quickly caused these roads to snarl up, necessitating the introduction of the much-dreaded Operation Stack.

First used in 1988 in response to a seamen's strike at Folkestone Docks, Operation Stack uses the coastbound carriageway of the M20 between Ashford and Folkestone as a *de facto* lorry park while locals are diverted on to the slower A20 route. In Easter 2005 a series of delays led to the closure of the entire 26 miles between Folkestone and Maidstone, providing space for over 7,000 lorries. By the time its impact was discussed in Parliament in 2007, Operation Stack had been used 74 times, sometimes for days at a time. Ashford MP Damian Green argued for a better solution than this stop-gap, stressing the need for free and plentiful lorry parking around the county while simultaneously blaming the French for the frequent road closures:

The combination of the notorious French attitude to industrial relations, which involves closing the port of Calais at the first available excuse, and the weather in winter, means that unless something is done, this policy will be a never-ending misery. I am not using exaggerated language. I could fill my entire time in this debate – and probably the Minister's – reading out letters and e-mails from my own constituents explaining how the closure of the M20 has affected them. Inevitably, it clogs up every main road in east Kent as people try to avoid it. People take hours to get to work. Appointments are missed. Contracts are lost. Business grinds to a halt.[46]

In response, local authorities in Kent formed the Channel Corridor Partnership, aiming to ensure that the county remained the 'Gateway to Europe' rather than a bottleneck. Rather than emphasising the benefits of the infrastructure associated with the tunnel, the Partnership argued that it was a financial burden that Kent could not be expected to bear alone, lobbying for additional government investment. Here, it was suggested that the costs of Operation Stack were compounded by illegal lorry parking, damage to verges and the expense of clearing up the large amounts of excrement and urine left at the roadside by drivers. Far from being the Garden of England, some suggested that the county was becoming the Toilet of England.[47]

While the Channel Tunnel, new international stations and the highspeed link were seen as important for job creation, on a day-to-day basis the overwhelming numbers of 'foreign-owned' lorries on Kent's roads served, at least in some minds, to cement the view that Kent was continuing to pay the price for Britain being in Europe. Talk of the 'chaos' on Kent's roads was frequently heard in the run-up to the Brexit referendum, mentioned in the same breath as the attempted migrant crossings at Calais that were rising in number. Responding, George Osborne pledged an additional £250 million for Kent's roads in November 2015, acknowledging the need for a bespoke lorry park to deal with the frequent backlogs caused by disruption to Channel crossings, including a four-day delay in the sweltering heat of July 2015. In early 2016 Boris Johnson was pictured in Dartford at a haulier's yard in an HGV emblazoned with the 'Take Back Control' message, and the pro-Brexit press began to assemble stories outlining the cost of Operation Stack for the national economy (often citing the improbable figure of £250 million a day). Another pre-referendum headline was generated by the Road Haulage Association of Great Britain suggesting that its members had been fined as much as £16 million in the period 2013–16 for unwittingly bringing illegal stowaways to the UK. Twenty-four Eritrean migrants were found alive in a lorry near Dover in September 2014, and another thirteen in a lorry at the Dartford crossing the same year. This raised the spectre of a repeat of the incident at Dover in June 2000 when 58 Chinese and East Asian immigrants were found dead in a lorry – the largest mass death of migrants in British history.

In this way, the humble HGV became oddly iconic in the run-up to the EU referendum, indicative of a botched European project that, on the one hand, was accused of making the UK's boundary more porous while, on the other, failing to deliver the speed and mobility promised by the TEN-T vision of a seamless Europe. Images of HGVs snarling up the roads of Kent thus became a key motif in Brexit debates, mirroring the anxiety about TIR (*Transports Internationaux Routiers*) juggernauts that Patrick Wright notes was prominent in the years immediately before the 1973 European vote. As he details, in the late 1960s and early 1970s, campaigners in villages including Boughton, Bridge and Harbledown near Canterbury became increasingly vociferous about the menace of lorries bound for Dover and Europe careering through what were inevitably described as 'medieval' settlements. But while significant damage was done to local buildings, and several pedestrians lost their lives in traffic accidents, Wright suggests that the nub of the issue was that these European 'motorway monsters' were viewed as 'out of place' in the Garden of England.[48]

However, following the decisive Brexit vote in 2016, it was the pro-Remain lobby that fixated on images of traffic chaos in Kent.

'Project Fear' had long argued that leaving Europe would require complex custom controls and create chaos at the border. Scare stories about shortages of medicine and food were commonplace, and the media headed to Kent to probe locals about their fears.[49] Operation Stack was also abandoned in favour of Operation Brock, the erection of a rigid steel barrier on the M20 between Ashford and Maidstone designed to hold lorries further from the port and allow for a contraflow of traffic. This was piloted from October 2018 through to January 2019 at a cost of £30 million. In October 2020 the government passed the Heavy Commercial Vehicles in Kent Order 2019, stipulating that from January 2021 any HGV entering Kent from another part of Britain would need to have a special ID. The plans to ring-fence Kent were immediately lambasted as the modern-day equivalent of the classic Ealing comedy *Passport to Pimlico*, in which a London borough declares independence. A satirical Twitter feed – 'The Kent Border' – began to spell out its 'Kexit' policies in its own 'News of the Weald', revealing that its stock of commemorative T-shirts (featuring the motto 'Our Quest is to Congest') was stuck somewhere outside Calais.

But for some Kent residents, the government's attempts to head off post-Brexit gridlock were no laughing matter. Back in Mersham, villagers awoke on 11 July 2020 to the news that a 1.2 million square foot parcel of land between the village and the southern orbital road around Ashford, earmarked for future warehouse development, had been purchased by the Department of Transport, part of a £705 million investment in border infrastructure designed to take UK border facilities 'to the next level' in readiness for Brexit.[50] For several months it had been rumoured that Amazon would be moving on to the site, with the newly completed Junction 10a providing easy access to the M20. While this had already raised fears of major disruption to local traffic, the proposed lorry park (with holding space for 2,000 HGVs) and inland customs facility escalated these. Local councillors complained bitterly about the daily disruption that would be caused by up to 11,000 vehicles entering and

5.5 Inland border facility, Sevington

leaving the facility: one predicted that 'it will be like Operation Stack every day'.[51] The fact that the news was broken by the press compounded the anxiety, with local MP Damian Green accusing his own government of negotiating a secret deal with no consultation. The Under-secretary of State for Transport later apologised when it transpired that the letter supposed to have been delivered to residents had never been sent.

Work on the new border facility began almost immediately, with the government claiming that planning permission was not required as there was already B8 (distribution) permission for the site. It later acknowledged that the use of the site as a lorry park would be unlawful without a Special Development Order, and, a full four months after clearance works had begun on the site, local people were finally consulted. Nevertheless, the Sevington Inland Border Facility gained Relevant Approval in December 2020 from the Secretary of State for Housing, Communities and Local Government, and opened in January 2021 despite waterlogging on site making part of the lorry park unusable. Almost immediately, Mersham became clogged with HGVs whose sat nav had inadvertently sent them trundling around country lanes, leaving them to attempt three-point turns in residential cul-de-sacs. Residents also reported sleepless nights due to the border facility's 24/7 floodlighting brightly illuminating the night skies. Through all of this, the government steadfastly refused to release details of an Environmental Impact Assessment of the site, with the Environment Agency responding curtly to FOI requests by stating that disclosure of details relating to the site was 'capable of adversely affecting public safety' – presumably because of concerns relating to people trafficking or terrorism.[52]

This pattern of poor government consultation and local frustration was repeated when, in November 2020, another border facility was announced for the village of Guston, near Dover, intended to deal with freight heading for the Port of Dover itself, including checks relating to live animal transport between the UK and Europe. As in the Sevington case, bulldozers started work on the 37-hectare facility before villagers had seen any detailed plans of the proposal, and before the consultation period for the proposal had finished. Fearing reductions in the value of their homes because of the noise and pollution, the villagers petitioned the government, angry with the lack of information provided. But the government pushed ahead, as at Sevington, looking to have Guston operational by July 2021.

In the event, the last-minute trade deal announced by Boris Johnson on Christmas Eve 2020 removed the threat of overly complex border tariffs, meaning that plans for the Guston facility were downsized in 2021 from 1,500 to 96 lorry parking spaces. But at the time of its initial announcement, the need for additional inland border facilities seemed pressing, made obvious first by five-mile queues on the M20 caused by the French authorities trialling post-Brexit procedures in November and then, on 20 December 2020, the unexpected closure of the French border as the 'Kent variant' of COVID-19 swept through the south-east of England. Electronic signs as far as one hundred miles from the border warned freight traffic not to head to the Channel ports, but traffic quickly built up around Dover and the Eurotunnel terminal. The next day, Johnson's COVID-19 press conference focused on the border closure, attempting to downplay the threat to UK imports and exports during the crucial Christmas period. Johnson stated that the number of lorries waiting on motorways had been reduced from 500 to 170 during the day (a figure immediately disputed by Highways England, which suggested that the figure was 950). Natalie Elphicke, MP for Dover, hit out at France's border closure, calling it 'unnecessary, unhelpful, and irresponsible'. She warned that the closure was causing 'serious traffic congestion', adding 'the longer that this goes on, the longer it will take to unwind, meaning that there could be queues past Christmas unless the French reopen the border soon'.[53]

The following day, over 1,500 lorries were queued. Operation Brock was implemented, and vehicles were directed towards the disused Manston Airport on the Isle of Thanet as the motorways filled up. By 23 December, even conservative estimates suggested that 4,000 lorries were parked across Kent, at which point France agreed to allow drivers with a recent COVID-19 test into the country. Angry continental drivers wanting to get home for Christmas clashed with police at Dover, frustrated with the lack of COVID-19 testing and basic facilities such as showers and toilets. Kent residents, who had often accused foreign lorry drivers of despoiling the local environment, took pity. Volunteers from the Guru Nanak Darbar in Gravesend made headlines by distributing 800 meals to lorry drivers stuck on the M20. Volunteers from Faversham took food parcels and provisions to Manston, passing supplies through holes in the perimeter fence to hungry drivers in desperate scenes, while on Christmas Day itself villagers from Mersham, including my mother, took it on themselves to lower bags of food and drink down to appreciative drivers stranded on the M20.[54]

With assistance from French police and thirty Polish doctors, rapid COVID-19 testing thankfully enabled the queues of lorries on Kent's motorway to be cleared before the New Year. But the

5.6 M20 lorry queues, from Mersham bridge

events of December 2020 seemed to symbolise the final and irreversible breakdown of the dream of seamless European mobility, barely twenty-five years after the opening of the Channel Tunnel. For many, dystopian images of lorry drivers stranded for days at a time, forced to live on meagre rations while missing out on Christmas at home, graphically illustrated the political fallout of Brexit. While the border closure was ostensibly about COVID-19 transmission, UK politicians accused President Macron of 'playing politics' with the lives of the lorry drivers. Downing Street was said to be incandescent, suggesting that the French were using the lorry chaos to 'strong arm' the UK into a trade deal.[55] Others argued that Britain was being punished for its 'world-leading' genomic research into coronavirus, implying that the French blockade was penalising the UK for its openness about the Kent variant. Here, the British media's coverage of the border blockade deployed familiar tropes to depict Britain's continental neighbours as devious, selfish and unreliable, a theme that returned during the vaccine dispute between London and Brussels early in 2021 (one notable headline in *The Daily Express* boasted that Britain had stockpiled enough COVID-19 vaccine and claimed 'We don't need EU!').[56]

In the shadow of the white horse

The Channel Tunnel has dramatically transformed the landscape of East Kent over the last twenty-five years, with the new road and rail networks that accompanied it overwriting existing infrastructure as the county became ever more incorporated into the European space of flows. Villages were split in two, homes destroyed and fields tarmacked over. Nationally, the economic benefits of this for the region were played up, but for local people the nuisances of HGV parking, Operation Stack and the periodic chaos created by the closure of the tunnel or ports often seemed to far outweigh these. In the fevered atmosphere around Brexit, discourses of environmental nuisance began to blur with more obviously xenophobic rhetoric, with the EU, France or foreign lorry drivers sometimes blamed for these local problems. Even the measures designed to ease local traffic issues – the new inland border facilities – have been controversial because the government rushed through their construction with few opportunities for local views to be registered: their rapid construction has often been justified with reference to the 'border chaos' caused by the French authorities rather than the obvious lack of preparation for Brexit on the English side. 'Taking back control' of the UK border has, then, come at a particularly high cost for those villagers living adjacent to what has been dubbed 'Farage's Garage'.

All this time, on the hillside next to 'Caesar's Camp', the Folkestone white horse has looked down on the Channel Tunnel terminal and the sometimes gridlocked M20 motorway, a witness to the sound and fury. It has been an essentially benign presence, a familiar local landmark helping cultivate a sense of place. The importance of the white horse in Kentish iconography is pivotal here. Indeed, it is hard to avoid the white horse in Kent given its contemporary prominence in road signs, statuary and iconography. Kent County Cricket Club's mascots are a pair of white horses, Victa and Victoria, and Gillingham FC, the county's only league football team, incorporates it in its badge. Yet no one is quite sure where this association comes from. William Lambarde's 1576 *Perambulation of Kent* provides perhaps the earliest explanation. Lambarde identified the megaliths at Kit's Coty in the Medway valley as the site of a key battle between Horsa and Categern, the son of the fifth-century Kentish king Vortigern. One of these megaliths subsequently became known as the White Horse stone, reputed to be the site where the Saxon standard was laid down.[57] Disputing this version, James Lloyd claims that there is actually little evidence that Horsa, Hengist or the kings of Kent ever used the white horse as a banner, and suggests that it is actually the white horse of Hannover and was adopted by the county to curry favour with royalty.[58] Indeed, it was in the seventeenth century that the 'Invicta' ('undefeated') white horse symbol was first incorporated into the county flag and the masthead of the *Kentish Post* newspaper.

While the significance of the white horse as a marker of local identity is unclear, traditions of carving white horses on English hillsides stretch back thousands of years (the most famous, at Uffington, Oxfordshire, originated in the late Bronze Age). This suggests that alongside its local, regional significance, it is also a symbol of national identity. This symbolism rests not so much on the figure of the horse, but the manner of its making. Chalk is a synecdoche for southern England, and, by extension, England itself. As Helen Gordon notes:

> Today in the south-east of the UK, much of the chalk has disappeared underneath sprawling towns and suburbs, but where it hasn't been built over it produces a landscape often viewed as quintessentially English. Smooth, rolling hills covered with short turf. Gentle slopes and steep escarpments, dry valleys and lonely beech hangers. Seen from a distance, it seems to ebb and swell like the ocean from which it once emerged. On postcards and tea towels, images of chalk landscapes perform a particular version of Englishness.[59]

Robert Macfarlane likewise claims that English chalk landscapes link British industry, architecture and imagination to the cycles of geological time. Suggesting that the first foot travellers to Britain crossed over on chalk, Macfarlane refers to 'chalky mysticism' – a mythology suggesting that chalk is a 'super-conductor of the sympathetic historical mind', connecting the present to the deep past.[60]

This connection is emphasised in some unlikely places. One example is the children's classic *Stig of the Dump*, authored by Clive King, who grew up in Ash in the North Downs in the 1930s. In the book, eight-year-old Barney falls to the bottom of an abandoned quarry and encounters a Neolithic caveman with whom he enjoys a series of adventures. The book makes much of the changing nature of the Kent landscape, contrasting the contemporary view from the Downs of enclosed fields and roads with the forest and heathland imagined to have existed in Neolithic times.[61] In some extraordinary passages, King evokes a sense of the geology and geography that underpins the construction of the 'cultural landscape', making reference to Barney's descent through layers of chalk and flint as he travels back in time. Standing with his caveman friend watching the sun rise above the standing stones (probably intended to be Kit's Coty near Maidstone), Barney is finally catapulted to the present: the Neolithic campfire vanishes and the 'distant chimney of a cement factory' comes into view.[62] The story hence speaks of continuity and change, with chalk the constant element.

Perhaps I am particularly prone to 'chalk mysticism'. Many of my direct ancestors – great-grandfathers and great-uncles – worked the chalk pits of North Kent, and until I was seven we lived on Dartford's Fleet Estate, where washing hung in the garden ended up coated in a thick layer of white dust thrown up by the Blue Circle cement lorries thundering by on Watling Street. But there are many others who have argued that chalk elicits deeply rooted feelings of national belonging.[63] For such reasons, chalk figures have become important symbols of the island-nation, their carving a re-enactment of rituals of scouring the earth connected to ideas of 'cleansing the nation'.[64] This theme is at the heart of G. K. Chesterton's epic poem *The Ballad of the White Horse*. Sometimes

5.7 The White Horse, Folkestone

radical in his politics, Chesterton was a committed Christian and distinctly parochial in his Englishness. His poem famously used the cleaning of the white horse overlooking the scene of the Danes' defeat at the hands of King Alfred (at Westbury in Wiltshire) as a metaphor for the need to protect the nation's borders and defend the 'hard-won' freedom of the English.[65]

In the same vein, it could be argued that the creation of the Folkestone horse at the turn of the millennium emphasised continuity over change, and the rights of English people to shape English soil. So while the Folkestone horse was ostensibly a celebration of the incorporation of Kent – and England – into a European space of flows, it was also an assertion of nationhood in an era when globalisation was seen to be challenging the significance of the nation-state.[66] In the post-Brexit era, and following the rupture with Europe, this intent seems clearer still. In stark contrast to the more encompassing sense of European identity promoted by the tunnel itself, its message appears unambiguous: This is England. This is not a statement of interconnection but one of distinctiveness and demarcation. It is less of a welcome, perhaps, than a valedictory statement, a two-fingered gesture in the direction of the continent.

Perhaps my reading of the white horse is overdetermined, a too convenient interpretation connecting the Kentish landscape to the negative politics of nationalism that accompanied the Brexit vote. But local ambivalence to the European project has at times been obvious, manifest in multiple episodes of opposition to the transport 'improvements' that have transformed this corner of England in the last quarter century, as well as the frequent accusation that foreign lorry drivers are despoiling the Kentish countryside. These protestations, sometimes accompanied by complaints about the cost of EU membership, have become conjoined with all manner of anxieties about migration and mobility. In Chesterton's patriotic vision of the island-nation, he recapitulated myths of King Alfred fending off 'heathen invaders' from Denmark: in recent times the media have served up a range of other figures as visceral threats to national sovereignty, iconic figures of non-belonging who must be repelled.[67] Foremost among these have been the asylum seekers and refugees who have arrived in Kent, sometimes in the back of lorries, but increasingly by boat. These migrants featured prominently in the Leave campaign's arguments about the need to 'take back control' of the border: subsequent government attempts to reduce asylum seeker numbers suggest that an exclusionary politics of Othering now irradiates official immigration policy. This has significantly changed the welcome visitors now receive at the Kentish border, meaning the white horse no longer embodies hospitality and welcome, but symbolises the 'hostile environment' England now offers to many overseas visitors.

6

Boat people

Their crews were from nowhere and anywhere. I'd been brought
up not to think about the Others in terms of where they came from
or who they were, to ignore all that – they were just Others.

John Lanchester, *The Wall*, 2019[1]

A few miles along the coast from Folkestone, Hythe is its sleepier,
smaller and more conservative neighbour. One of the original
Cinque Ports, given privileges by a twelfth-century royal charter,
its role diminished as longshore drift created a shingle bar across
the town's haven (harbour). Despite continuing efforts to maintain
the harbour, by the eighteenth century it was abandoned, with
those employed as seamen switching to fishing, marine salvage,
brewing and, in some cases, smuggling (always important in this
corner of Kent). Today the former harbour is lost beneath multiple
housing and industrial developments. Coastal retreat also means
that the town's attractive, long High Street stands a considerable
distance from the shore, separated from it by elegant Victorian
sports pitches and Edwardian villas, as well as the 92-bedroom
Imperial Hotel. This hotel, opened by the Prince of Wales in 1880,
was requisitioned as a gun emplacement by the Home Guard in
World War II, at which point the neighbouring golf course was
turned into a minefield. Today, the restored golf course is a selling
point for a new 'lifestyle' seafront development of three-storey
townhouses aimed squarely at the retirement market, with lifts
integrated as standard: semi-detached three-bedroom homes here

sell for upwards of £600,000. Another controversial development of 150 homes has been approved further along Prince's Parade, suggesting that additional gentrification of this part of the coast is imminent.

Behind this flat coastal strip, the town rises dramatically towards the Saxon church of St Leonards, most famous for its macabre ossuary, a collection of 1,200 human skulls exhumed from the town's churchyards as they fell out of use in the fifteenth century, long rumoured to include the remains of men who fell in the Battle of Hastings as well as Danish pirates slain by locals. Between the town centre and the seafront is the Royal Military Canal, dug between 1803 and 1809 as a defensive work, stretching some 28 miles between Hythe and Pett Level (located on the Sussex border). Three squat Martello Towers also remain on the seafront, intended to be the defensive frontline in the Napoleonic War. The Hythe Ranges, built to support the school of musketry pioneered by Pitt Rivers in the 1850s, likewise remain as testament to Hythe's military past. When opponents of the new housing development on Prince's Parade lobbied the local council, they argued that Hythe seafront had 'successfully defended us against Napoleon, the Kaiser and Hitler' and was 'definitely worth fighting for'.[2] Despite this, and a judicial review in 2020, work on the site began in 2021, with a new artificial badger sett constructed to accommodate the several clans displaced by construction work.[3]

Despite the occasional planning controversy, Hythe has the reputation of being a town where nothing much happens. In his 1900 account of the Cinque Ports, Kent-based Ford Madox Ford (named after his maternal grandfather, the pre-Raphaelite painter Ford Madox Brown) wrote that

> the pervading charm of the town is that of sleep ... One is back in a century – some beatific century which one cannot name – where– nothing is hurried, nothing passion-worn, nothing strove, when everyone was at peace with his neighbours and when the greatest of crimes was sitting up too late o' nights.[4]

A century or so later, Hythe retains its comfortable and sleepy air: the unexplained theft of eleven skulls from the church ossuary in 2018 was the biggest shock to the community in years. Despite oozing old-world charm, Hythe rarely witnesses the crowds that descend on Whitstable or Margate on hot summer days, partly because of its lack of train connections, and partly because of a dearth of obvious tourist attractions. Though it was briefly a fashionable resort, with a Venetian fete on the Royal Military Canal a draw for tourists in the Victorian era, there are now few seafront facilities catering for visitors beyond ice cream vans, some occasional food trucks and a couple of fish restaurants. There are no amusement arcades or fairground rides, and though the clean, massive shingle beach is probably the best for swimming on the Kent coast, the front is more popular with dog walkers and fishermen than sunbathers and pleasure-seekers.

Although Hythe's town centre has been going through some difficult years – its once bustling antique shops now outnumbered by charity outlets and vape shops – it still appears a content town,

6.1 Moyle Court, Marine Parade, Hythe

popular with the retirees who buy properties along the seafront. Among these properties is Moyle Court, a nondescript 1990s postmodern retirement complex. This sits on the site of Moyle Tower, a gothic mansion built in 1877 by Irish architect and one-time mayor of Hythe, Frederick William Porter, named in honour of his wife, Sarah Moyle.[5] Frederick travelled between Dublin and Kent for a number of years: his father William, also an architect, was responsible for Kent Terrace, a Regency revival development in one of the more affluent suburbs of Dublin.[6] A rambling seaside residence, Moyle Tower was built to be Frederick and Sarah's retirement home. Frederick suffered with poor health and died in 1901; when Sarah died in 1912, their home was requisitioned by the army to house members of the Devonshire Regiment. In 1923 it was purchased by the Holiday Fellowship (an organisation founded by church minister and social reformer Thomas Leonard to provide affordable holidays for the working classes). Used for that function for many years, in 1979 the building was bought by the British Council of Aid to Refugees as one of forty UK reception centres for Vietnamese boat people before they were rehoused elsewhere in the country.

One of those who passed through Moyle Tower was Hahn Tran, who fled Saigon when the North Vietnamese army arrived in 1975, fearing that his father's migration from the communist north some years before would make his family a target.[7] After going into hiding, he and another brother fled the country in 1979 in an 11-metre boat with 86 others. Attacked by Thai pirates just three days into their journey and turned away from Singapore and Malaysia by armed forces, Hahn was picked up by a British merchant vessel from a deserted island after a violent storm, becoming one of the estimated 19,000 Vietnamese refugees resettled in the UK between 1979 and 1990. While the Thatcher government was initially not keen to take in these refugees, privately predicting riots if they were offered council housing, their traumatic journeys were widely covered in the media and generated great sympathy in the UK, with local authorities, church groups and local reception committees making major efforts to support arrivals.[8] After refugees were met at the airport by government officials, reception centres such as Moyle Tower were used to resettle them, provide language training and acclimatise them to British life while jobs and homes were found for them. Despite Hythe's reputation as an inherently conservative and elderly town, there appeared to be very little local opposition. Thanh Cherry, director of the Hythe reception centre, recalls that 'locals saw the Vietnamese as the best thing that ever happened to Hythe', recounting to historian Jordanna Bailkin that the presence of boat people in the town not only gave the townsfolk an opportunity to engage with difference, but also made them feel that they were 'doing good'.[9]

The porous border

Fast forward to 2020. A new population of 'boat people' are arriving in Kent. These are the asylum seekers taking increasingly risky journeys in small boats, ranging from glass-fibre rowing boats and sea kayaks to larger rigid inflatable boats with outboard motors and even jet skis. The majority attempting the crossing are originally from the Middle East, Iranians, Iraqis and Syrians being the most numerous.[10] Most – around 60% – are men, but many are women, with entire families sometimes making the journey together. Before 2014 the numbers attempting to cross the Channel by boat were thought to be insignificant, although in 2002 a Russian national died attempting to cross in a canoe, and in 2003 two unknown men were discovered drowned in the sea and assumed to be asylum seekers.[11] But from 2014 the European migrant 'crisis' associated with the conflict in Syria and continuing war in Iraq, coupled with increasing securitisation of the borders of the EU, witnessed ever more desperate and risky journeys being undertaken. Though this was most evident in the Mediterranean (where over 3,000 drowned in attempting the crossing to Europe in 2014 alone), the media began to document increasing numbers crossing the English Channel by boat as the authorities clamped down on other clandestine methods of travel by road and rail.

In their analysis of media coverage at this time, Kara Dempsey and Sarah McDowell show that there were very rapid shifts in the portrayal of these asylum seekers. They note that the UK press initially highlighted the humanitarian dimensions of the 'migration crisis', personalising the migrants' plight with stories of their difficult journeys. But gradually this began to shift with the emergence of language that dehumanised the displaced, describing them variously as a wave or swarm.[12] Compared with their European counterparts, the British media were more likely to describe migrants as 'illegal' and less likely to highlight the geopolitical instabilities that caused them to migrate.[13] Given this emerging construction of asylum seekers as a threat, the British government made repeated attempts to reassure the public that it was tightening control of the border, beefing up security checks and investing in new security infrastructure to deter clandestine entry to the UK.[14]

Seeking to demonstrate this enhanced control, the Home Office boasted that British and French border patrols had prevented around 39,000 illegal crossings in 2014–15, with most of these attempts involving asylum seekers breaking into lorries at the Port of Calais. However, the media began to fixate on more audacious attempts to cut or climb perimeter fences to access Eurostar trains, while in the summer of 2014 a group of two hundred stormed a ferry, causing significant disruption to services. Such incidents allowed the media to talk not just of the increasing desperation of asylum seekers but their recklessness, stressing the danger that their behaviour posed to others. Significant in this respect was the 2015 coverage devoted to Abdul Rahman Haroun, a migrant from Sudan who managed to walk all the way through the Channel Tunnel, successfully claiming asylum the following year after a nine-month sentence for obstructing rail services. Many others were not as lucky: multiple deaths were recorded in 2015 as determined migrants attempted to jump on to moving trains near the Calais Coquelles terminal, partly because the double security fence erected around the Port of Calais made accessing the port increasingly difficult.[15] Of the 28 refugee fatalities known to have occurred in 2015 on the French/English border, twelve occurred on or near the French Eurostar terminal.

The Channel Tunnel – once heralded as a site of seamless European mobility – hence became the focus of anxieties about the porosity of the border, as Chenchen Zhang describes:

> The Channel Tunnel … provided a focal point for visualising the idea of border threats … made real through the circulation of numerous images in newspapers and TV news shows depicting 'would-be' illegal migrants wandering in the terminal area or found hidden under lorries. The images are often accompanied by dehumanising descriptions referring to unauthorised travellers as 'flood' or 'swarm' … The visual thus 'speaks' through interacting with other visual and textual discourses, which have also been used by government ministers.[16]

Downplaying the human cost of the crisis and externalising much of the blame to the French authorities, the British media also highlighted the economic consequences of regular migrant incursions into the Channel Tunnel, and, for the first time, the stacking of lorries on the M20 for reasons not related to industrial disputes or bad weather. One lengthy delay, in July 2015, was caused by the death of a Sudanese man under the wheels of a lorry at Calais. The following day, Prime Minister David Cameron stated, 'I have every sympathy with holidaymakers who are finding access to Calais difficult because of the disturbances there and we will do everything we can to work with the French to bring these things to a conclusion.'[17] He neglected to pass on any condolences to the victim's family.

With the British press narrating a 'crisis in Calais' during the summer of 2015, Theresa May and her French counterpart Bernard Cazeneuve signed the agreement that resulted in the infamous

'Wall of Calais', alongside increased police patrols and CCTV surveillance. Eurotunnel also cleared 100 hectares of vegetation between the Sangatte camp and its terminus to remove hiding places, flooding part of this land to discourage attempts at incursion. This securitisation made crossing via the tunnel or ferry port less of an option. With the 2016 destruction of the Calais camp and the dispersal of its occupants, it became increasingly likely that crossings would be made via other routes.[18] A spate of small boat crossings in November and December 2018 (amounting to 138 people) confirmed this and led then Home Secretary Sajid Javid to organise a coordinated response by the Border Patrol and Immigration Control. Nonetheless, in 2019 an estimated 2,000 migrants successfully made the crossing to the UK in small boats, most landing around Dover and Folkestone, but some towards Walmer and Deal to the north and as far south as Fairlight and Winchelsea in Sussex.

Images of these crossings were widely circulated, becoming the dominant visual dramatisation of irregular migration to the UK. Suddenly, the focus shifted from France and the tunnel to the busy waters of the Channel, so often the setting for national mythmaking, and a space laden with the 'material legacies of colonialism'.[19] Images of rubber dinghies crammed with wet, cold migrants, many of them not wearing lifejackets, became a news staple, variously evoking pity, anxiety or fear. Stories highlighted the ill-preparedness of those crossing, many of whom were simply provided with a boat and basic information about suitable landing sites. First-hand accounts, such as this provided by a Dover fisherman, emphasised the danger:

> I looked through my binoculars and I could see something. It was ten in the morning on a flat, calm, sunny day. We were four miles off Dover. As we got closer, I could see they were waving a white T-shirt tied on an oar. It was obvious they were in distress … I got alongside, and one of them leapt for the boat. He was hanging on my railing as we were still moving. There was panic in the dinghy.

> They'd obviously been out there a while. They didn't speak English
> so I pointed towards France and a woman nodded … The lady was
> being quite ill. There was a bloke bringing up blood, that might
> have been through dehydration. My anglers actually gave them
> some of their clothes, because the dinghy was half-full of water.[20]

The emphasis here is clear: even on good days, when the sea is
flat calm, these crossings are dangerous when attempted by inex-
perienced crew. Coupled with images of ill-prepared migrants
rowing unseaworthy boats with spades or arriving drenched to the
skin in overcrowded rib boats, such coverage establishes the idea
that these are irresponsible people, risking their lives as well as the
lives of others.[21] Particular condemnation is reserved for those
travelling with young children. Few articles note that those crossing
are seeking a better future for their children, or that it is the UK's
securitisation of the border that has forced these families to undertake
this dangerous journey. No one suggests that easier routes should
be opened to allow the migrants to seek asylum in the UK, or that
they should be brought to the UK for their claims to be assessed.

Geographer Nicholas De Genova argues that the state and the
law use this 'border spectacle' to reaffirm sovereignty, making those
who dare to cross borders via unapproved routes hyper-visible
through surveillance and media coverage, illegalising them in the
process.[22] Images of this 'spectacle' became relentless in 2020 as
the press highlighted growing numbers crossing the Channel,
depicting them as migrants to be repelled rather than refugees to
be welcomed. On one day alone in January 2020, 102 refugees
were picked up by the Border Force, most in rubber dinghies
attempting to cross in treacherous conditions, and another nine
were detained on a beach near Folkestone. The numbers increased
further during the clement summer weather of 2020, with the
suspension of ferry crossings during the COVID-19 lockdown and
calm conditions coinciding with new records in the number of
migrants intercepted in the Channel. As Joseph Maggs notes, in

a standard news report the headline typically identified a particular crossing as another episode in a 'summer of crossings', informing the reader about the number of people involved, and explaining in cold bureaucratic language that they had been 'intercepted', 'found' or 'caught' by the authorities.[23] Images of patrol boats also abounded, the English Channel depicted as a battleground where migrant boats played cat and mouse with border patrols. At times, refugee boats were also circled by the media: remarkably, both BBC and Sky carried live pictures of the crossings in the summer of 2020, migrants cowering away from cameras as journalists asked them where they were from.

This grotesque reality TV was fuel to the fire and helped whip up a veritable moral panic about the crossings, something easily done in a summer when COVID-19 and Brexit was focusing minds on the border as never before. Parts of the press reported that French politicians were encouraging crossings by suggesting that life in England was easy for migrants; others argued that racism in France was a major push factor for those making the journey. Countering, the Minister for Immigration Compliance Chris Philp stated that he shared 'the anger and frustration of the public at the appalling number of crossings … they are totally unacceptable and unnecessary as France is a safe country'.[24] However, Sir David Normington, former permanent secretary at the Home Office, argued that the 'only solution' was for French officials to 'intensify their efforts' to stop the migrants leaving France.[25] Irrespective of this, the numbers increased: 145 on 8 May 2020 (the VE Day Bank Holiday); 166 on 3 June; 180 on 12 July; 202 on 29 July; 235 on 6 August; and a record (at that time) 416 people on 2 September. Responding to the latter figure, Home Secretary Priti Patel argued that 'the situation simply cannot be allowed to go on', appointing a former Royal Marine as a 'clandestine Channel threat commander' and sending drones to the French to help in surveillance operations.[26] The battleground metaphors were stepped up.

But something else was shifting in the coverage of the sea cross-ings. Before 2020 most of the coverage was about the boats rather than individual asylum seekers. The spectacle of dinghies and ribs crowded with a huddled, faceless mass of migrants supported the narrative of a crowd or 'flood' heading in the direction of the UK. This started to change as names were put to those whose journeys ended in tragedy. Most notably, the death of a family of five Kurdish-Iranians, including a 15-month-old boy, was given prominent media coverage in October 2020, with headlines quoting charities which claimed that the Channel risked becoming a 'graveyard for death'. As with the drowning of Alan Kurdi, the three-year-old Syrian photographed washed up on a Turkish beach, the death of Artin Iran Nejed and his family highlighted the dangers of the Channel crossing, allowing refugee charities to evoke compassion among those otherwise unsympathetic to the plight of those seeking asylum in the UK.[27] However, this was immediately countered by coverage that put the blame for these and other deaths like them on the unscrupulous people smugglers who were 'forcing' refugees on to crowded boats at 'gun-point'. Precious little attention was devoted to the UK's securitisation of the border which made crossing the Channel by boat the only real option for those wanting to seek asylum in the UK.[28]

Thankfully, the majority of those who are not picked up by the French border forces make it to the UK, either being escorted to Dover Harbour in boats or being picked up on Kent's beaches by the police who are tipped off by locals. But the fact that increas-ing numbers managed to evade cross-Channel patrols and were pictured standing on Kent beaches allowed some sections of the media to talk of a *de facto* 'invasion' (one article in *The Sun* carried a photo that it claimed captured 'The Moment Migrants Storm Kent Beaches', invoking militaristic metaphors of national defences having been breached). This type of representation embodies the 'myth of encroachment' that Patrick Wright argues has proved so important in recent debates about English identity.

For Wright, such myths produce a 'Manichaean understanding' of England as a virtuous nation constantly under threat from the outside:

> To the considerable extent that this resurgence of English identity has been engineered by partisan politicians, campaigners and journalists, it has also been activated by the deployment of allegorical narratives that work by simplification and polarisation. In these encroachment narratives, the traditional nation and its way of life is typically squared off against a vividly imagined and probably advancing threat – be it immigrants, bureaucrats, Europe, 'experts' etc. Where the reality addressed is likely to be complex and full of nuance, encroachment narratives of this kind press that reality into a brutally simplified and prejudged opposition between good and evil.[29]

The British press was evidently not concerned with such nuance and continued to present accounts deploying myths of invasion. Perhaps this was not surprising in the febrile atmosphere engendered by COVID-19 and pre-Brexit anxiety. After all, in the run-up to the Brexit referendum, the spirit of 1945 was regularly invoked by those arguing that it was time for Englanders to 'take back control', and a facile equation was often drawn between the Nazi threat and a contemporary politics in which the white working class were being forgotten by a cosmopolitan Remainer elite who embraced the idea of open borders.[30] As such, Brexit was fuelled by a cultural manipulation of ideas of Englishness which incorporated white nostalgia for the British imperial project as well as the class resentments emerging in an era of austerity.[31] Brexit was, then, a vote against London, globalisation and multiculturalism as much as it was a vote against Europe, a combination having particular appeal for many older, white voters living outside the capital.[32] As subsequent coverage of the 'boat people' in Kent shows, images of immigration were deployed to suggest that everything that is good about England is threatened by everything that comes from elsewhere, with the Channel crossings depicted as an existential threat to sovereignty.

Suspicion and surveillance

Predictably, perhaps, the figuration of Kent as the frontline in the 'migrant crisis' witnessed increasing numbers of 'proud patriots' (white, right-wing extremists) taking it upon themselves to patrol the Kent coast. In September 2019 the far-right group Britain First started beach patrols on Samphire Hoe, the country park created from the Channel Tunnel excavations, in what they dubbed 'Operation White Cliffs'. In 2020 its members blocked the Port of Dover, causing gridlock, and also launched their own patrol boat *Alfred the Great*, helmed by an ex-Navy veteran who patrolled the waters around Dover, promising to stand firm 'against the unprecedented invasion by economic migrants'.[33] Though branded as racist vigilantes by many, and repeatedly confronted by the police, their efforts to survey the beaches of Kent looking for bodies and boats was arguably encouraged by the government's own rhetoric, which has demanded that coastal populations be constantly vigilant. Project Kraken, launched by the Home Office in 2016, implored people to report unusual behaviour off the coast. The campaign's poster, 'Seen Something Suspicious?', appeared to be modelled on World War II propaganda posters, the image of a lighthouse shining its light into the murky gloom suggesting the importance of constant surveillance. For criminologist Duncan Walker, Kraken constructs a 'surveillance community':

> UK waters contain remote 'blind spots' that elude local and national security attention, and which are prone to illegal incursion by traffickers of humans, drugs, weapons and terrorist thought and resources. Such spaces of seclusion are marginal to high politics of national security. They tend to be 'seen' and trodden not by state personnel but by the public, and particularly those whose lives and livelihoods are conducted, to some degree, 'on the edge' of land/water. Such people are often peripheral to high-security politics yet endowed with the intuition – the ability to filter (ab)normalities during their daily encounters of land/water – that the UK government needs. [34]

Walker argues that Project Kraken narrates 'a sense of foreboding at those unknowns lurking on or beyond the terranean visual horizon'.[35] This is the sort of thinking played up in John Lanchester's dystopian novel *The Wall*, published in 2019, which depicts a future in which climate change and sea-level rise has forced increasing numbers to seek entry to the UK, and where young conscripts are forced to pace the bleak concrete of the National Coastal Defence Structure, endlessly staring out into the gloom for the nameless Others who might appear at any time, rising from the sea.

The involvement of right-wing vigilantes, known to have attacked some of those landing at Kent, further contributed to the 'spectacle' of the border. Their members spread rumours about landings, filmed the refugees coming ashore, accused the state of inaction and identified pro-refugee campaigners as traitors. They also fuelled Islamophobia by invariably labelling all migrants, irrespective of their background, as 'Muslim men', depicting them as economic

6.2 Project Kraken

migrants and potential threats to 'English values'. I witnessed this first-hand on a visit in September 2020 when I was able to use the loosening of the COVID-19 lockdown to take a brief camping trip to Kent. For mainly nostalgic reasons I wanted to return to a campsite I had been to in 1978, in Kingsdown, immediately to the south of Walmer, a village sitting at the foot of the north end of the cliffs of Dover. My memory of the campsite was of a long sloping field with a spectacular view of the English Channel, ringed by dense woodland and just a short walk from the beach. My recollection was remarkably accurate, and the campsite was largely unoccupied despite the dry, sunny September weather. Kingsdown itself is often described as idyllic, with quaint, whitewashed fishermen's cottages on the beach, many of these holiday lets, and larger, well-kept, period properties in the village proper, which boasts an old-fashioned village butcher, a post office and several well-regarded pubs, including the Zetland Arms, ever popular with walkers on the English Coastal Path.

I travelled with my partner, and we had the campsite more or less to ourselves, bar a few caravans and one or two solitary campers nearby. We pitched our tent next to a clump of blackthorn trees hung with plump, purple sloe berries, facing due east so we could wake with the sun rising over the sea. On the second, bright, windless morning, I accordingly awoke early, poking my head out of the tent to take in the view over the Channel. Even before six in the morning, the Channel appeared busy with what I first took to be mainly inshore fishing vessels and netters, as well as the usual parade of tankers and container ships mid-Channel. But one ship stood out, a larger vessel that appeared to be towing another small boat. Struggling to focus through the early morning haze, I retrieved my binoculars, confirming my initial suspicions. This was the large, grey Border Force cutter *Seeker*, going along the Channel picking up migrant boats. Zooming in I could see groups of people huddled to the front of the boat, their inflatable dingy tethered to the rear. I also realised I was not the only one watching through binoculars, and that fifty or so yards away, a solo camper was also showing a lot of interest in what was going on, with notebook in hand.

Over the next sixty minutes or so I watched the boat move up and down the coast picking up another three small ribs or dinghies, before I retreated to the shower block to prepare for the day. There, as I showered, I overheard a woman washing up outside: 'Is that another lot coming in?' Then another voice: 'It's been every day this week, yesterday the police ended up chasing them through the golf course, running through gardens.' The first voice again: 'It's terrible … if it was down to me I'd put mines on the beach, that would soon stop them.' Both laughed. When I came out of the shower a few minutes later and returned to my tent I could see the boat they were talking about – a large inflatable boat with perhaps ten people sitting on each rib, just pulling on to the wide, private beach at the foot of the cliff below the golf club. Ten minutes later, another smaller rib arrived and another group waded ashore just a few hundred yards away. It was at this point that I noted that the solo camper who was our nearest neighbour on the campsite, some fifty yards away, had packed up and left.

Leaving the campsite an hour or so later, I made a wrong turn and found myself driving towards the golf club rather than towards the main Dover Road. Cursing my own incompetence, I suddenly spotted a cluster of figures huddled at the side of the road, wet and bedraggled, wearing what looked like quite traditional Kurdish clothes, with a woman in a headscarf cradling a child in her arms, two older children alongside her and an older bearded man. My instinct was to slow down, and my mind raced as to how we could help them, whether we had food left from the previous night we could share with them. But before I could stop, I spotted a police car parked at the junction, and a masked policeman who waved me on insistently. I drove on before I realised I was going the wrong way. I turned round and had to drive past the bedraggled group again, the policeman glaring at me accusingly. We finally arrived at the main road at Ringwould, but not before passing another group sitting in a lay-by who looked as though they had made it about a mile inland before being intercepted by the police and what looked like immigration control staff. Again, they appeared to be a family group, surrounded by officials in disposable facemasks who were handing them drinking water. Seeing so many individuals arriving, visibly dazed and confused after the crossing, with no possessions, was profoundly upsetting. My partner fell silent; I did not know what to say. We drove on in silence, holding back tears. The voices I heard at the campsite earlier kept coming back to me: how, I wondered, could people who have witnessed this kind of suffering have such little regard for human life that they would even joke about turning the beach into a minefield?

We continued to drive, my partner checking their phone. They started looking for any coverage of the landings we had just witnessed and started scrolling through Twitter. On it they found a series of recent postings of pictures of some of the asylum seekers we had seen landing, and their dinghies abandoned on the beach at Kingsdown. I stopped the car and scrolled through the images. They were not of the family groups we saw, but mainly of well-dressed younger male migrants in designer jackets and Western sportswear. In other photos, women and children had been cropped out. Being charitable, I suggested that the photographer obviously felt it wrong to publicly post photos of vulnerable women and children, but carrying on scrolling I saw that the same person had posted a steady stream of photos and images detailing the landings, alongside other posts about 'illegal' immigrants, anti-masking and the 'state-sanctioned' child abuse in Rochdale and Rotherham perpetuated by 'Muslim men'.[36] His comments suggested that the media were fixating on ill and vulnerable refugees, but that 90% of migrants were young men, and therefore 'economic migrants'. The photos he posted were designed to back this up and support his accusation that politicians are making Britain a soft touch. As I looked through the photos, I realised that one of the most recent was taken from the same campsite we had stayed at. It slowly dawned on me that the 'proud patriot' regularly documenting the arrival of 'illegals' in Kent was the same middle-aged man who was our neighbour on the campsite.

A million miles from home

Later that day we were back in Folkestone, where I wanted to photograph a piece of art designed to celebrate the 25th anniversary of Eurotunnel in 2019. Yseult Digan, a French-based street artist better known as YZ, was chosen to create a 50-metre-wide image on the tunnel entrance at Calais of a young girl looking towards the other side of the Channel, with the twin tunnel entrances serving as *de facto* binoculars. On the Folkestone side, she painted the girl's eyes looking out from two of the arches above Folkestone's Sunny Sands. Designed as a metaphor for the connection between two nations, and the past and future of the tunnel, YZ's project (*I Will Always See You*) involved local pupils on both sides of the Channel, and was inspired by her own experience of having been in Folkestone on exchange trips and able to see France from the beach.[37] However, when I arrived at Sunny Sands, the artwork had, perhaps predictably, been graffitied over by locals with a series of scrawled tags, something I was tempted to read as a comment on Anglo-French relations.

So, instead, we decided to head out to the harbour arm, recently restored following the dereliction that followed the axing of the ferries in 2000 and the closure of Folkestone Harbour railway station in 2001. During its years of abandonment, it was mainly used by anglers, though I also occasionally found methadone bottles in the ruined railway station, suggesting that the area had other less salubrious uses. In many ways the state of the harbour arm encapsulated the fortunes of the town. Once Folkestone was a fashionable Edwardian resort, with the harbour arm, the departure point of the Orient Express, overlooked by the majestic Grand and Metropole hotels on the Leas Cliff promenade, designed by Decimus Burton in the mid-1800s. But the decline of local tourism,

155

hastened by the destruction of the pier in the 1940s, the closure of the Leas Tea Pavilion in 1986 and the demolition of the Rotunda Amusement Park in 2003, meant the town became shabby and partly derelict:

> By the advent of the millennium, Folkestone had evidently lost a clear sense of its purpose and identity as a place to live, let alone visit. Many of the buildings in the central area surrounding Payers Park, above all on the main arteries of Tontine Street, which leads down to the harbour front, and the cobbled Old High Street, were dilapidated and boarded up. Local unemployment was high, with key industries, services and businesses in the town having gone to the wall. Educational achievement was statistically of the lowest standard in the country, which pointed to bleak post-school prospects for young people regardless of whether or not they chose to remain in the town. A seemingly unstoppable downward spiral of Folkestone's general fortunes was the gloomy order of the day.[38]

It was also a town divided between the genteel streets of West Folkestone and the more rough and ready areas of East Folkestone, blighted by unemployment. However, the harbour was bought by Roger de Haan, former Saga chairman, in 2004, and from 2014 the harbour arm underwent a dramatic transformation, spruced up, adorned with public art and linked to the town via a 'green' viaduct which is now Folkestone's stylish equivalent of Manhattan's High Line. In lockstep with De Haan's vision of a regenerated, creative Folkestone, the formerly bleak harbour is now home to any number of pop-up eateries and food shacks, many frequented by DFLs keen to explore Folkestone's Creative Quarter and its sprawling, permanent collection of contemporary urban art, which includes public artworks and installations by Tracey Emin, Antony Gormley, Yoko Ono and Mark Wallinger.[39]

Even in a time of COVID-19 and social distancing, the harbour arm was relatively busy in the early autumnal sun of a September afternoon. As in Margate, the sprinkling of creative dust over the town appears to have attracted the affluent, with the Book Festival (from 2002) and the Folkestone Triennial (from 2004) placing

6.3 Harbour arm, Folkestone

Folkestone firmly on the cultural map and generating favourable headlines in the colour supplements. A 2021 *Harper's Bazaar* article described Folkestone as Kent's 'rough diamond', 'genuine and hardy' as opposed to Margate's 'gentrified hipster parody', while *The Independent* suggested that it is 'cooler than Margate' and 'more inclusive to boot'.[10] Not all agree. Jon Ward, lecturer in cultural and creative industries, has argued that both towns have failed to tackle social problems through art, noting that although the Creative Foundation has secured affordable arts spaces, much of the regeneration is predicated on precarious labour.[11] Moreover, despite the depiction of De Haan as a philanthropic cultural benefactor, few of the 1,000 or so apartments being constructed on the land owned by the Folkestone Harbour Company will be affordable, their prices no doubt inflated by the town's cachet as a cultural destination. This has led some to identify Folkestone as a prime example of 'artwashing', the process whereby art is used to smooth over social tensions and hide gentrification behind a carefully aestheticised façade.[42]

Irrespective, the harbour arm was once an unlovely expanse of concrete and broken glass, but in September 2020 was busy with people enjoying drinks and food by the sea. At the very end of the harbour arm, the quirky Lighthouse champagne bar was especially lively with groups tucking into stone-fired Italian pizzas and Basque tapas washed down with prosecco, jazz music drifting out. Picnic tables and deckchairs were organised to allow diners to luxuriate in views up the Channel towards the white cliffs of Dover. But behind them, and the only boat moored alongside the harbour arm, was the *Seeker* cutter. The sight of champagne being drunk in front of the same patrol boat I had witnessed picking up dishevelled migrants earlier the same day was unnerving. No doubt many of those sitting in the sunshine were aware of its presence and were perhaps discussing the rights and wrongs of the British response to the 'border crisis' themselves, not least because news had just broken that a new asylum centre was planned for the town.

In recent years, most asylum seekers arriving at the Kent coast have been escorted to short-term detention holding facilities in Dover (at Tug Haven) or Folkestone (at Frontier House or Longport, a freight shed described in a 2015 inspection as a 'wholly unacceptable environment in which to hold people').[43] From here, destitute asylum seekers are typically taken to facilities in other parts of the country, including Yarl's Wood in Bedfordshire. Yet the increasing numbers arriving in 2020, coupled with the problems of social distancing and hygiene during the COVID-19 pandemic, led to an announcement that, for up to a year, a maximum of 431 adult male asylum seekers would be housed at a former Ministry of Defence property in Folkestone. Shorncliffe Heights, the staging post for so many who left for the Western Front in World War I, was to become an asylum holding centre, with the Napier Barracks blocks, built in the 1890s, being adapted by the Clearsprings Group to accommodate the refugees.

Boat people

The local response to the news was largely negative. The local
MP Damian Collins wrote to Home Secretary Priti Patel to suggest
that the decision had been 'exceptionally poorly communicated'.[44]
The local council was first informed about the plan on Thursday
10 September (the day before I was in Folkestone photographing
on the harbour arm), with work beginning on site the following
Monday and the first refugees arriving, remarkably, just a week
after that. The fact that the residents would be free to come and
go as they pleased (albeit with a voluntary 10 p.m. curfew and
signing-in scheme) raised local hackles. Social media was abuzz
with rumour and anxieties about the possible security implications
of housing asylum seekers in the town. A decade or so before, I
had listened to and read the objections of villagers in Newton,
Nottinghamshire, faced with the prospect of a local ex-RAF base
being used as an asylum detention centre. There, complainants
argued that young men brought up in 'foreign cultures' would not
understand local customs or ways of life. Discourses emphasising
the dangers of housing asylum seekers near family housing were
prominent, and the idea of the asylum seeker as sexual threat was
to the fore.[45] In the Napier case, these concerns resurfaced, with
Home Office assurances that the asylum seekers were law-abiding
dismissed by many residents on the basis that they had entered the
country illegally and therefore could not be trusted. Some suggested
that they were potential murderers and rapists, arguing that women
and children living locally would no longer feel safe. Others voiced
the threat of terrorism, stressing that local people used to keep
their doors unlocked but would not do so any more.[46] Added to
this were concerns about COVID-19, and the idea that new arrivals
would transmit coronavirus to one another and to the wider community. When news of the Kent COVID-19 variant emerged in
December 2020, some were quick to suggest, erroneously, that the
most likely source of the infection was Napier.

The housing of asylum seekers at Napier Barracks clearly aroused
deep passions, and the opposition cause was quickly taken up by

right-wing groups, some of whom turned up at Napier on the day the first residents arrived.[47] On social media there was talk of raising a militia to 'take back the country'. One participant – a 'proudly British' Twitter user – argued that the soldiers of the barracks had 'wasted their time defending the country only for them [immigrants] to invade us, rape our wives and bleed us dry'. Others spoke of 'freeloaders', suggested that placing 'Muslim men' in accommodation opposite nearby war graves was 'totally disgusting', and talked of asylum seekers 'grooming 13-year-old girls' online using the 'iPhones given to them by the government'.[48] Throughout, familiar gendered tropes were deployed to present white, English, working-class families as threatened by religious and racial others, with the fragile masculinities of right-wing extremists on display for all to behold.[49] This was far from the welcome afforded to the Vietnamese at Moyle Tower in Hythe in the late 1970s, the seaview guest house traded for a bleak, institutional setting with right-wing vigilantes skulking outside. Of course, not all locals were so unfriendly. Invoking a discourse of hospitality, local charity activists, the Kent Refugee Action Network (KRAN), organised a counter-protest in October 2020, with up to 200 attending a 'welcome event' where banners and placards were used to show that not all locals were against the centre, albeit a small group of far-right protestors also turned up on the day. Members of KRAN have returned frequently to protest about the conditions at the camp.

Napier has, then, exposed the fault-lines of intolerance and generosity evident in this corner of Kent. But along with a similar asylum centre in Pembrokeshire, Wales, Napier has become a wider signifier, held up by some as emblematic of contemporary attitudes to asylum seekers, and described as Britain's first modern-day (i.e. post-Brexit) migrant camp.[50] Its prison-like, militarised appearance, with security provided by private for-profit companies, appeared deeply dystopian to some, along the lines of the (imagined) internment camp in Alfonso Cuarón's 2006 sci-fi drama *Children of Men*, or the eugenic concentration camps in Russell T. Davis's 2019

Years and Years (in which a social worker accompanying his gay asylum-seeking partner across the Channel drowns a mile offshore, and washes up on a Kentish beach). Stories of mass COVID-19 infection in overcrowded dorms, with some residents sleeping outside to avoid becoming ill, began to circulate, and migrants spoke to the press about poor sanitation, a lack of showers and generally abysmal conditions. One, Nima, who came from Iran, spoke of his experience:

> When I arrived in the camp I saw someone being beaten up by racist people who started shouting at us, yelling that we should leave England and go back to where we came from. We're not welcome. We're unwanted. It seems people are repulsed by us. There are around 400 people living here. We queue for food. We're surrounded by fences. It's a prison camp. It's a trap. Some people self-harm. Someone claimed he'd hang himself unless he was transferred soon. I had to translate his words and listen to his devastating story. It hurt me, I could understand his frustrations. He magnified my hopelessness.[51]

In January 2021 178 people tested positive for COVID-19 at Napier. A major fire the next month was said to have been started by five COVID-free asylum seekers unhappy that they were not to be moved out of this insalubrious environment, providing further evidence of the unsuitability of Napier for vulnerable asylum seekers, many already traumatised by their journey to the UK. Later in February, a two-day joint inspection by the Prison Inspectorate and the Chief Inspector of Borders and Immigration found Napier to be 'impoverished, run-down and unsuitable for long-term accommodation', noting that residents had little to do with their time, little privacy and limited information about what would happen to them. It concluded that this was having 'a corrosive effect on residents' morale and mental health'.[52] The Home Office responded by halving the numbers at the camp and promising improvements, but in April 2021 plans were announced to increase numbers again to 337, with each asylum seeker expected to be there for up to 90 days.

6.4 Napier Barracks, Folkestone

Amid legal arguments that holding asylum seekers at Napier was contrary to their human rights, and the All-Party Parliamentary Group on Detention ordering a public inquiry, Priti Patel insisted that 'this site [Napier] has previously accommodated our brave soldiers and army personnel ... it is an insult to say that it is not good enough for these individuals'.[53] Her language echoed many right-wing extremists in maintaining that these immigrants do not have any entitlements, and that they are lucky to be provided with accommodation at all. Nigel Farage, writing in *The Daily Telegraph*, argued coldly against improving Napier and other similar facilities:

> The bigger problem is that more and more people want to come to soft-touch Britain. The expectation of the life on offer has reached the point where some who arrived this year have been protesting angrily about the conditions of the former army barracks where they are being held. These people have claimed asylum in Britain having supposedly fled war-torn countries, yet some seem to think that they can automatically move into their own room in a four-star hotel. They represent a very different kind of asylum seeker to those who have come before them.[54]

The periodisation offered by Farage suggests that contemporary migrants are economic opportunists, unlike, for example, the Vietnamese boat people who came to the UK in the 1970s and 1980s. Others seemingly agree. In March 2021 a *Daily Mail* reporter spoke to Hythe residents about the fact that some of those moved out of Napier because of the COVID-19 outbreak were being temporarily housed in the Stade Court Hotel on Hythe's Marine Parade, some 150 yards from Moyle Court.[55] *The Daily Mail* reported that they were quarantined because they had COVID-19, whereas they had actually been moved because they had tested negative.[56] Little of the hospitality shown in the 1970s was reported, with locals angrily suggesting that the asylum seekers were not observing the lockdown, were mixing with others, and were walking along the front with 'no regard for families'. Others took to social media to moan about them being rewarded for burning down Napier by being moved to the luxury of a three-star hotel with 'wonderful sea views' (ignoring the fact that they were moved before the fire). Some proposed a boycott of the hotel, others demanded a council tax rebate. On social media there was a further tirade of contempt and scorn: 'They've got our hotels, what do they want next? Our homes?'

Britain is a nation built on a mythology that it shelters those fleeing persecution. But this depiction of asylum seekers as parasites on the nation's hospitality suggests that important shifts have occurred in the imagined relationship between 'host' and 'guest'.[57] The welcome extended to the stranger appears more conditional than it was in the recent past, those coming 'without invitation' now subject to sanction and suspicion. Here, the media's discourse of a 'migrant crisis', coupled with the Conservative government's creation of a hostile environment for undocumented migrants, has created fear and mistrust. In this respect, the distinction sometimes made between the 'genuine refugee' of the 1970s and the modern-day 'economic migrant' seems to ignore the continuities between then and now: continuing wars and religious persecution, natural disasters fuelled by environmental exploitation and capitalist processes of exploitation that require illegal migrants to perform precarious, expendable and compliant labour. The processes that encourage people to flee to the UK in search of a better life have not fundamentally changed, but the reception they receive has.

But not everyone regards asylum seekers with suspicion, and in Folkestone, as in Margate, there are notable public artworks celebrating immigration and the fusion of cultures it creates. One is Varga Weisz's five-headed sculpture *Rug People*, which I first saw in the dilapidated harbour station in 2011, one of the public art installations commissioned for that year's Triennial. Entitled *A million miles from home*, and focusing on displacement and travel, the Triennial's theme seemed particularly apposite for Folkestone, a town whose history has been shaped by refugee journeys, from the arrival of those fleeing Belgium during World War I to the present 'wave' of boat people. Nicholas Wybrow writes that 'this Triennial had obvious ambitions to show how art could open up unseen, unsuspected, through-the-looking-glass worlds that might appear tangential, "far away" or even fantastical, but were actually related immediately to the life of the town'.[58]

Weisz's sculpture originally sat on a rug, suggesting a body or bodies keeping warm in blankets or rags, the multiple heads showing people of different ethnicities and evoking notions of multiculturalism. For a while the sculpture sat opposite Tim Etchel's neon installation behind it, spelling out 'The coming and going is why the place is there at all', underlining the idea of Folkestone as place of transit. Viewed alongside the quote, *Rug People* spoke of speed and slowness, of the varied mobilities that characterise the contemporary world, and the divide between those who can legally cross borders and the kinetic underclass who cannot. The sculpture is simple and affective: it depicts a group of travellers waiting for a train that will never come. The carpet is now long gone, rotted by years of rain, but the sculpture remains, no longer in rusted ruins but in a beautifully restored railway station, redolent of the

6.5 Varga Weisz, *Rug People*, Folkestone Harbour Railway Station

elegant days of the Orient Express. This imbues the sculpture with new meanings, contrasting those who have crossed the Channel smoothly, and in style, with those for whom the Channel represents a dangerous and fraught passage. Here, it is important to note that German-based Weisz was inspired to make the installation following her own journey to Folkestone, having witnessed refugees in the camps of Calais.[59] As someone whose own family fled Nazi Germany, the existence of these camps obviously struck a chord with her. A decade or so later, the installation seems more relevant than ever.

But my favourite of Folkestone's artworks is sculptor Richard Wentworth's *Racinated*, which has survived from the original 2008 Triennial. This consists of ten navy blue plaques, dotted through the town, indicating the presence of non-native plants: the privet, the weeping ash, the white poplar, the holm oak, the eucalyptus and so on. Some plaques are prominent, others less so. Finding all ten requires an energetic stroll around the town, from the Bayle and Old Town to the Leas and beyond. One was alongside a

Buddleja davidii, the purple-flowered plant that has colonised many derelict plots because of its tolerance of mortar and calcium-rich soil. Its roots are also coated in a peppery fungicide which makes it resistant to many grubs and microfauna. It is now a familiar sight in the UK, especially along railway lines, where its seeds are dispersed by the airflows created by passing trains, and it is widely known as the 'butterfly bush' or summer lilac. The plaque details how this plant, native to China, was brought to the UK in the nineteenth century, and describes the plant as an escapee that colonises vacant land.

Buddleja is a divisive plant species in the UK. Its ubiquity has led some to proclaim it our national flower, and it does important work in attracting pollinators. Others condemn it as a fast-growing weed that has little place in traditions of British horticulture, a sign of neglect and abandonment. Like the distinction between native and imported oysters, the fraught position of the buddleja

6.6 Richard Wentworth, *Racinated*, Shellons Street, Folkestone

in national imaginaries indicates how the distinction between native and non-native can take on an ideological charge.[60] It seems an effective metaphor for the presence of migrants in our midst. They enrich our country, do useful work and make their homes here, yet their presence continues to disturb some. And migrants, like weeds, can often be uprooted, removed as 'out of place'. Geographer Tim Cresswell notes the frequent depiction of weeds as 'mobile fugitives' that breed abundantly, stressing that the weed metaphor is often used to signify populations regarded as somehow undesirable or harmful.[61]

Richard Wentworth's deep blue enamel signs around the town do not seem to attract much attention these days, and at least one of the plaques seems to have been removed. I recall that the buddleja sign was on the junction of Dover Road and Shellons Street, just round the corner from the Banksy *Art Buff* mural that created so much furore as an unofficial part of the Triennial in 2014. The Banksy is no longer there, chiselled off the wall and placed in storage. However, returning in 2020, I find that the buddleja sign is still there, albeit partially obscured behind some council rubbish bins on the corner of an unloved traffic intersection. In a town full of photogenic public artworks, it is hard to imagine it turning many heads. But it is, I think, an important statement about the importance of opening our nation to Others. I watch butterflies dancing around the plant in the autumn sun and listen to the buzz of bees as they flit from flower to flower. For me, the buddleja on the corner of a dreary traffic intersection in Folkestone is not just another weed growing in an urban interstice, but a salutary reminder of the way the nation is enriched by non-natives.

7

The strange coast

The ocean with its vastness, its blue green,
Its ships, its rocks, its caves, its hopes, its fears,
Its voice mysterious, which whoso hears
Must think on what will be, and what has been
John Keats, 'To My Brother George', written in Kent, 1816¹

In a town bursting with public art, *The Folkestone Mermaid* is perhaps
the most iconic sculpture of all. Completed by Cornelia Parker
for the 2011 Triennial, this life-size bronze cast was famously modelled
on Georgina Baker, 38-year-old mother of two, chosen from fifty
local applicants. The mermaid sits at the edge of the harbour, atop
a boulder, staring out at the sea in all weathers. An obvious homage
to the Copenhagen sculpture commissioned in 1909 as a tribute
to Hans Christian Anderson's fairy tale, the mermaid punctuates
the harbour and provides a good photo opportunity for tourists.
She overlooks the beach where the annual sandcastle building
competition is held, and where those participating in the annual
Boxing Day swim are cheered on by large crowds. Invoking the
power of the sea, the mermaid's presence reminds the viewer of
the dangers that are ever-present at the coast, and the unruly nature
of a body of water that, while often appearing benign and shallow,
has claimed many lives over the centuries. Perhaps the worst disaster
in living memory was the 1971 collision of the *Texaco Caribbean*
tanker and a Peruvian freighter, with the wreck of the former then

7.1 Cornelia Parker, *The Folkestone Mermaid*, Sunny Sands

hit by a German ship, *Brandenberg*, and, improbably, a Greek steamer
Niki. In all 51 lives were lost, and oil slicks washed up on Kent
beaches for months.

But as well as acknowledging the destructive power of the English
Channel, the mermaid also stands as a tribute to one of Folkestone's
most celebrated residents. Visionary writer H. G. Wells's health
was poor throughout his life, and this prompted him to move to
the Folkestone suburb of Sandgate in 1896 to avoid the polluted
air of London. He found Kent an inspiring setting, writing *The
Invisible Man* and *The War of the Worlds* while living in Beach House,
not far from Sandgate Castle. Wells moved in a fashionable circle
of Kent-based writers and artists – Joseph Conrad, Ford Madox
Ford, George Bernard Shaw and others – and felt Beach House
was inadequate for hosting such luminaries. Hence, in 1901 he
commissioned renowned Arts and Crafts designer and architect
C. F. A. Voysey to construct a spacious family home closer to
Folkestone at a cost of £1,760. Although Wells left Kent in 1909,
Spade House still stands elegantly perched half-way up Sandgate
Hill, a cream-coloured house with broad eaves, small-mullioned

windows and tall rough-cast chimney stacks. For a while in the 1960s the house was a vegetarian restaurant, but today it is Wells House nursing home, with a blue plaque indicating its former resident.

The Sea Lady (1902), first serialised in *Pearson's Magazine*, was written by Wells while at Spade House, though it is thought to have been influenced by his time at Beach House, a property 'so close to the sea, that in rough weather waves crashed over it'.[2] The tale appears to be inspired by the proximity of the sea, but writing later Wells revealed that his direct inspiration was the sight of May Nesbit, the orphan daughter of a former journalist friend of his, emerging from the surf wearing a 'close-fitting bathing dress' which led to a 'rush of sexual desire'.[3] Although she was only 'fifteen or sixteen' at the time, Wells – a serial philanderer whose wife tolerated innumerable extramarital affairs – reportedly courted the girl. In the novel *The Sea Lady*, May becomes Wells's 'Folkestone Mermaid', a vamp feted by high society and hounded by journalists, who finally tempts the protagonist of the story, Henry Chatteris, to his demise:

> Did he look back, I wonder? They swam together for a little while, the man and the sea goddess who had come for him, with the sky above them and the water about them all, warmly filled with the moonlight and set with shining stars. It was no time for him to think of truth, nor of the honest duties he had left behind him, as they swam together into the unknown. And of the end I can only guess and dream. Did there come a sudden horror upon him at the last, a sudden perception of infinite error, and was he drawn down, swiftly and terribly, a bubbling repentance, into those unknown deeps? Or was she tender and wonderful to the last, and did she wrap her arms about him and draw him down, down until the soft waters closed above him into a gentle ecstasy of death?[4]

On one level *The Sea Lady* is light social satire, showing how an 'alien' figure can adopt the airs and graces of polite society and ingratiate themselves. But given the sexual imagery so overt in the novel, it also speaks to male fantasies about the sea as a feminised space, the mythic-monstrous mermaid a siren drawing men to their death.

Parker herself has described how she developed the concept for *The Folkestone Mermaid* in 2009 during the Copenhagen Climate Conference, suggesting that the Copenhagen and Folkestone mermaids are not connected through their sexual imagery per se, but through their placement on coastlines threatened by climate change. *The Folkestone Mermaid* is, then, part of a more general renaissance of the mermaid in popular culture which legal scholar Emily Barritt suggests symbolises the search for a better, more sustainable model of ocean stewardship. As she notes, with sea levels rising, oceans acidifying and microplastics accumulating unabated, contemporary society's impact on the oceans has been 'as devastating as many mermaid myths foretold'.[5] In this sense, *The Folkestone Mermaid*'s watchful gaze over the horizon alludes to the threat of rising sea levels for populations living by the sea, and fact that while the government has spent untold millions on border infrastructure, anti-terrorism measures and migration control, its track record on tackling climate change remains desultory.

As an example of environmental public art, *The Folkestone Mermaid* is a layered and subtle articulation of the relationship between culture and nature. In this respect, the gaze of the mermaid is important as it draws our attention to the shifting and uncertain boundary of land and sea. The beach at Folkestone is, in this sense, neither one thing nor another. It is a liminal zone of sand, mud and waves, that is sometimes sea, sometimes land, always transitory and on the threshold between one realm and the other. As geographer Leah Gibbs notes, the coast is a zone where 'terrestrial environments and processes influence marine ones, and vice versa', a continuously changing space where 'land's seeming solidity and stability meet the liquidity and constant motion of water'.[6] So despite attempts to render the distinction between land and sea clear cut, and juxtapose the safety and sturdiness of land with the unruliness of the ocean, the sea always threatens to undermine these physical (and cultural) divides.[7] *The Folkestone Mermaid* embodies this: when the tide is out on a flat calm summer's day, she sits serene, far from the sea, but when the spring tides crash in, she is obscured by foamy plumes of spray. But elsewhere on the Kent coast there are other equally potent symbols of the constant battle of land and sea.

The fragile coast

Tom Selwyn, in a wonderful essay on the topographies of Rye Bay, on the margins of Kent and Sussex, writes that a 'walker cannot but be aware at every turn of the ubiquitous sea defences that speak materially, metaphorically and accurately enough of anxieties about rising sea levels and the propensity for parts of the land behind the coast to be flooded'.[8] All around the Kent coast there are sea walls, sluices, groynes and breakwaters designed to prevent coastal inundation. But behind these there are often signs of previous inundations and the destructive force of the sea. For example, Sandgate Castle's perimeter walls began to collapse into the sea as early as 1616, and, despite repeated attempts to shore it up, around half of the castle was swept out to sea by storms in 1927 and 1950 before a new sea wall helped secure its survival as a private home. Another of Henry VIII's fortresses, Sandown Castle (north of Deal), was not so lucky, demolished in the 1890s following repeated collapse caused by coastal erosion. It was recorded as uninhabitable as early as 1793, and only a small commemorative plaque and gardens now register its location, much of its building material having been reused elsewhere for sea defence. On the north Kent coast at Reculver the Roman fort was lost to the sea thanks to the rotational slumping of the cliffs in periods of storm surge. As geologist Charles Lyell noted in his 1830 *Principles of Geology*, the fact that the church minster erected on the site of the old fort was also undermined by coastal erosion pointed to the dynamism of sea level change:

> On the coast to the east of Sheppey stands the Church of Reculver, upon a sandy cliff about twenty feet high. In the reign of Henry

VIII. it is said to have been nearly a mile distant from the sea. In the *Gentleman's Magazine*, there is a view of it about the middle of the last century, which still represents a considerable space as intervening between the north wall of the churchyard and the cliff. About twenty years ago, the waves came within one hundred and fifty feet of the boundary of the churchyard, half of which has been washed away. The church is now dismantled and is in great danger; several houses in a field immediately adjoining have been washed away.[9]

Dynamited by the Admiralty in 1809, only the imposing twin priory towers ('The Sisters') were allowed to remain standing as an aid to navigation. The salvageable building material was used to build a replacement parish church on higher ground at Hillborough, though within a few short years Trinity House took steps to ensure that the twin towers were not undermined further, putting large ragstone blocks between wooden groynes on the beach, a partially successful solution. Some of the subsequent measures proposed to prevent further erosion appeared somewhat drastic: local lore suggests that a letter was sent to the Strand Board of Works in the 1850s suggesting that the pauper dead of London could be encased in concrete sarcophagi and transported to Reculver to form the basis of a sea wall. There is no evidence of any reply.

In the 1800s the archaeological ruins at Reculver, Sandown and Sandgate were presented as enigmatic and romantic sites as part of the Victorian 'ruin craze': Reculver's towers, for example, notably featured in some of J. M. W. Turner's seascapes, as well as William Daniells's popular engravings of scenes around the British coast. Today, they are freighted with different meanings, symbolic of the vulnerability of the coast at a time of unprecedented sea level change. As geographer Lucas Pohl argues, 'the perception of the world as ruin seems a suitable approach to face the end times we live in today', suggesting that when we look upon sites like these, they are indicative of the ontological condition of a world in the grip of an inescapable climate crisis.[10] Commenting on such ruinscapes,

7.2 Reculver Towers

geographer David Matless likewise draws on Bruno Latour to suggest
that they are apocalyptic in the sense that they offer a revelation
not of things in the past but of things rushing towards us. With
the growing recognition of our climate emergency, this rush seems
headlong. Indeed, these coastal ruins fall into the category of what
Matless terms the *anthroposcenic* – landscapes emblematic of sea
level change and coastal erosion, encountered as uncanny sites of
memory and loss.[11]

Matless, alongside others, identifies the East Anglian coast as
particularly prominent in contemporary debates about sea level
change, noting the human drama of huge swathes of land being
lost to the sea at Hemsby and Happisburgh. Erosion is less immediately evident on the Kent coast, perhaps, but the problems of
sea level change are no less real, with rises of up to 2 mm a year
this century, double that of any year in the last.[12] With 10% of
Kent's population (160,000 people) at risk from coastal flooding, a
projected 30 cm rise in sea level by 2050 or 80 cm by 2100 would
have devastating implications.[13] Already, the coastline of the Isle

of Thanet is constantly changing thanks to the undercutting of chalk cliffs, repeated falls, and longshore drift transporting beach material around the headland. On the north Kent coast, where London Clays are prevalent, slumping and slipping caused homes to fall into the sea at Eastchurch, Sheppey, in 2020, and there has been major coastal defence work and groyne renewal at Whitstable, Hampton and Seasalter to prevent further erosion along the lower-lying stretches of this coastline, which flooded catastrophically in 1953.[14] Substantial sea defence works have also been undertaken recently at Deal, with millions of tonnes of Norwegian rock moved into place to reduce wave energy, while shingle is regularly recycled and regraded along the beaches of Folkestone and Hythe. At Dover, the famous white cliffs erode at an average rate of 20 cm per year but are left largely to the mercy of the elements. A major fall in February 2021, after months of rain, was read portentously by some Remainers as a symbol of post-Brexit national decline.[15]

7.3 Cliff erosion, St Margaret's at Cliffe

The 2021 novel *Dreamland* by Rosa Rankin-Gee takes some of the familiar landmarks of the Kent coast, most notably Margate's Arlington House and the funfair next door, to speculate on the impacts of climate change.[16] Part of an emerging tradition of ecocritical 'cli-fi', Rankin-Gee's novel borrows the conceit of Russell Hoban's 1980 novel *Riddley Walker* that sea level change will ultimately cut off Thanet ('Ram' in his novel) from the mainland.[17] Hoban's novel is set some 2,500 years after a nuclear catastrophe: Rankin-Gee grounds her narrative in a more recognisable near-future, a 'post-boom' Margate from which the DFLs and gentrifiers have departed as the town begins to be pummelled by regular tsunamis. Temperatures, and tensions, rise as the government cuts off essential services, with new Localisation Acts forcing residents to fend for themselves. Looting is endemic, and food banks are relied upon by most. 'Kem' is rife on the streets, a 'roughed up British Meth' that becomes the locals' drug of choice as they try to cope with rising sea levels and winter temperatures approaching 40 degrees.[18] Enter representatives of the mysterious company LandSave, who, while lodging at the boutique Sands hotel, recruit locals to building projects along the edge of Thanet, promising to improve housing and build sea defences to keep the tide at bay. It is only later that the novel's protagonist, Chance, realises that the wall being constructed is not to keep the tide out, but the people in, with the Isle of Thanet's population regarded as expendable by the London-based elite. The premise of the novel is perhaps not as far-fetched as it might seem: the Isle of Thanet was separate from the mainland as recently as the eighteenth century before the Wantsum channel finally silted up. In 2020 US think tank Climate Central produced an interactive map showing that by 2050 a combination of fluvial flooding and sea level rise will again turn Thanet into an island, while much of central Margate, including the low-lying Dreamland theme park, built alongside the Tivoli brook, will be regularly flooded.[19]

But it is on the low-lying land of Romney Marsh that fears of coastal inundation are most acutely felt. This part of Kent owes its existence to the vast shingle spit that grew across the mouth of the River Rother, and ultimately up towards Hythe, around 4,000 years ago. This barrier beach of flint shingle stopped alluvial deposits from being washed away to sea and encouraged the gradual silting up of the land behind. Today, the marsh is Kent's famous 'fifth continent', a reclaimed land of drainage ditches and pasture where sheep outnumber people and trees are few. It boasts distinctive wildlife, with marsh frogs, leeches, water voles and crested newts found in prodigious numbers in the complex ditch network, and wildfowl wintering on the flooded fields between. It is a flat landscape of big skies and changing light, punctuated by distinctive church towers, many serving settlements that have long since disappeared, washed away by thirteenth-century storms or depopulated by the Black Death. In his series of motor adverts for Shell in the 1950s, Sir John Betjeman opined:

> Romney Marsh, where the roads wind like streams through pasture and the sky is always three-quarters of the landscape. The sounds I associate with Romney Marsh are the bleating of sheep and the whistle of the sea wind in old willow trees. The sea has given a colour to the district: it has spotted with silver the oak posts and rails, it gives the grass and rushes a grey, salty look. [20]

The marsh has changed notably since Betjeman's day, and no doubt he would baulk at the sight of the twenty-six 100-metre-high wind turbines at Little Cheyne Court, on the Brenzett to Rye road, visible from as far away as the North Downs. He might also have regrets for the loss of substantial areas of pasture to arable, with ploughing accelerating land erosion by leaving areas susceptible to the wind as the peaty soil desiccates. Most of the land remains two or three metres above sea level, but there are parts where even modest sea level change would cause almost constant flooding without remedial action.

But despite recent change, Romney Marsh retains a unique sense of place. This is a Marmite, love-it-or-hate-it identity that attracts a particular breed of people – marshlanders – who revel in the area's peculiar geography, its reminders of past inhabitation and portents of potential disaster to come. These are the type of people who have started up the Romney Marsh Mountain Rescue service as an in-joke and circulate stories of the real and imagined beasts that haunt the marshes.[21] Here, myths are layered on myths. With its bleak and windswept vistas, remote villages and malarial marshes, Romney Marsh was the setting for actor Russell Thorndyke's series of *Dr Syn* novels (published between 1915 and 1944). As a ten-year-old, I thought the novels, read to us by our schoolmaster alongside *Moonfleet* and *The Hobbit*, were based on historic events, including the exploits of the notorious Aldington gang. I am probably not alone in that, with the evocative tales of the masked leaders of the local smuggling gangs trading shots with Revenue troops having helped mythologise the marsh as somehow beyond the law. It is a conceit that continues in the Kentish noir of William Shaw, whose crime thrillers *Salt Lane*, *The Birdwatcher* and *Grave's End* play on the bleakness of the landscape, with detective Alex Cupidi forced to engage with its environmental histories as she unravels tales of corruption, revenge and greed.[22] In *Salt Lane* a woman's body is found dead in a drainage ditch and a migrant labourer in a nearby slurry pit; in *Grave's End*, badgers exhume a body hidden under a new housing development; and *The Birdwatcher* sees the eponymous title character murdered in a remote cottage on a bleak, rain-lashed beach.

As both littoral and liminal landscapes, marshlands such as Romney Marsh have long been imagined as culturally problematic, neither solid land nor flowing water, a shifting, permeable zone of presence and absence. At Romney Marsh this indeterminacy is also evident in the settlements that stand between marsh and sea, many of which appear rather thrown-together, partly due to the coastal processes that have greatly altered the shoreline over recent centuries. Dymchurch is a case in point. Once the administrative centre of the marsh, it straggles along the coastal road between Hythe and St Mary's Bay. Writing in 1989, Derek Jarman described

7·4 Fairfield Church, Romney Marsh

it as 'strangely old-fashioned'.[23] Little has changed. At its centre are the vestigial traces of a bucket and spade tourism industry that flourished from the 1930s through to its heyday in the 1960s. It boasts a couple of amusement arcades with coin pushers and pinball machines, badly named fish and chip shops ('The Codfather') and a small, dated fairground. The main tourist attraction, set back a little from the centre of the village, is the station, one of eight stops on the thirteen-mile narrow-gauge Romney, Hythe and Dymchurch Railway. Opened in the 1920s, the 'little' railway was the brainchild of 'Count' Louis Zborowski, Canterbury-based racing driver, owner of the original Chitty Chitty Bang Bang and heir to part of the Astor fortune. Around the village are three caravan parks with upwards of six hundred caravans, many of them semi-permanent, and a motley assortment of interwar homes, many on unadopted, potholed roads. A few grander, older houses remain, hinting at the village's medieval wealth, with the 1575 New Hall at the centre of the village having once served as court and gaol for convicted smugglers. Most of the village's properties are but a stone's throw from the beach, but only a handful have any sea view. Instead, most look out on the grassed bank that rises twenty or so feet to the sea wall. On windy days, the main beach car park, next to Martello Tower 25, is often full of people parked up with flasks of coffee, staring out, not at the sea, but at the wall.

The wall

Fully four miles long, Dymchurch Wall was begun by the Romans, who built up clay banks behind the shingle beach. However, after the great storms of the thirteenth century breached it, and longshore drift shifted the shingle towards Hythe, the flat sandy beach offered little defence against spring tides. New taxes were raised, and the wall improved, built this time of wooden piles and faggots (bundles of sea buckthorn branches, thought to be impervious to water). Groynes, supported by rocks, were used to prevent further shingle depletion, with the maintenance of the wall requiring a small army of labourers permanently stationed in the village. In the nineteenth century the sea wall was faced with Kentish ragstone, with the whole wall rendered with concrete in 1899. It was this wall that began to fail in the 1990s, notably at points where it had been weakened to the rear by burrowing animals. Given predictions of sea level change, the Environment Agency decided to spend £60 million on a new sea wall, including 1,700 new stepped sections designed to dissipate the energy of the waves, each weighing twenty tonnes, arrayed in front of an improved wall to the rear. Opened in 2011, the wall was proclaimed as guaranteeing the safety of 2,400 local homes, reducing a 1-in-10 annual flood risk to a 1-in-50. The pale concrete walkway along the top of the wall is augmented by elegant art deco flourishes, such as porthole viewing platforms, and is popular with walkers. But the stepped sections below are notoriously slippery and often slimy with green algae, with several serious injuries having occurred when unwary dog walkers have fallen.

Dymchurch, and Romney Marsh as a whole, owes its existence to the wall. One person who realised this was Paul Nash, contemporary

7.5 Dymchurch Wall

of Eric Ravilious and Stanley Spencer. Most famous as a war artist, Nash was a formidable painter of 'soil and sea' whose sometimes abstract and surreal landscapes provide an important link between the British Vorticists and the European *avant-garde*.[24] During World War I, Nash tripped and injured himself in the trenches, being evacuated to Britain while his comrades were slaughtered at the Battle of Passchendaele. Returning as an official war artist, he produced some of the most haunting images of the conflict. Few of these paintings depicted combatants, as this was art emphasising desolation and despair by focusing on the primal qualities of landscape: these were elongated, near-architectural images of flooded trenches, broken tree stumps and brooding skies.

After the war Nash was diagnosed with post-traumatic stress disorder, and moved to the Kent coast, like so many others before him, to recuperate. Renting a former Dymchurch pub, Rose Cottage, with his wife Margaret in 1920, Nash found himself a war artist with no war to paint. Instead, he turned to the sea wall as subject matter, producing a remarkable series of sketches and paintings that pitched nature against culture in an elemental battle of sea against land, as if opponents in a war. These are remarkable perspectival images: Dymchurch Wall is frequently viewed as if from above, an angular, massive modern structure attempting to hold out the more fluid sea. Often the sky is dark and threatening, holding portents of impending disaster. For Nash, this landscape clearly resonated with the battlefields of World War I, as Andrew Causey notes:

> The waterlogged Flanders landscape had been a danger apart from the fighting, with the risk to men and horses of becoming trapped in mud and even drowning, and at Dymchurch there is a possible reading of the wall both as a defensive and protective element against the sea and also as a reprise, more solidly constructed, of the fragile lines of duckboards across the Flanders' wastes.[25]

Given these intimations of conflict, and his own fear of water (he once nearly drowned as a child), it is perhaps not surprising that Nash referred to Dymchurch as the 'strange coast', rendering it a stark borderland between life and death.[26] For Nash, the sea wall stood on the threshold of past and present, his paintings alluding to the ways that the sea threatened to return him to the nightmares of his youth. In his autobiography, Nash described the seas off Dymchurch as 'cold and cruel waters, usually in a threatening mood, pounding and rattling along the shore'.[27] He left for East Sussex in 1925, writing of his time documenting the Dymchurch shoreline that 'I shall never work there anymore … a place like that and its effect on me – one's effect on it. It's a curious record formally and psychologically when you see the whole set of designs together.'[28]

After his Dymchurch sojourn, Nash turned his gaze towards other landscapes, and increasingly towards the threat from the sky. During the Battle of Britain he produced powerful images of German bombers crashed in quintessentially English rural landscapes.[29] Nevertheless, he continued to work on some of his

Dymchurch paintings until his death in 1946. In these later pictures, monochromatic imagery emphasising the stark geometry of the wall was replaced by more colourful and complex renderings inspired by the surrealism of Giorgio de Chirico. *Nostalgic Landscape*, for example, was started in 1923 as a simple perspective of the wall, but was changed by Nash in the 1930s through the inclusion of a (now-demolished) sluice gate, with its doorway leading to a seemingly endless, dark tunnel beyond.[30] The sluice gate in this painting resembles a watchtower, but it also appears to serve as a repository of Nash's memories at the point where the fluidity of the sea met the solidity of the sea wall. Paul Hendon offers a Freudian interpretation of the painting, arguing that 'the watch-tower on the sea wall is so represented that it offers a path that evades the sea/land dialectic of the [earlier] Dymchurch paintings and its associated oppositions of feminine and masculine, erosion and resistance'.[31] This hints at an alternative reading of the threat of coastal inundation, one that suggests that we should 'not put too much faith in the stability and dependability' of the distinction between land and sea, and recognise that land reclamation is always fragile and temporary.[32]

An alien land

Moving south from 'Dymchurch-under-the-Wall', the coastal path follows the shoreline, and is flat and unrelenting, betraying that much of the land here was reclaimed from the sea. Littlestone-on-Sea, for example, stands on land reclaimed in the nineteenth century as Romney Bay silted up. It was originally planned by King's College alumnus and Liberal MP Sir Robert Perks as a fashionable resort for the Victorian upper classes. Herbert Gladstone MP once owned a home there, but only a few, elegant townhouses were ever constructed, hinting at what might have been. Henry Tubbs' plans for a pier, electric tramway and promenade were also never realised. Further down the coast at Greatstone, boxy four-storey retirement apartments give way to a motley assortment of functional retirement bungalows from the 1960s and occasionally more stylish homes from between the wars. Here, the sand has drifted over the shingle beach and created large dune systems that need constant stabilisation to prevent wind erosion, with the planting of sea buckthorn the traditional method used to hold the dunes together. Greatstone was a hugely popular resort in the 1950s and 1960s, with Maddieson's Holiday Camp the centre of attention: it is now demolished, though traces of its swimming pool can still be found in the bushes. Today, Greatstone's wide, flat beach is popular with windsurfers and dog walkers, but Londoners seeking sun and sand generally head for Camber Sands, over the Sussex border. A notable exception was an illegal cookout 'rave' organised on Greatstone beach by a London jerk chicken shop during the COVID-19 lockdown. Participants were accused of urinating in local driveways, leaving rubbish strewn on the beach and failing to observe social distancing rules: deploying familiar anti-metropolitan sentiments, one local resident vented their spleen on social media: 'I think there must be something in the air in the big stink that makes Londoners just plain daft.'[33]

To the south of Greatstone, things begin to get even more motley as one walks towards the lighthouse at Dungeness that marks the south-eastern tip of Kent. The lighthouse, erected in 1961, is the tallest building in this flat landscape at 141 feet, and stands only a few hundred yards from the slightly smaller 'old' lighthouse dating from 1904, open to the public through the summer months. This in turn is only 50 yards from the base of the 1792 tower, demolished following violent storms. This was the third of no less than five lighthouses built since the seventeenth century. Each of the five lighthouses was, in its day, an important signifier of modern science, safety and rationality at the edge of the sea. Notably, Dungeness had the first lighthouse in Britain to be powered by an electrical generator, installed in 1862, and the 1961 lighthouse was the first to incorporate a strobe beam to prevent nocturnal bird kills.[34] The fact that each new lighthouse has been constructed successively closer to the sea underlines that coastal change here is a dynamic process, with coastal retreat having also required foghorns to prevent ships running aground on the shingle banks around the headland, the first an experimental Daboll foghorn installed by Michael Faraday in 1863. Today, the lighthouse is a constant reminder of the threat of sea level change, its verticality at odds with the horizontal, low-lying landscape.

Often erroneously identified as a desert, Dungeness is a large cuspate headland, twelve square miles of constantly shifting shingle, pockmarked with sea kale, gorse and buckthorn, sheltering Denge Marsh to the rear (one of the earliest portions of Romney Marsh, reclaimed from the sea in the eighth century). Apart from lighthouses, the headland is home to the nuclear power station opened in 1983, Dungeness B, alongside the decommissioned Dungeness A, opened in the 1960s. There are also former radar and coastguard stations, some sound mirrors, a couple of pubs and many shacks, bungalows and plotlander homes, several of which were converted from railway carriages in the 1920s.[35] Elsewhere, rusted winches and decaying fishing huts remain from a time when fishing was bigger business, and there are occasional fragments of broken railway track along the shore, indicating how fish were transported up the coast before the main road was completed in 1938. The fishing industry is still present, with a small fleet of boats moored on the beach, and cod, whiting and conger caught in relative abundance on spring tides. Sea anglers are particularly drawn towards the stretch of coast known as the 'boils' where the power station cooling water flows out into the Channel. Here, the combination of warm effluent and the dead fish that get caught in the power station's filtration system attract sizeable numbers of whitebait and the bigger fish that feed on them. These in turn attract gulls and terns, with the RSPB reserve established to the rear of the headland in 1932 providing an observatory for watching these as well as migratory populations of swallows, warblers and wheatears, together with less frequently spotted visitors including Kentish plover and bittern.

7.6 Dungeness beach

With its large skies, unrelenting acres of shifting shingle that are difficult to walk on, and the constant, brooding presence of the power station, Dungeness is frequently written about in terms of its wild, inhospitable nature. Even more so than the marshes behind it, the Dungeness headland exudes an eerie quality, appearing devoid of life despite the obvious presence of signs of inhabitation in the form of recently renovated homes and cabins on the beach. Mark Colquhoun, former student of cultural theorist Mark Fisher, describes Dungeness by invoking Fisher's distinction between the weird and the eerie:

> The simplest way to get to this difference is by thinking about the (highly metaphysically freighted) opposition – perhaps it is the most fundamental opposition of all – between presence and absence … The weird is constituted by a presence – the presence of *that which does not belong*. In some cases … the weird is marked by an exorbitant presence, a teeming which exceeds our capacity to represent it. The

eerie, by contrast, is constituted by a *failure of absence* or by a *failure of presence.* The sensation of the eerie occurs either when there is something present where there should be nothing, or there is nothing present when there should be something.[36]

For Colquhoun, Dungeness embodies the eerie by virtue of being a landscape devoid of human figures yet full of human traces. In Fisher's work, the radical potentiality of the eerie is that it unsettles and decentres the human subject, revealing how society structures our expectations of the way things are and the way they should be.

 In the twenty-first century, this sense of the eerie has had considerable draw for visitors who have repeatedly documented Dungeness in photography, art and music.[37] Like Folkestone, Margate and Whitstable, Dungeness is now a 'must-see' destination for Londoners on a day out, with newspaper travel writers waxing lyrical about its quirky but transformative qualities. Nick Hunt, for example, describes a week in Dungeness as 'like falling into the clear light of another world', paraphrasing W. H. Auden by proclaiming it 'a place that was altogether elsewhere'.[38] The peculiar appeal of Dungeness has also unleashed an unlikely wave of gentrification. Architectural students and landscape designers alike descend on Dungeness to marvel at how new designer homes relate to their surroundings, making the most of views which frame not the seascape per se, but the power station and lighthouse. Plotlander shacks change hands for big money and even the former coastal pumping station is now an AirBnB that charges over £700 a night. One three-bedroom conversion, featured in Kevin McCloud's *Grand Designs* in 2016, attracted media headlines when it was put on the market for close to one million pounds, making it Britain's most expensive 'shed'.

 The idea that people now pay a premium to live, or holiday, a stone's throw from a nuclear power station inverts many of the assumptions that exist about contemporary 'green' or eco-gentrification. Equally, it is difficult to see the appeal of living in a place that feels dreadfully isolated, open and exposed to the elements, especially in winter when bitter winds can swing in from the East. At other times, fog envelops the headland even when the rest of Kent basks in sunshine. But Dungeness continues to be sought after by those attracted by its liminal character. It was this that brought the BBC *Doctor Who* production team to Kent in January 1971 to film the episode 'The Claws of Axos', a story that was originally going to be filmed at Battersea power station but was moved to the Kent coast after it was proposed as a suitably 'other-worldly' location that might amplify fears of the alien Other. The fact that the location filming was blighted by incredibly changeable weather, from bright sunshine to thick fog and light snowfall, heightened the unearthly nature of the setting.[39] 'The Claws of Axos' is a pretty standard 1970s *Doctor Who*, with a plot involving aliens crash-landing on earth, but subsequent positive evaluations of the story note how the filming exploited the stark, primal beauty of the Dungeness landscape, with the monumental nuclear power station 'standing out like a large film set front against the horizontally-arrayed gradations of shingle, sea and sky'.[40]

When I visit Dungeness, I am not sure whether my response to it is still informed by watching 'The Claws of Axos' as an impressionable child. Like many who grew up in the early 1970s, for me *Doctor Who* was *the* television event of the week, with Jon Pertwee, and then Tom Baker, taking me on journeys that were fantastical but still rooted in the landscapes I saw around me in North Kent, an edgeland of gravel pits, disused cement works and electrical substations. Juxtaposing these everyday settings with threats of invasion, contamination or body horror, *Doctor Who* played on ideas of liminality to change the meaning of these places and suggest that they might be in some way connected to irruptions of alien life. In that sense, it is perhaps not surprising that these settings appear prominently in a range of twenty-first-century art and media that could be described in some way or another as hauntological. This is a term regularly used, often alongside 'folk horror', to describe media which carry with them a 'sense of troubled nostalgic reverberation from another time and place', often Britain of the early 1970s.[41] This was a Britain of the three-day week and oil shortages, a time when the white heat of industrial modernity was burning out. It was also during the Cold War, a period of considerable nuclear anxiety, a theme played up in 'The Claws of Axos' when the alien Axons threaten to turn Dungeness power station into a gigantic nuclear bomb.

As Kate Shaw notes in her overview of hauntological literature, there has been a lot of attention given to the legacy of early 1970s sci-fi and fantasy TV, especially programmes portraying the past returning to haunt the present (for example *Penda's Fen*, *The Tomorrow People*, *The Owl Service*), or those, like earth-bound *Doctor Who*, that explore the parallel worlds that exist slightly out of synch with our own. Remembrance of these programmes (and sometimes their misremembering) informs modes of place-writing that Robert Macfarlane argues imbue the landscape with alternative meanings:

> We are, certainly, very far from 'nature writing', whatever that once was, and into a mutated cultural terrain that includes the weird and the punk as well as the attentive and the devotional. Among the shared landmarks of this terrain are ruins, fields, pits, fringes, relics, buried objects, hilltops, falcons, demons and deep pasts. In much of this work, suppressed forces pulse and flicker beneath the ground and within the air (capital, oil, energy, violence, state power, surveillance), waiting to erupt or to condense.[42]

In many hauntological works there is reference to ancient pasts just beneath the surface of the perceptible, and the presence of malign influences shaping the present. In 'The Claws of Axos', the notion of malevolent influence took a specific inflection: the Axon spaceship, embedded in the shingle of Dungeness, is not that of an invading force, but of aliens seeking fuel to get home. It is the involvement of a government official, 'little Englander' Horatio Chinn, that antagonises the situation, with Chinn seeing the opportunity to exploit the aliens to ensure British economic supremacy on an international stage. As the story unfolds it is the power plant, not the aliens, that becomes the main threat, with the spectre of nuclear disaster foregrounded. The landscape does active work here in emphasising this threat – the impending nuclear disaster is presaged by previous scars on the landscape, with Dungeness appearing as already somehow post-apocalyptic.

Given the way 'The Claws of Axos' plays with themes of nuclear anxiety, it is perhaps not surprising that it has informed a range of hauntological interventions that use it as a critical tool for comprehending the post-millennial and post-nuclear era. For example, sound-artist Nick Edwards/Ekoplekz released tracks on his *Intrusive Incidentalz* which directly cite Brian Hodgson's memorable electronic soundtrack for the episode. Perhaps more notably given his role in popularising Derrida's notion of hauntology, k-punk (Mark Fisher) argued that 'The Claws of Axos' exploited the Dungeness landscape of rotting shacks, WWII relics, power stations and 'the strange Picabia-like machines left on the beach like detritus abandoned by a departed civilization whose intentions are now opaque to us'.[43] These traces led Fisher to term Dungeness a *scurf space*, flakily encrusted with the detritus of different phases of occupation. Fisher also referred to the work of Brian Dillon, who proposes that Dungeness is a palimpsest of the twentieth century's technological development, from the mid-century sound mirrors and radar station through to the 'pallid, misty expanse of a nuclear power station' and a 'fenced-off spike of a mobile-phone mast'.[44]

Adam Scovell, author of *Folk Horror*, concludes that Dungeness exhibits 'topographical schizophrenia', much of this deriving from the presence of the nuclear power station. Here, he notes the pleasures of being both spatially close to, but temporally distant from, a power station that represents the white heat of 1960s optimism.[45] He insists that while a power station might be viewed as a dangerous place, it also draws us in, as if its danger is in the past. The opening of the Dungeness power station visitor centre in 2013 underlines the capacity of nuclear power to generate ambivalence, the visitor experience somewhere between dark tourism

7.7 Dungeness power station, lighthouse and radar station

and the hauntological desire to exorcise the ghosts of the past.[46] Gareth E. Rees, who runs the *Unofficial Britain* website, has also written about being haunted by Dungeness power station. Moving to Hastings from Hackney in the 2000s, he purchased a painting of the power station, entitled *Ghostbox*, from Bristol-based artist Hollis. Acquainting himself with his new Hastings home, he realised that the power station depicted in the painting is visible from the town on a clear day. With the cliffs at Hastings collapsing into the sea, battered by winter storms, Rees writes that 'the Power Station was out there on the edge of England, exposed to the forces of long-shore drift, climate change and rising seas'.[47] In Rees's 2018 book *The Stone Tide*, it becomes 'symbolic of the world's end', and Rees's 'own rapidly approaching personal apocalypse'.[48] In the last chapter of Rees's hallucinogenic account, the power station begins to melt down as rising seas overwhelm the shingle spit and flood the reactor. Tellingly, Rees's book was written in the wake of the 2011 Fukushima disaster, which suggested that the risks posed by flooding were much higher than previously imagined: remedial flood defence work was announced by EDF Energy in 2014, but serious corrosion of pipework in the turbine halls led Dungeness B to be decommissioned in 2021, some eight years ahead of schedule.[49]

Life at the end of the world

The nuclear borderlands of Dungeness have inspired a rich range of artistic and musical responses. In Rees's account, Dungeness is located on the edge of England, and stands for the end times, its brutal block of a power station standing on 'a shifting bed of stones beneath a duplicitous blue sky'.[50] But it is arguably in the work of Derek Jarman that we find the clearest articulation of the connections between the nuclear uncanny, Englishness and questions of identity. Jarman's home at Dungeness is arguably the principal reason why the area has gentrified, his reputation as *avant-garde* film-maker, painter, queer activist and writer having grown significantly since his death of AIDS-related illness in 1994 (he is buried in Old Romney church, a few miles from Dungeness). Jarman moved to Dungeness in 1986 following his HIV diagnosis, using £32,000 left to him by his father to buy Prospect Cottage. Dungeness had appeal for Jarman, being close enough to London that he could continue to see friends but isolated enough that he could live anonymously among the plotlanders and fisherfolk, to whom he was just Derek.[51] But more than this, Dungeness became Jarman's muse, prompting an outpouring of art, poetry and film in the last years of his life. Luke Turner concludes that here, 'on the edges of England', Jarman explored Englishness in terms of 'its paradoxes, the repression and homophobia, prejudice and conservatism, but also its twisted humour, complex relationship to the erotic and a history that might be up for reclaiming'.[52]

Jarman was much inspired by the local landscape, writing that 'Dungeness has luminous skies: its moods can change like quicksilver. A small cloud here has the effect of a thunderstorm in the city;

the days have a drama I could never conjure up on an opera stage.'[53] Elsewhere, he enthused about the lack of light pollution in this remote corner of the country: 'The night sky here is a riot that outshines the brightest lights of Piccadilly; the stars have the intensity of jewels. So flat is the Ness that those stars that lie at the horizon touch your very feet and the moon tips the waves with silver.'[54] For Jarman, this was the antithesis of the English rural idyll, but one that he found sublime: 'Dungeness is a premonition of the far North, a landscape Southerners might think drear and monotonous, which sings like the birch woods in Sibelius' music.'[55] In *Modern Nature*, published from his journals, he recalls a conversation with a journalist from the *Folkestone Herald*. When she asks how he can live in such a bleak environment, he quips back, 'It's much more interesting than Folkestone.' The conversation continued with her asking whether he liked having a nuclear power station in his backyard. He retorted that the Chernobyl disaster had made it obvious that we all have a nuclear power station in our backyard, and that at least he could see it.

Prospect Cottage, Jarman's home at Dungeness, is now a place of pilgrimage for many in the LGBTQ community, Jarman being the nearest it has to a secular saint.[56] But the modest, black, clapboarded shack attracts many others, principally because of its celebrated garden. This is in an unpromising location, more beach than land, and brutally exposed to the salty winds that whip up the Channel. But Jarman produced something unique at Prospect Cottage, combining different elements to create a garden that has often been described as heterotopic by virtue of its startling juxtapositions.[57] Jarman wandered daily on the beach collecting flotsam and jetsam – rusted fishing poles and old railway sleepers – to provide an overall structure for the garden. He imported soil to create shallow beds, bordering these with pebbles to prevent the soil from drying out, transplanting varied cuttings and nursery plants despite the seeming unsuitability of the environment. As renowned gardener and writer Christopher Lloyd described it:

His garden lies around the house, but mostly fore and aft in roughly equal proportions. The principal feature in a flat landscape is the Dungeness nuclear power station. It is not a romantic scene, being scattered with huts and sporadic habitations, with pylons and overhead cables and power lines. But it is open and it smells good. Mainly of the sea, of course, but also of flowers and plants in their season.[58]

Jarman was interested in plant diversity, irrespective of whether the plant was local or not, and experimented liberally, bringing plants and seedlings in from elsewhere. Foxgloves, gorse, yellow Californian poppies, lavender, stocks, dog rose, lovage and fennel sit higgledy-piggledy alongside ragwort, valerian, sea kale, white campion and toadflax, plants conventionally described as weeds. 'So many weeds are spectacular flowers' was Jarman's view.[59]

In *Modern Nature*, Jarman contemplates the future of his garden, and his own mortality, in relation to the constant presence of the power station. In a diary entry from 1989, he notes an unseasonable May heatwave, and presciently refers to the greenhouse effect setting in. He writes that Dungeness will disappear in a hundred years' time beneath the waves, along with its power station, which, he notes, will take a hundred years to dismantle. He continues: 'A

7.8 Derek Jarman's garden, Dungeness

meteor passes close to the earth, and the ozone hole shifts over southern Australia.'[60] Here, his awareness of environmental damage is intertwined with his sense of the destruction associated with the AIDS pandemic. Melissa Zeigler suggests that through its placement and methods, his garden generated 'allusions to AIDS, war, nuclear power, the environment, and queerness'. She continues:

> Its noncompliance with assumptions about garden aesthetics appears instantly. Plants are allowed to wander; weeds are as welcome as cultivars; and in contrast to what defines almost all gardens, no walls or fences mark the property's beginning or end, a feature that makes some visitors uncomfortable: how close to the house may one venture?[61]

As Jarman recorded in his diaries, 'There are no walls or fences. My garden's boundaries are the horizon.' Written in 1991, these words pre-empt Giovanni Aloi's 2019 insistence that there should be no distinction made between the native and the invasive, given that 'plants infiltrate new territories at every opportunity, utterly disrespecting legal borders and trespassing human-erected boundaries'.[62] Indeed, Jarman's wilful ignorance of the conventions of garden design indicated his enthusiasm to develop what has latterly been termed 'queer ecology', a notion of 'being-in-common' deployed against univocal, bounded understandings of nation, nature and heritage.[63]

This queer imaging of Dungeness as the outward-looking edge of England goes against the more frequent allusion to coasts as the territorial boundaries of contemporary nationhood, spaces where fragile (and often white, straight and masculine) selves are reconstituted or reclaimed.[64] This queer reading also allows us to make unexpected parallels between 1970s *Doctor Who* and Derek Jarman's garden. In 'The Claws of Axos', the Doctor is called to Dungeness to deal with an alien threat to the nation-state. But gradually, the story disrupts this conventional narrative by depicting the threats as within. Thus, the state is not so much countering threats but producing new dangers. An ontological displacement takes place, with the conventional narrative of the external enemy threatening the boundaries of the body politic inverted. In 'The Claws of Axos', the Doctor ultimately exposes the small-minded jingoism of the government official Chinn and questions the emotional complex of anger, resentment and envy which fuels a corresponding cycle of violence towards the alien Other.

Here, Lisa Blackman's post-humanism offers an interesting perspective on the figure of the alien. As she argues, 'the trope of visitation presumes an entity not of this world, which encroaches and even disrupts what might count as life, and particularly those forms of life which might challenge human sense-making and grids of intelligibility'.[65] Rejecting the idea that the alien is an Other, she proposes instead that 'human life is always co-evolved with other objects and trajectories, existing at the nexus of different scales of matter, including the planetary, biological and the popular, disclosing a cosmos that exceeds current systems of thought as well as displacing the human from its apparent centre'. This takes us very close to the symbolism of Jarman's garden, a 'textual-botanical memorial' that poses questions about the taken-for-granted distinctions between culture and nature (and host and alien) by suggesting an openness to the world.[66] What would Jarman have made, I wonder, of the asylum seekers who have landed at Dungeness in recent years, using the lighthouse as a beacon to guide their journey? I like to imagine that he would have extended the hand of welcome. After all, in Jarman's garden there are no weeds, in the same way that for the Doctor there is no such thing as an alien species (the Doctor being an alien living in exile). And, as Blackman asks, if we are all aliens then perhaps this will provide the grounds for 'an ethics that can counter the barbaric articulation of difference as otherness, which has marginalised, persecuted, discriminated against and drawn lines around who and whose lives count, and come to matter within the context of the category of the human'.[67]

All of these thoughts are swimming in my head as I arrive, blistered and tired, at the tip of Dungeness on 29 March 2019 after a four-day coastal walk undertaken in the run-up to the Brexit-that-never-was. My right knee had twisted when I fell part way down a sea wall at Sandwich two days before, and I was hobbling rather than walking. But during evenings spent, feet up, in hotels *en route* I had watched the sorry Brexit saga unravel. Theresa May's Brexit agreement was voted down on three separate occasions, necessitating frantic negotiations with Donald Tusk and the European Council, and an extension of the Leave date to May, then, a few days later, to October. By then, of course, Boris Johnson would be Prime Minister. But when I planned my walk from Whitstable to Dungeness in late 2018, I could have predicted little of this. Instead, I thought I would be walking the coast when the UK would finally leave the European Union after forty-six years. I knew I wanted to be at the Kent coast when this happened, to witness this moment of separation. I also had a finishing line in mind: not the power station or the lighthouse at the tip of the peninsula, but a more recent addition to the landscape, Joe Sweeney's *Leave a Message for Europe* installation. This was a 1980s British Telecom phone box of the type that often stands vandalised on British high streets. Installed at Dungeness throughout March 2019, this installation encouraged visitors to leave a phone message for Europe. For Sweeney, the synergy between the location and the artwork was clear:

> Dungeness's location enhances the metaphorical implications of the sculpture as a modern relic – an isolated and fading fixture of daily British life that stands as a bastion against change and regeneration … While it is installed in this wild and unsheltered environment, the sculptural replica of a near-extinct urban motif will be subjected to natural elements that will cause the untreated metallic components to naturally age and rust. This slow but certain degradation of the sculpture will cause it to emerge over time as a physical record of its difficult environment.[68]

Using a strangely familiar relict of British life – the phone box – Sweeney was adding another layer to what Jarman described as the 'landscape of past endeavours' at Dungeness.[69] Standing incongruously at the edge of the car park of The Pilot inn, a pub known for its excellent fish and chips, the phone box also made oblique reference to the Doctor's TARDIS police box, the space-time machine that has lost its ability to merge into its surroundings, yet which seldom excites comment despite its seeming oddness.

As I sat in the pub eating my cod and chips, washed down with Kentish ale, I watched people crunching across the shingle, approaching the phone box warily and picking up leaflets about the project. These explained that Sweeney's installation invited people to leave their opinion on Brexit, whether positive or negative, via a website. However, most passers-by ignored the phone box, probably regarding it as just another piece of cultural detritus that had somehow ended up at Dungeness, that weirdest of places. Munching my food and staring out to sea, I thought about using my mobile to leave a message of my own. But what had I learned from my walk down the coast that could be summarised in a single pithy phone message? What could I say about borders and bordering that would help others make sense of Brexit? My mind raced through the different forms of exclusionary nationalism – social, cultural, political, environmental – that I had witnessed, and my emerging conviction that Britain was turning away from Europe at a time of immanent and inescapable global change that requires cooperation, not isolationism. I struggled as I considered how I could best capture the essence of this strange coast or explain how it encapsulates the ambivalent relationship between Britain and its continental neighbours. I hesitated as I rehearsed different versions of my message for Europe, each sounding too trite, too lacking in nuance or too contrived. So, instead, I finished my drink, went home, and started to write this book.

7.9 The author at Dungeness, 29 March 2019

Afterword: the Kent variant

From the Garden of England to the slums of Calcutta, our Kent COVID variant is now theirs ... There is a strong possibility that the devastating wave of the coronavirus sweeping across India is being propelled not by the so-called Indian but rather by the strain that originated in Kent.

Ben Spencer, *The Sunday Times*, 25 April 2021[1]

This is not the book I wanted to write. In 2019, following my walk on the Kent coast, I had taken notes, visited libraries and read umpteen papers on borders, identity, nationhood and Europe. But the extension of Brexit via the Article 50 agreement, and a transitional period until 31 December 2020, meant that the Kent coast remained in the media spotlight, its futures and pasts still debated. I began to plan further visits, and fieldwork involving interviews with local stakeholders and residents. But it was not to be. In February 2020 I was standing on a picket line handing out flyers to international students explaining why their lecturers were on strike, noting an increasing number wearing face masks and recoiling as we thrust leaflets upon them, aghast that we could be so irresponsible in the face of an impending global pandemic. On 12 March I helped run a stakeholder event at the Greater London Assembly on the demolition of housing estates in London, from which many of the attendees stayed away, worried about the increasing number of COVID-19 cases being diagnosed in the UK.

Afterword: the Kent variant

The following day, I travelled to Kent to see my mother with food and provisions, mindful that cases were spiralling and that washing hands might not be enough to prevent a national catastrophe. On the same day in Cheltenham, thousands attended the Gold Cup, unknowingly accelerating the spread of the virus. By the following Monday, Boris Johnson was imploring people not to travel unless it was essential, and maintaining that Britain could 'turn the tide' on coronavirus in twelve weeks by observing good sense and basic hygiene. A week later Britain entered full lockdown.

Given travel restrictions and 'stay local' advice, my best-laid plans fell to pieces. But in many ways the pandemic provided fresh impetus for this book. Pre-COVID-19, Kent featured prominently in media coverage of the impacts of EU withdrawal, with much discussion about its potential role in harming or, conversely, boosting the local economy. In that respect it was not alone, with the press also descending on other Brexit 'strongholds' – most notably declined industrial towns such as Stoke-on-Trent and Hartlepool, as well as those areas of Eastern England with large numbers of A8 migrants, especially towns such as Boston and King's Lynn. The border between Northern Ireland and the Republic was also the subject of widespread speculation, with proposals to draw a new *de facto* border in the Irish Sea drawing extensive criticism and threatening to accelerate devolution. But in 2020 everything seem-ingly changed. Remarkably, in the face of a global pandemic, 'island-thinking' became more, rather than less, prominent. For example, following the arrival of COVID-19 in the UK, Johnson's cod-Churchillian bluster invoked the wartime spirit, and many compared the crisis to World War II. One elderly caller to a radio phone-in, who recalled the London Blitz of the 1940s, surprised the host by suggesting that living through coronavirus was tougher than living through the bombing. Others were sceptical about this, but this did not stop the nation emerging from the first lockdown into the bright May sunshine to the strains of Vera Lynn, with street parties and BBQs to celebrate the 75th anniversary of 'Victory in Europe'. National hero Captain Tom Moore was number one in the charts at the time, his duet with Michael Ball, 'You'll never walk alone', making him the oldest artist ever to score a top ten hit (he died of COVID-19 in February 2021).

The fact that Boris Johnson survived coronavirus himself, and emerged from intensive care in time for the birth of his sixth child, seemed to further fuel what Mark Juergensmeyer terms 'COVID nationalism'.[2] This was a populism that spun in different, unpredictable directions, from the well-intentioned but often hypocritical 'Clap for Carers' through to anti-masking protests (sponsored by Nigel Farage's UK Reform party) and the pathetic spectacle of drunk, ageing, white racists 'protecting' the Churchill statue in Whitehall in the face of the Black Lives Matter movement. And with Britain becoming the first nation in the world to approve a coronavirus vaccine, COVID nationalism subsequently begat vaccine nationalism. Britain stockpiled vaccines from an early stage, and when the EU tried to prevent the export of EU-produced vaccine from Ireland to Northern Ireland early in 2021, the battlelines were drawn for an undignified scramble to be at the front of the international queue for vaccines. In this sense, not much had changed from pre-Brexit spring 2020, when Johnson had refused to join EU schemes to procure ventilators, and July 2020 when he rejected the opportunity to join an EU cooperative scheme to work on vaccine production and distribution.[3] Britain's self-proclaimed role in leading 'humanity's charge against the disease' – to quote UK Business Secretary Alok Sharma – bolstered the idea that Britain should be the master of its own destiny, stoking exclusionary nationalisms in the process.[4]

Throughout the pandemic, those from other nations were often depicted as threatening outsiders importing the virus, meddling in UK affairs, or, worse, freeloading from 'our' NHS.[5] Unlikely stories circulated about unscrupulous foreign travel agents arranging holidays for 'vaccine tourists' to visit the UK to get vaccinated; conversely, those overseas governments that banned UK travellers were labelled disproportionate and scaremongering. Concerns were also raised that post-Brexit border checks would create bottlenecks in the supply of vital COVID medicines, a fear that was heightened following the French trials that caused five-mile tailbacks on the M20 in October 2020. At the same time as these stories circulated, media coverage of the 'migrant crisis' – admittedly already ubiquitous in the run-up to the Brexit vote – was also ramped up. First it was the bureaucratic incursion of EU law that the UK had fought off. Then it was the peril of COVID-19 that threatened national health and security. Now, the UK had another invasion that it needed to quell – the migrant tide that washed up on our beaches. Pictures of young men striding casually past swimmers, fishermen and dog walkers on the Kent coast, abandoning their rubber dinghies behind them, consolidated discourses of contagion and threat. The government's response was that it was time to pull up the drawbridge on this invading force: in September 2020 trials were held using Border Patrol and Royal Navy boats to block the path of migrants and refugees crossing the Channel, following the Australian 'turn back the boats' model.

The refugee landings, lorries queueing on motorways, and the battle between Britain and Europe over COVID-19 vaccines were all presented by Brexiteers as *de facto* evidence that the decision to sever ties with Europe had been the right one. Significantly, all these stories took tangible and sometimes iconic form on the Kent coast. In my brief visits to Kent, squeezed between lockdowns and online teaching in 2020, I attempted to come to terms with what was happening. There was almost too much to comprehend, the layering of discourses reinforcing some of the ideas I had already developed about Kent's borderscape, but confounding others. And then, in December 2020, a new announcement. NERVE-TAG (the New and Emerging Respiratory Virus Threats Advisory Group) concluded that rapidly rising coronavirus infection rates in the South-East of England were associated with a new COVID-19 variant, 50% more transmissible and 60% more deadly than the dominant strain. A third lockdown followed, and Christmas was effectively cancelled, but by then the so-called 'Kent variant' was already widespread. As Ben Spencer noted in *The Sunday Times*, by the spring of 2021 this variant was not just dominant in the UK, but globally prevalent, thought to be contributing to an intense and deadly second wave in India. Far from a 'developing' nation with a floundering health system being responsible for importing an aggressive COVID-19 variant to the UK, this was a post-colonial boomerang of a different kind. Before this, the UK was more focused on the need to monitor the border, enforce quarantine on visitors and ban tourists from nations including South Africa and Brazil where more deadly variants were thought to be present. Now it was clear that, like the refugees on the beaches of Kent, the 'enemy' was already here, in the form of a homegrown super-spreading COVID-19 variant.

In raising parallels between the visibility of 'economic migrants' on the beaches of Kent and the rise of a new COVID-19 variant, it is important to stress that few blamed the refugees for bringing the variant to Kent (though inevitably, some did). In the absence of an accurate track and trace regime, the search for the origins of the Kent variant instead focused on those areas where rates appeared to be galloping out of control, six or seven times the national average.[6] Swale (especially Sittingbourne and Sheppey) and Thanet (Margate, Ramsgate and Broadstairs) were the two areas initially fingered as the potential source by Public Health England, which worked from assumptions that they possessed pockets of deprivation where social distancing rules were not being closely followed. By December 2020 genomic analysis had found a prevalence of the alpha mutation B.1.1.7 in these areas, suggesting that behavioural factors were not to blame for the rapid uptick in local cases. Most likely, it was concluded by the authorities, the Kent variant resulted from the mutation of the coronavirus in an immunocompromised individual with multiple existing medical conditions, possibly because of other medication they were taking.

Afterword: the Kent variant

Even so, when commenting on the Kent variant a full six months after its first known case, Patrick Cockburn highlighted the possible links between the socio-economic character of these coastal communities and the spread of the virus:

> It wasn't surprising that Swale and Thanet should be badly affected: these are areas notorious for their poverty and likely to provide an ideal breeding ground for the virus. They are prime examples of coastal Britain, depressed places where failed hotels and B&Bs have been chopped up into one-room flats and where few can work from home because their jobs won't allow it; the homes, in any case, are too small to work in. Years of austerity had already cut back the funding and benefits on which such towns depended. People were vulnerable to the virus here because their health was poor before the pandemic and their access to healthcare limited: in Swale the ratio of GPs to residents is lower than anywhere else in England. Inequality is extreme: a woman living in the most affluent ward in Thanet will live on average 22 years longer than a woman living in the most deprived ward.[7]

In making these connections, Cockburn suggested that certain towns on the Kent coast were places on the margin where people are forced to take multiple jobs or could not afford to take COVID-19 tests for fear of losing pay. While not suggesting that migrants brought the virus to the region, he notes that there are good reasons to suppose that COVID-19 might have spread quickly among the Czech, Pole and Roma workers who are employed in the Kentish coastal hinterland, mainly in fruit and vegetable picking but also in hotels and retirement homes in the coastal towns themselves. Packed into HMOs (houses in multiple occupation) or caravans, there is little chance that such precarious workers would be able to socially distance from an infected co-worker.

These arguments reproduce widespread and common-sense understandings of the Kent coast as part of 'left behind' Britain. Indeed, if we buy into the idea that poor people are less likely to socially distance or mask-up than the wealthy, and more likely to live in close proximity to others, there appears to be evidence that the spiralling transmission of the new COVID-19 variant in Kent was indeed accelerated by poverty. But, as I have shown, Kent is nothing if not contradictory. Both Swale and Thanet are well connected with London, and possess pockets of gentrified wealth (Margate's old town, Faversham's Standard Quay) alongside areas of deprivation (Blue Town in Sheerness, Cliftonville in Margate). Both are associated with DFLs, people either escaping London's overheated rental market or cashing in by buying up affordable second homes and seasonal AirBnB lets. So, while it is certainly true that poorer people in precarious employment have been more exposed to COVID-19, it is inequality, not poverty per se, that is arguably to blame for high rates of COVID-19 on the Kent coast, with its labour markets often polarised between a mobile class of second homeowners and a poorer, servicing class who do 'dirty' and seasonal work. Indeed, a wealth of UK evidence now shows a correlation between inequality, social problems and health outcomes, suggesting that simple steps up the income ladder do not always result in equal gains. Related to this is the fact that it is harder to be poor in places where the gap between the haves and have-nots is getting wider, not least where gentrification is displacing long-established local businesses and pushing decent housing beyond the thresholds of affordability for many.[8]

The Kent coast is, then, a swirling mass of contradictions. This is a borderscape characterised by both poverty and prosperity, with recent pockets of gentrification a stone's throw from some of the poorest neighbourhoods in the South-East of England. It is socially, economically and politically divided. It is home to those who welcome refugees and those who demand that they are prevented from ever arriving. There is virulent racism but there is also strident anti-fascism. For some the coast represents a bulwark shore, repelling those who would threaten us; for others, it is merely a bridging point on the short journey that links Britain and the continent, and integrates us into a European space of flows. For the former, it is apprehended as a borderscape of castles, forts and defensive formations which have stood proud in times of national crisis. During Brexit, when so much was uncertain, it was perhaps not surprising that these sites, and the Kent coast in general, were seized upon as part of the mythology of the 'island fortress'. The white cliffs in particular became increasingly figured as the vulnerable boundaries of an island-nation, in need of protection.[9] The 'proud patriots' who descended on Kent during the 'migrant crisis' were hence involved in a modern-day re-enactment of the 'beating of the bounds', staking out an insular version of Englishness as they patrolled the 'white walls of Albion'. But looking beyond such displays of exclusionary nationalism is vital to avoid stereotyping the Kent coast as a repository of racism and intolerance: the coast at Kent also embodies more radical, inclusive and cosmopolitan visions of Englishness. This is the Kent of Derek Jarman and *The Folkestone Mermaid*, a county where refugees from Belgium made a home during World War I and Vietnamese boat people in the 1970s and 1980s. This is a county where backwards-looking versions of Englishness, drawing on stories of the white horse, Horsa, Hengist and the Kentish kings, coexist with a growing recognition that the greatest threat we face today is not immigration, but an impending climate emergency that will scorch the land at the same time as it floods our homes.

In this book I have dwelt on some of these contradictions and the way they manifest in struggles concerning identity and belonging along the Kent coast, travelling from the muddy flats of Whitstable round to the shingle expanses of Dungeness via the soaring chalky foreland of Folkestone and Dover. At each juncture, I have argued that the Kentish coastal landscape, and its refraction in media, culture and art, speaks to broader debates about nationalism, identity and belonging at a time of Brexit. But in arguing this, I have never intended to suggest that the Kent coast is a microcosm of England, a bellwether that stands for the whole. Nor have I argued that the Kent coast is the only site where bordering occurs; on the contrary, we need to recognise that the UK border now exists at different spatial scales, both within and beyond the territory of the state. But this noted, I have shown that Kent's borderscape has come to occupy an important yet contradictory position in the contemporary national imaginary, being a frontline that is also somehow on the margins, a site of ordering and Othering where national identities are often fluid, messy and contested. The conjuncture of COVID-19, Brexit and the 'migrant crisis' brought this borderscape into sharper focus, but it is unlikely to be the last time the coast closest to continental Europe is entwined in debates about national identity and belonging.

Figures

1.1   The view from the white cliffs (Paul Barker Hemings
      CC BY-SA 2.0)   2
1.2   Jason deCaires Taylor, *Pride of Brexit* (courtesy of the
      artist)   6
1.3   Projection on Dover cliffs (Jess Hurd/Global Justice
      CC BY 2.0)   21
2.1   Faversham Creek (Phil Hubbard)   27
2.2   Whitstable beach (Neal Theasby CC BY-SA 2.0)   33
2.3   Trestles on foreshore, Whitstable (Phil Hubbard)   38
2.4   Beach hut for sale, Whitstable (Phil Hubbard)   39
2.5   Beach signage, Whitstable (Phil Hubbard)   41
2.6   Rachael Louise Bailey, *The Black Stuff*, Whitstable
      (courtesy of Foundation François Schneider and
      Rachael Louise Bailey)   43
3.1   Margate sands (courtesy of Lyanne Wylde)   53
3.2   Arlington House, Margate (courtesy of Lyanne
      Wylde)   56
3.3   Cliftonville Lido, Margate (Phil Hubbard)   61
3.4   The Turner Contemporary, Margate (Phil Hubbard)   66
3.5   Dreamland, Margate (Phil Hubbard)   70
3.6   Michael Rakowitz, *April is the Cruellest Month* (courtesy
      of Thierry Bal)   75

Figures

4.1 Dan Tweedy, *The Sheerness Mermaid* (Luke McKernan CC BY-SA 2.0)   79

4.2 Pillboxes, Warden Point (Metal123 CC BY-SA 2.0)   82

4.3 Dover Castle (Michael Coppins CC BY-SA 4.0)   85

4.4 Sound mirror, Abbot's Cliff (Phil Hubbard)   89

4.5 Battle of Britain memorial, Capel-le-Ferne (Phil Hubbard)   93

4.6 Poppies on beach, Folkestone (Phil Hubbard)   98

5.1 Channel Tunnel terminal, Cheriton (Phil Hubbard)   110

5.2 Eurostar Meadow, Mersham (Phil Hubbard)   117

5.3 Former cattle market, Ashford (Phil Hubbard)   120

5.4 Shared space, Elwick Place, Ashford (Phil Hubbard)   123

5.5 Inland border facility, Sevington (Phil Hubbard)   129

5.6 M20 lorry queues, from Mersham bridge (Phil Hubbard)   132

5.7 The White Horse, Folkestone (Phil Hubbard)   136

6.1 Moyle Court, Marine Parade, Hythe (Phil Hubbard)   140

6.2 Project Kraken (Phil Hubbard)   151

6.3 Harbour arm, Folkestone (Phil Hubbard)   157

6.4 Napier Barracks, Folkestone (Phil Hubbard)   162

6.5 Varga Weisz, *Rug People*, Folkestone Harbour Railway Station (Phil Hubbard)   165

6.6 Richard Wentworth, *Racinated*, Shellons Street, Folkestone (Phil Hubbard)   166

7.1 Cornelia Parker, *The Folkestone Mermaid*, Sunny Sands (Phil Hubbard)   169

7.2 Reculver Towers (G. Weston CC BY-SA 2.0)   174

7.3 Cliff erosion, St Margaret's at Cliffe (Phil Hubbard)   175

7.4 Fairfield Church, Romney Marsh (Tim Firkins CC BY-SA 3.0)   179

7.5 Dymchurch Wall (Phil Hubbard)   181

7.6 Dungeness beach (Phil Hubbard)   186

7.7 Dungeness power station, lighthouse and radar station (courtesy of Lyanne Wylde)   191

Figures

7.8 Derek Jarman's garden, Dungeness (courtesy of
     Lyanne Wylde)   194
7.9 The author at Dungeness, 29 March 2019 (Phil
     Hubbard)   199

Acknowledgements

This book had a long gestation, and it is hard to recall when my ideas about the relationship between the Kent coast, nationhood and identity began to solidify into a book project. But here I think much of the blame rests with my former colleagues at the University of Kent with whom I had dialogues about the nature of the coast, not least those who co-organised the 'Topographies' seminar at Whitstable in 2015, Anne Bottomley and Ben Hickman first and foremost. Other Kent colleagues who deserve mention here include Tim Brittain-Catlin, Dawn Lyon, Chris Pickvance, Tim Strangleman, David Nettleingham, Vince Miller, David Garbin, Ellie Jupp, Alex Stevens, Chris Rootes, David Herd, Axel Klein, Adam Burgess and the many others who I had conversations with about the changing Kent coast. I also wish to thank George Laurence QC and Rodney Stewart Smith, New Square Chambers, and Elaine Sherratt, Clinic Solicitor at the Kent Law clinic, for their patient explanation of the Whitstable beach case. Andrew Brooks, my colleague at King's College London, is to be particularly thanked for his insightful contributions and insights on Whitstable's gentrification. Other colleagues, past and present, at King's College also need to be acknowledged for their support and insight, including Johan Andersson, Adam Elliott-Cooper, Katie Meehan, Jon Reades, Richard Schofield and especially Lyanne Wylde (for the fabulous photos and Kent anecdotes). Andrew Kerr, also in the Department of Geography at King's, deserves special thanks for his careful proofreading and chasing of references. Thomas Dark at MUP is also to be thanked for his encouraging and close reading of the manuscript. I should also acknowledge those at Canterbury City Council, Kent County Council and Folkestone & Hythe Council who responded patiently to my inquiries. Other people I need to thank for information and insight include Rachael Louise Bailey, John Baker, Jonathan Davies, David Hanbury, The Whitstable Beach Campaign group, Jacob Paskins, Nick Edwards (Ekoplekz), Sonia Overall, Jason deCaires Taylor, Trish Morrissey, James Sidaway and Patrick Wright. Jon Ward, former PhD student at University of Kent, deserves especial thanks in relation to the material on Margate and Folkestone, and I'd also like to thank Jason Lim for his critical comments on the initial proposal. Finally, I want to thank Livvy and Lucy for coming to the beach with me, Eleanor for the swimming, Corinne for forcing me to walk great distances, and Brian and Joy for starting all this off.

This book is dedicated to the work of the Kent Refugee Action Network (KRAN), which supports asylum seekers in Kent: my royalties from this book are being donated to them in recognition of the important work that they do at a time when so many are increasingly hostile towards Others.

Notes

Notes to Chapter 1

1 Julian Baggini, 'Why the White Cliffs of Dover are so special', *The Guardian*, 19 October 2012, https://www.theguardian.com/commentisfree/2012/aug/19/white-cliffs-of-dover (accessed 23 November 2021).

2 Richard Ford, 'Great Wall of Calais to deter Jungle migrants', *The Times*, 7 September 2016, http://www.thetimes.co.uk/article/great-wall-of-calais-to-deter-jungle-migrants-k570pxj66 (accessed 23 November 2021).

3 These are estimates: the UK government does not routinely publish figures relating to number of refugees coming to the UK by route or mode of arrival.

4 See Nicholas De Genova, 'Spectacles of migrant "illegality": the scene of exclusion, the obscene of inclusion', *Ethnic and Racial Studies* 36(7) (2013): 1180–1198. On the Channel crossings as spectacle, see Joseph Maggs, 'The "Channel crossings" and the borders of Britain', *Race & Class* 61(3) (2019): 78–86.

5 See, among others, Harriet Gray and Anja K. Franck, 'Refugees as/at risk: the gendered and racialized underpinnings of securitization in British media narratives', *Security Dialogue* 50(3) (2019): 275–291.

6 Tobias Heidenreich, Fabienne Lind, Jakob-Moritz Eberl and Hajo G. Boomgaarden, 'Media framing dynamics of the "European refugee crisis": a comparative topic modelling approach', *Journal of Refugee Studies* 32 (2019): 1172–1182.

7 Chris Grey, *Brexit Unfolded: How No-one Got What They Want (and Why They Were Never Going To)* (London: Biteback, 2021).

8 Satnam Virdee and Brendan McGeever, 'Racism, Crisis, Brexit', *Ethnic and Racial Studies* 41(10) (2017): 1802–1819.

9 John Agnew, 'Taking back control? The myth of territorial sovereignty and the Brexit fiasco', *Territory, Politics, Governance* 8(2) (2019): 259–272.

10 Paul Readman, *Storied Ground: Landscape and the Shaping of English National Identity* (Cambridge: Cambridge University Press, 2018).

11 Ruth Pitman, 'On Dover Beach', *Essays in Criticism* 23(2) (1973): 109–136.

12 Walter Jarrold, *Folkestone and Dover* (London: Blackie, 1920), 6.

13 Luke O'Reilly, 'Moment WW2 plane drops 750,000 poppies over White Cliffs of Dover', *Evening Standard*, 10 November 2019, https://www.standard.co.uk/news/uk/remembrance-sunday-2019-moment-world-war-2-plane-drops-750-000-poppies-over-white-cliffs-of-dover-a4283311.html (accessed 23 November 2021).

14 Maxwell Uphaus, ''The chalk wall falls to the foam': reimagining littoral space in the poetry of the Dover cliffs', *Comparative Literature* 73(2) (2021): 209–224.

15 Bonnie Christian, 'SOS signal beamed onto White Cliffs of Dover calling for Brexit delay', *Evening Standard*, 4 April 2019, https://www.standard.co.uk/news/politics/sos-beamed-across-the-channel-to-europe-calling-for-brexit-extension-a4109626.html (accessed 23 November 2021).

16 Jason deCaires Taylor, 'The Pride of Brexit', Floornature.com, 2019, https://www.floornature.com/blog/pride-brexit-jason-decaires-taylor-15069/ (accessed 23 November 2021).

17 Jason deCaires Taylor cited in Stuart Jeffries, 'Three lions on a beach', *The Guardian*, 17 November 2019, https://www.theguardian.com/artanddesign/2019/nov/17/three-lions-pride-of-brexit-sculptor-jason-decaires-taylor-protest (accessed 23 November 2021.)

18 Natalie Bannerman, 'Equinix to build new subsea cable across the English Channel', Capacitymedia.com, 2018, https://www.capacitymedia.com/articles/3822365/equinix-to-build-new-subsea-cable-across-the-english-channel (accessed 23 November 2021).

19 Adrian Favell, *Eurostars and Eurocities: Free Movement and Mobility in an Integrating Europe* (Oxford: Blackwell, 2008).

20 Bastian A. Vollmer, 'Categories, practices and the self – reflections on bordering, ordering and othering', *Tijdschrift voor economische en sociale geografie* 112(1) (2021): 4–10.

21 See Elena dell'Agnese and Anne-Laure Amilhat Szary, 'Borderscapes: from border landscapes to border aesthetics', *Geopolitics* 20(1) (2015): 4–13; Chiara Brambilla, 'Exploring the critical potential of the borderscapes concept', *Geopolitics* 20(1) (2014): 14–34; Dina Krichker, 'Making sense of borderscapes: space, imagination and experience', *Geopolitics* 26(4) (2019): 1224–1242.

22 See, among others, Denis E. Cosgrove, *Social Formation and Symbolic Landscape* (Madison, WI: University of Wisconsin Press, 1998); John Wylie, *Landscape* (Abingdon: Routledge, 2006); W. J. Thomas Mitchell, *Landscape and Power* (Chicago: University of Chicago Press, 2009); Trevor J. Barnes and James S. Duncan, *Writing Worlds* (Abingdon: Routledge, 2013).

Notes

23 Don Mitchell, 'Cultural landscapes: just landscapes or landscapes of justice?', *Progress in Human Geography* 27(6) (2003): 787–796.

24 Michael Billig, *Banal Nationalism* (London: Sage, 1995).

25 Peter J. Taylor, 'The English and their Englishness: "A curiously mysterious, elusive and little understood people"', *Scottish Geographical Magazine* 107(3) (1991): 146–161.

26 Agnew, 'Taking back control?'.

27 On Englishness, exclusion and identity, see especially Sarah Neal, *Rural Identities: Ethnicity and Community in the Contemporary English Countryside* (Abingdon: Routledge, 2016), 134.

28 Divya P. Tolia-Kelly, 'Narrating the postcolonial landscape: archaeologies of race at Hadrian's Wall', *Transactions of the Institute of British Geographers* 36(1) (2011): 75. See also Ben Pitcher, 'Belonging to a different landscape: repurposing nationalist affects', *Sociological Research Online* 21(1) (2016): 77–89 for a response to Tolia-Kelly's work.

29 Alex Niven, *New Model Island: How to Build a Radical Culture beyond the Idea of England* (London: Repeater, 2019).

30 Christine Berberich, 'This green and pleasant land: cultural constructions of Englishness', in Robert Burden and Stephan Kohl (eds), *Landscape and Englishness* (New York: Rodopi, 2006), 207–224.

31 Sidney William Wooldridge, *London's Countryside: Geographical Field Work for Students and Teachers of Geography* (London: Methuen, 1957), 45.

32 Similar points have been made in relation to other Sunday night fare. See Tom Mordue, '*Heartbeat* country: conflicting values, coinciding visions', *Environment and Planning A: Economy and Space* 31(4) (1999): 629–646; Martin Phillips, Rob Fish and Jennifer Agg, 'Putting together ruralities: towards a symbolic analysis of rurality in the British mass media', *Journal of Rural Studies* 17(1) (2001): 1–27.

33 Sean O'Grady, 'ITV's *Darling Buds of May* adaptation is a Brexit television abomination', *The Independent*, 11 October 2021, https://www.independent.co.uk/arts-entertainment/tv/reviews/the-larkins-review-bradley-walsh-b1934987.html (accessed 23 November 2021).

34 Patrick Wright, 'The English Fix – Series 1 – the Common Market in the Garden of England', *BBC Sounds*, 2017, https://www.bbc.co.uk/sounds/play/bo8fdwfq (accessed 23 November 2021).

35 Frances Heather Robbs de la Hoyde, *The Impact of the Loss of Land to Urban Development on Agriculture in Kent* (2017), https://cprekent.org.uk/wp-content/uploads/2013/05/Urbanisation-and-Agriculture-in-Kent.pdf (accessed 23 November 2021).

36 Marion Shoard, 'Edgelands', in Jennifer Jenkins (ed.), *Remaking the Landscape: The Changing Face of Britain* (London: Profile Books, 2002), 117–147. This is often proclaimed as an important work in the attempt to reassess England's liminal spaces, and one that has done much to highlight their role as

spaces of 'accidental' ecological richness. See also Paul Farley and Michael Symmons Roberts, *Edgelands: Journeys into England's True Wilderness* (London: Random House, 2012).

37   On the relation of landscape and 'islandness', see John Wylie, 'Landscapes', in Paul Cloke, Philip Crang and Mark Goodwin (eds), *Introducing Human Geography* (London: Taylor and Francis, 2013), 262–274.

38   Matthew Gandy, 'Unintentional landscapes', *Landscape Research* 41(4) (2016): 433–440.

39   Paul Readman, '"The cliffs are not cliffs": the cliffs of Dover and national identities in Britain, c.1750–c.1950', *History* 99(335) (2014): 241–269.

40   Here it is important to stress that I am not focusing solely on the coast-scape but the wider borderscape. On coastscape as a concept, see Martin Döring and Beate Ratter, '"I show you my coast…" – a relational study of coastscapes in the North Frisian Wadden Sea', *Maritime Studies* 20 (2021): 317–327.

41   Daniel Burdsey, *Race, Place and the Seaside* (Berlin: Springer, 2016).

42   Kate Oakley, Jonathan Ward and Ian Christie, 'Engaging the imagination: "new nature writing", collective politics and the environmental crisis', *Environmental Values* 27(6) (2018): 687–705.

43   On edgelands, see especially Farley and Symmons Roberts, *Edgelands*. Other examples of recent works that have an interest in such quotidian landscapes include Rob Cowen, *Common Ground* (London: Hutchinson, 2015); Gareth Rees, *Marshland: Dreams and Nightmares on the Edge of London* (London: Influx, 2013); Esther Woolfson, *Field Notes from a Hidden City* (London: Granta, 2013); John Grindrod, *Outskirts* (London: Sceptre, 2018); and Melissa Harrison, *Clay* (London: Bloomsbury, 2013).

44   For such reasons, Wylie favours the term 'landscape writing' over the 'new nature writing' – see John Wylie, 'Vanishing points: an essay on landscape, memory and belonging', *Irish Geography* 50(1) (2017): 3–18.

45   See Joe Moran, 'A cultural history of the new nature writing', *Literature & History* 23(1) (2014): 49–63.

46   See Melanie Pryor, 'Eco-autobiography: writing self through place', *A/B: Auto/Biography Studies* 32(2) (2017): 391–393. There are clear parallels between the new nature writing and more established traditions of psychogeographically inflected urban writing: see Alastair Bonnett, 'The dilemmas of radical nostalgia in British psychogeography', *Theory, Culture & Society* 26(1) (2009): 45–70.

47   It would be remiss here not to also mention Tom Bolton, *Low Country: Brexit on the Essex Coast* (London: Penned in the Margins, 2018). There are many similarities between the Kent coast – especially the low-lying areas of the North Kent Marshes and the Dungeness peninsula – and coastal Essex, and some of these translate into political parallels: for example, the UKIP victories in Rochester and Clacton in 2014–15. However, while

wary of inflaming long-held Kent–Essex rivalries, my claim in this book is that in the pre- and immediate post-Brexit years, Kent has become far more totemic in debates about the relationship of Europe and the UK, with the conjuncture of Brexit, COVID-19 and the 'migrant crisis' in 2020 arguably putting Kent in the spotlight as never before.

48 Maano Ramutsindela, *Cartographies of Nature: How Nature Conservation Animates Borders* (Cambridge: Cambridge Scholars Publishing, 2014).

49 Ben Pitcher, 'Belonging to a different landscape: repurposing nationalist affects', *Sociological Research Online* 21(1) (2016): 77–89.

50 Sarah Whatmore and Steven Hinchliffe, 'Living cities: making space for urban nature', *Soundings* 12(1) (2003): 37–50

51 Farley and Symmons Roberts, *Edgelands*.

52 Hannah Lilley, 'New British nature writing', *Oxford Handbooks Online*, 2017, https://www.oxfordhandbooks.com/view/10.1093/oxfordhb/97801 99935338.001.0001/oxfordhb-9780199935338-e-15 (accessed 23 November 2021).

53 David Matless, *In the Nature of Landscape* (Oxford: Wiley Blackwell, 2014); Shelley Trower, *Rocks of Nation: The Imagination of Celtic Cornwall* (Manchester: Manchester University Press, 2015); Sophia Davis, *Island Thinking* (Basingstoke: Palgrave Macmillan, 2020).

54 David Matless, 'The anthroposcenic', *Transactions of the Institute of British Geographers* 42(3) (2017): 363–376.

55 David Matless, 'Describing landscape: regional sites', *Performance Research* 15(4) (2010): 72–82.

56 John Wylie, 'A single day's walking: narrating self and landscape on the South West Coast Path', *Transactions of the Institute of British Geographers* 30(2) (2005): 245.

57 Kate Shaw, *Hauntology: The Presence of the Past in Twenty-First Century English Literature* (Berlin: Springer, 2018).

58 See Phil Smith, 'The contemporary dérive: a partial review of issues concerning the contemporary practice of psychogeography', *Cultural Geographies* 17(1) (2010): 103–122.

59 For a broad overview, see Merlin Coverley, *Psychogeography* (Harpenden: Oldcastle Books, 2018). See also Kirsten Seale and Emily Potter, 'Wandering and placemaking in London: Iain Sinclair's literary methodology', *M/C Journal* 22(4) (2019), https://doi.org/10.5204/mcj.1554.

60 David Overend, Jamie Lorimer and Danielle Schreve, 'The bones beneath the streets: drifting through London's Quaternary', *cultural geographies* 27(3) (2020): 453–475; see also Tom Chivers, *London Clay* (London: Doubleday, 2020).

61 Doreen Massey, 'Landscape/space/politics: an essay', *The Future of Landscape and the Moving Image*, 2008, https://thefutureoflandscape.wordpress.com/landscapespacepolitics-an-essay/ (accessed 23 November 2021).

62 See Will Ashon, *Strange Labyrinth: Outlaws, Poets, Mystics, Murderers and a Coward in London's Great Forest* (London: Granta, 2017); Carol Donaldson, *On the Marshes* (Beaminster: Little Toller Press, 2017); Justin Hopper, *The Old Weird Albion* (London: Penned in the Margins, 2017); Sonia Overall, *Heavy Times: A Psychogeographers' Pilgrimage* (London: Penned in the Margins, 2021); Nick Papadimitriou, *Scarp* (London: Hachette, 2012); Gillian Tindall, *The Tunnel through Time: A New Route for an Old London Journey* (London: Chatto and Windus, 2016); Luke Turner, *Out of the Woods* (London: Weidenfeld and Nicolson, 2019).

63 Anita Sethi, *I Belong Here: A Journey along the Backbone of Britain* (London: Bloomsbury Nature, 2021).

64 David Seabrook, *All the Devils are Here* (London: Granta, 2002); Ben Myer, 'Nightmare on sea: a strange, once-forgotten history of the Kent coast is a cult favourite', Newstatesman.com, 2018, https://www.newstatesman.com/culture/books/2018/02/nightmare-sea-strange-once-forgotten-history-kent-coast-cult-favourite (accessed 23 November 2021).

65 See Will Self, 'The deep topography of Nick Papadimitriou', 2011, https://will-self.com/2011/02/18/the-deep-topography-of-nick-papadimitriou/ (accessed 23 November 2021).

66 Tim Edensor, 'Walking through ruins', in Jo Lee Vergunst and Tim Ingold (eds), *Ways of Walking* (Abingdon: Routledge, 2016), 135–154.

67 Overall, *Heavy Times*, 113.

68 Tolia-Kelly, 'Narrating the postcolonial landscape'.

69 James Sidaway, 'Shadows on the path: negotiating geopolitics on an urban section of Britain's South West Coast Path', *Environment and Planning D: Society and Space* 27(6) (2009): 1109.

70 Len Platt, *Writing London and the Thames Estuary* (Leiden: Brill, 2017).

71 Maighna Nanu, 'Veterans project love letter to EU on White Cliffs of Dover', *The Independent*, 31 January 2020, https://www.independent.co.uk/news/uk/politics/brexit-world-war-two-veterans-eu-dover-soldiers-a9311761.html (accessed 23 November 2021).

Notes to Chapter 2

1 Charles G. Harper, *The Kentish Coast* (London: Chapman and Hall, 1914).

2 Halford Mackinder, *Britain and the British Seas* (London: William Heinemann, 1902).

3 Rachel Lichtenstein, *Estuary: Out from London to the Sea* (Harmondsworth: Penguin, 2016).

4 Patrick Wright, *The Sea View Has Me Again: Uwe Johnson in Sheerness* (London: Repeater Books, 2020).

Notes

5   See also Mary Gearey, Andrew Church and Neil Ravenscroft, 'Wetlands as literary spaces: off kilter, off grid, off the wall', in Mary Gearey, Andrew Church and Neil Ravenscroft (eds), *English Wetlands* (Cham: Palgrave Pivot, 2020), 91–118.

6   Carol Donaldson, *On the Marshes* (Beaminster: Little Toller Press, 2017).

7   See Carol Donaldson, 'Walk the North Kent Marshes – while the solitude lasts', *The Guardian*, 21 December 2017, https://www.theguardian.com/travel/2017/dec/21/walking-north-kent-marshes-hoo-peninsula-charles-dickens (accessed 23 November 2021).

8   Gary Budden's *The Hollow Shore* deserves mention here as an example of 'wyrd' fiction that builds on the uncanny nature of the marshes. Starting as a short story about a bear-type figure stalking the marshes, it was ultimately published as a book that uses the distance between London and the north Kent coast as the basis of a novel exploring the relationship between father and son. See Gary Budden, *The Hollow Shore* (London: Dead Ink, 2017).

9   Brian Dillon, *The Great Explosion* (Harmondsworth: Penguin, 2015); Historic England, 'Memorials to the victims of the 1916 Faversham munitions explosion, Faversham – 1261010', 2016, https://historicengland.org.uk/listing/the-list/list-entry/1261010 (accessed 23 November 2021).

10 Brian Dillon, '"The ghost of an awful energy" – the Great Kent Explosion of 1916', *The Guardian*, 16 May 2015, https://www.theguardian.com/books/2015/may/16/brian-dillon-the-great-explosion-munitions-factory-uplees-faversham-kent-1915 (accessed 23 November 2021).

11 Initial reviews of *The Great Explosion* suggested it was something of a companion to David Seabrook, *All the Devils are Here* (London: Granta, 2002), but in many ways it bears closer comparison to Philip Hoare's account of the now-demolished Victoria Hospital at Netley, Southampton, a biography of a building that allows Hoare to deal with themes of masculinity, identity and his own past: see Philip Hoare, *Spike Island* (London: Fourth Estate, 2001).

12 Charles Dickens, *Great Expectations* (London: Chapman and Hall, 1861), ch. 23.

13 See David Nettleingham, 'Beyond the heartlands: deindustrialization, naturalization and the meaning of an "industrial" tradition', *The British Journal of Sociology* 70(2) (2018): 610–626.

14 See also Les Roberts, 'Landscapes in the frame: exploring the hinterlands of the British procedural drama', *New Review of Film and Television Studies* 14(3) (2016): 364–385.

15 Harper, *The Kentish Coast*.

16 Michael Watkins, 'Cakes and ale but no oysters', *The Times*, 23 August 1986, 7.

17 Gareth Davies, 'A stone's throw from Islington', *The Sunday Times*, 2 September 2000, 12.

18 C. J. Stone, 'Style: Whitstable – the new Chelsea?', *The Independent*, 12 December 1999, https://www.independent.co.uk/life-style/style-whitstable-new-chelsea-1131848.html (accessed 23 November 2021).

19 Tom Dyckhoff, 'Let's move to Whitstable, Kent: pockets of peace on the gentrified seaside', *The Guardian*, 5 April 2019, https://www.theguardian.com/money/2019/apr/05/lets-move-to-whitstable-kent (accessed 23 November 2021).

20 Andy Beckett, 'Albion Ltd', *The Guardian*, 23 May 2005, https://www.theguardian.com/lifeandstyle/2005/may/23/shopping.fashion (accessed 23 November 2021).

21 David Brooks, *Bobos in Paradise* (London: Simon and Schuster, 2001).

22 Tim G. Acott and Julie Urquhart, 'Sense of place and socio-cultural values in fishing communities along the English Channel', in Julie Urquhart, Tim G. Acott, David Symes and Minghua Zhao (eds), *Social Issues in Sustainable Fisheries Management* (Dordrecht: Springer, 2014), 257–277.

23 The oyster produces gentrification in at least three ways. First, it is a visceral object whose affective qualities create hierarchies of taste and dis-taste through processes of desire and disgust; secondly, it is a marker of class change that positions the 'local' within wider circuits of consumption; and, thirdly, it is a labouring body that reconstitutes the coastal ecosystem on which aquaculture depends.

24 See John Sheail, 'An historical perspective on the development of a marine resource: the Whitstable oyster fishery', *Marine Environmental Research* 19(4) (1986): 279–293; pollution concerns resurfaced in the twenty-first century, with Southern Water fined £90m in July 2021 for repeated illegal dumping of sewage at Whitstable (and other sites on the South East coast) linked to the possible *E. coli* contamination of oyster stocks.

25 These numbers are disputed, with varied maps and interpretations of the number of trestles presented at Planning Inquiry C/18/3209297, July 2021.

26 Jason Holland, 'Aquaculture has put the oysters back in oyster town', *Global Aquaculture Alliance*, 7 January 2019, https://www.aquaculturealliance.org/advocate/aquaculture-put-oysters-back-in-oyster-town/ (accessed 23 November 2021).

27 See https://www.comparemymove.com/coastal-relocations (accessed 23 November 2021).

28 See Phil Hubbard, 'Legal pluralism at the beach: public access, land use, and the struggle for the "coastal commons"', *Area* 52(2) (2020): 420–428.

29 *Whitstable Society v Canterbury City Council* [2017] EWHC 254 (Admin).

30 This legal term, also referred to as 'time out of mind', is taken to indicate any practice that is thought to predate 1189.

Notes

31   As cited in the 2004 Whitstable Oyster Fishery Company Bill, House of Commons, https://publications.parliament.uk/pa/cm200405/cmprbill/006/05006–a.htm (accessed 23 November 2021).

32   See https://publicaccess.canterbury.gov.uk/online-applications/application Details.do?activeTab=neighbourComments&keyVal=_CANTE_DCAPR_117205 (accessed 5 March 2019).

33   Thanet District Council, 2018, 'Pacific oysters in the NE Kent MPA', http://www.thanetcoast.org.uk/projects-and-issues/pacific-oysters-in-the-ne-kent-mpa/ (accessed 23 November 2021).

34   C. J. Stone, 'Whitstable vs Whitstable Oyster Fishery Company', *Whitstable Views*, 8 July 2021, https://whitstableviews.com/2021/07/08/whitstable-vs-whitstable-oyster-fishery-company/ (accessed 23 November 2021).

35   Jennifer L. Ruesink, Hunter S. Lenihan, Alan C. Trimble, Kimberly W. Heiman, Fiorenza Micheli, James E. Byers and Matthew C. Kay, 'Introduction of non-native oysters: ecosystem effects and restoration implications', *Annual Review of Ecology, Evolution, and Systematics* 36(1) (2005): 643–689.

36   There is, however, some evidence that a tiny proportion of triploid oysters may lose one set of chromosomes and revert to diploid reproductive state, albeit this tendency is more pronounced in warmer water. See Roger Herbert, John Humphreys, Clare Davies, Caroline Roberts, Steve Fletcher and Tasman Crowe, 'Ecological impacts of non-native Pacific oysters (*Crassostrea gigas*) and management measures for protected areas in Europe', *Biodiversity and Conservation* 25(14) (2016): 2835–2865.

37   Juliet Fall, *Drawing the Line: Nature, Hybridity and Politics in Transboundary Spaces* (Abingdon: Routledge, 2017).

38   Jonathan Davies, 'Brexit and invasive species: a case study of the cognitive and affective encoding of "abject nature" in contemporary nationalist ideology', *Cultural Studies* (2021), 1–30, https://doi.org/10.1080/09502386.2021.1882520 (accessed 23 November 2021).

39   Roger Herbert, Caroline Roberts, John Humphreys and Steve Fletcher, *The Pacific Oyster (Crassostrea gigas) in the UK: Economic, Legal and Environmental Issues Associated with its Cultivation, Wild Establishment and Exploitation* (London: The Shellfish Association of Great Britain, 2012), http://www.shellfish.org.uk/files/PDF/73434Pacific%20Oysters%20Issue%20Paper_final_241012.pdf (accessed 23 November 2021).

40   Ben Pitcher, 'Belonging to a different landscape: repurposing nationalist affects', *Sociological Research Online* 21(1) (2016): 77–89.

41   Muzna Rahman, 'Consuming Brexit: alimentary discourses and the racial politics of Brexit', *The Open Arts Journal* 8 (2020): 71–82.

42   Stijn Billiet, 'Brexit and fisheries: fish and chips aplenty?', *The Political Quarterly* 90(4) (2019): 611–619.

Notes

43 See Jeremy Phillipson and David Symes, '"A sea of troubles": Brexit and the fisheries question', *Marine Policy* 90 (2018): 168–173.

44 *Hansard*, Official Report, 3 June 2015 596, c. 675, https://hansard.parliament.uk/commons/2015-06-03/debates/15060324000002/DevolutionAndGrowthAcrossBritain (accessed 1 February 2022).

45 Hannah Jones, 'More in common: the domestication of misogynist white supremacy and the assassination of Jo Cox', *Ethnic and Racial Studies* 42(14) (2019): 2431–2449.

46 Patrick McGuire, 'Chris Grayling: British countryside "will be ruined by migrant homes"', *Daily Express*, 30 May 2016, https://www.express.co.uk/news/politics/675034/chris-grayling-green-belt-migrants-countryside-eu-referendum-brexit-david-cameron-uk (accessed 23 November 2021).

47 For further discussion of the entanglement of social and environmental histories in Brexit, see also Lenka Vráblíková, 'Othering mushrooms: migratism and its racist entanglements in the Brexit campaign', *Feminist Encounters: A Journal of Critical Studies in Culture and Politics* 5(1) (2021), https://www.lectitopublishing.nl/Article/Detail/othering-mushrooms-migratism-and-its-racist-entanglements-in-the-brexit-campaign-9742 (accessed 23 November 2021).

48 John Nurden, 'Cockle pickers are "raping" Kent beaches', *Kent Online*, 4 June 2020, https://www.kentonline.co.uk/sheerness/news/hordes-of-cockle-pickers-are-raping-kents-beaches-228278/ (accessed 23 November 2021).

49 In July 2021 raw sewage dumped into the sea by Southern Water was linked to a possible outbreak of *E. coli*, with harvesting of Whitstable oysters suspended for a week. See Jack Peat, 'Diners poisoned by sewage at Whitstable oyster festival', 27 October 2021, https://www.thelondoneconomic.com/news/diners-poisoned-by-sewage-at-whitstable-oyster-festival-298464/ (accessed 23 November 2021).

50 Adam Payne, 'Shellfish businesses say government plan to build purification centres won't help most exports', *Politics Home*, 10 March 2021, https://www.politicshome.com/news/article/shellfish-purification-centres-exports (accessed 23 November 2021).

51 This portmanteau term acknowledges the role of tourism in gentrification; see Kevin Fox Gotham, 'Tourism gentrification: the case of new Orleans' vieux carre (French Quarter)', *Urban Studies* 42(7) (2005): 1099–1121.

Notes to Chapter 3

1 The Libertines, 'The Good Old Days' (Doherty/Barat), from the album *Up The Bracket* (Rough Trade, 2002).

Notes

2 See Nigel Barker, Allan Brodie, Nick Dermott, Lucy Jessop and Gary Winter, *Margate's Seaside Heritage* (Swindon: English Heritage, 2007).

3 Opened to the public in 1830s, and containing multiple sacred symbols, the origins of this are much speculated upon, with some even suggesting a link with the Phoenicians and their goddess Tanit. See Gary Budden, 'The shell grotto', *Unofficial Britain*, 2014, http://www.unofficialbritain.com/the-shell-grotto/ (accessed 23 November 2021).

4 Charles G. Harper, *The Kentish Coast* (London: Chapman and Hall, 1914).

5 David Jarratt and Sean Gammon, '"We had the most wonderful times": seaside nostalgia at a British resort', *Tourism Recreation Research* 41(2) (2016): 123–133.

6 The Introduction to Chris Rojek and John Urry, *Touring Cultures* (London: Routledge, 1997), notes that many English seaside resorts appear empty of time or slowed down.

7 Paul Watt, '"This pain of moving, moving, moving": evictions, displacement and logics of expulsion in London', *L'Annee Sociologique* 68(1) (2018): 67–100.

8 Charlotte England, 'Heaven Kent? Margate's regeneration', *Inside Housing*, 16 June 2017, https://www.insidehousing.co.uk/insight/insight/heaven-kent–margates-regeneration-50912 (accessed 23 November 2021).

9 Nick Hodgson, 'Lambeth council plans to move homeless families to Margate', *Evening Standard*, 4 April 2013, https://www.standard.co.uk/news/london/lambeth-council-plans-to-move-homeless-families-to-margate-8559292.html (accessed 23 November 2021).

10 Alan White, 'Thousands of homeless families drift to the end of the track', *New Statesman*, 21 November 2012, https://www.newstatesman.com/alan-white/2012/11/thousands-homeless-families-drift-end-track (accessed 23 November 2021).

11 See especially Melanie Griffiths, 'Out of time: the temporal uncertainties of refused asylum seekers and immigration detainees', *Journal of Ethnic and Migration Studies* 40(12) (2014): 1991–2009.

12 Fiachra Gibbons, 'Meet me in Margate', *The Guardian*, 9 March 2001, https://www.theguardian.com/film/2001/mar/09/culture.features (accessed 23 November 2021).

13 Steven Allen, 'British cinema at the seaside – the limits of liminality', *Journal of British Cinema and Television* 5(1) (2008): 53–71.

14 There are parallels here to writing on commercial leisure spaces, cafés and takeaways as sites of everyday multiculturalism. See Emma Jackson, 'Valuing the bowling alley: contestations over the preservation of spaces of everyday urban multiculture in London', *The Sociological Review* 67(1) (2019): 79–94; Hannah Jones, Sarah Neal, Giles Mohan, Kieran Connell, Allan Cochrane and Katy Bennett, 'Urban multiculture and everyday encounters in semi-public, franchised café spaces', *The Sociological Review* 63(3) (2015): 644–661.

Notes

15 See Les Roberts, 'Welcome to Dreamland: from place to non-place and back again in Pawel Pawlikowski's *Last Resort*', *New Cinemas: Journal of Contemporary Film* 1(2) (2002): 78–90, and Alice Bardan, 'Welcome to Dreamland: the realist impulse in Pawel Pawlikowski's *Last Resort*', *New Cinemas: Journal of Contemporary Film* 6(1) (2008): 47–63.

16 *Second Report of the Communities and Local Government Committee on Coastal Towns* (2007), http://www.publications.parliament.uk/pa/cm200607/cmselect/cmcomloc/cmcomloc.htm (accessed 23 November 2021).

17 See Thanet District Council, Selective Licensing Scheme (2021), http://www.thanet.gov.uk/housing/selective_licensing_scheme/the_profile.aspx (accessed 23 November 2021).

18 See the Centre for Social Justice, *Turning the Tide* (2013), https://www.centreforsocialjustice.org.uk/core/wp-content/uploads/2016/08/Turning-the-Tide.pdf (accessed 23 November 2021).

19 Marion Shoard, 'Edgelands', in Jennifer Jenkins (ed.), *Remaking the Landscape: The Changing Face of Britain* (London: Profile Books, 2002), 117–147.

20 Here I borrow from Tim Edensor, 'The ghosts of industrial ruins: ordering and disordering memory in excessive space', *Environment and Planning D: Society and Space* 23(6) (2005): 829–849.

21 See Rachel Johnson, 'The Venus of Margate: fashion and disease at the seaside', *Journal for Eighteenth-Century Studies* 40(4) (2017): 587–602.

22 See, for example, '28 Days Later, report – Margate Lido and the Vortgern Caves, 2010', cited at https://www.28dayslater.co.uk/threads/margate-lido-and-the-vortigern-caves-5-5-10.50061/ (accessed 23 November 2021).

23 See Ben Hickman, 'Listening to lidos', 14 July 2016, https://blogs.kent.ac.uk/criticalkent/2016/07/14/listening-to-lidos-cliftonville-2016/ (accessed 23 November 2021).

24 See Philip Hubbard, *The Battle for the High Street* (Basingstoke: Palgrave, 2017).

25 Selby Whittingham, 'J.M.W. Turner, marriage and morals', *The British Art Journal* 15(3) (2015): 119–125.

26 See also John E. Thornes, 'Cultural climatology and the representation of sky, atmosphere, weather and climate in selected art works of Constable, Monet and Eliasson', *Geoforum* 39(2) (2008): 570–580.

27 Iain Aitch, 'Gallery 0, North Sea 1', *The Guardian*, 2 February 2005, https://www.theguardian.com/artanddesign/2005/feb/02/architecture (accessed 23 November 2021).

28 Jonathan Glancey, 'On the waterfront', *The Guardian*, 29 October 2001, https://www.theguardian.com/culture/2001/oct/29/artsfeatures.arts (accessed 23 November 2021).

29 Cabinet Minutes, Thanet District Council, 15 July 2004 https://democracy.thanet.gov.uk/Data/Cabinet/20040715/Agenda/$Agenda%20Enclosure%202.doc.pdf (accessed 23 November 2021).

Notes

30   Cited in William Shaw, 'Windows of opportunity', *New Statesman*, 2 April 2009, https://www.newstatesman.com/culture/2009/04/windows-opportunity (accessed 23 November 2021).

31   Andrew Jackson, Amy Nettley, Joanne Muzyka and Tim Dee, *Turner Contemporary: Art Inspiring Change. Social Value Report (15/16)* (Margate: Turner Gallery, 2016).

32   House of Lords Select Committee, *The Future of Seaside Towns* (2019), House of Lords Paper 320, https://publications.parliament.uk/pa/ld201719/ldselect/ldseaside/320/320.pdf (accessed 23 November 2021).

33   *Summary of Conclusion and Recommendations, Final Report of the Select Committee on The Future of Seaside Towns* (2019), https://publications.parliament.uk/pa/ld201719/ldselect/ldseaside/320/32010.htm#_idTextAnchor141 (accessed 23 November 2021).

34   Michael Smith, 'How Margate became the new hipster's paradise', *Esquire*, 3 April 2015, https://www.esquire.com/uk/food-drink/travel/news/a8101/how-margate-became-the-new-hipsters-paradise/ (accessed 23 November 2021).

35   Cited in https://www.filmfeeder.co.uk/exclusive-interview-with-jellyfish-director-james-gardner/ (accessed 23 November 2021).

36   Nick Laister, 'Delivering the dream: saving Britain's amusement park heritage and the reawakening of Margate's Dreamland', in Jason Wood (ed.), *The Amusement Park* (Abingdon: Routledge, 2017), 203–227.

37   Around the same time, ex-Clash bassist Paul Simenon teamed up with Damon Albarn (Blur), Tony Allen and Simon Tong for *The Good, The Bad & The Queen* project, which mined similar myths of nationalism and decline through a William Blake-inspired exploration of Englishness; interestingly, their second album *Merrie England* (2018) begins with a short extract from Powell and Pressburger's *Canterbury Tales*, set in wartime Kent.

38   Here I am indebted to Alexandra Kolesnik, 'Popular culture and history: representations of the past in British popular music of the 2000s', *Higher School of Economics Research Paper No. WP BRP 54* (2014), http://dx.doi.org/10.2139/ssrn.2472893 (accessed 23 November 2021).

39   The idea of the urban pastoral emerges in the work of Julian Stallabrass and is developed in the context of gentrification by Andrew Harris, 'Art and gentrification: pursuing the urban pastoral in Hoxton, London', *Transactions of the Institute of British Geographers* 37(2) (2012): 226–241.

40   Andrew Trendall, 'An update from Pete Doherty on The Libertines' hotel: "It's never going to be hipster because you've got that smell that the sea gives out"', *NME*, 1 May 2019, https://www.nme.com/news/music/libertines-hotel-margate-albion-rooms-studio-pete-doherty-interview-smell-july-opening-2483011 (accessed 23 November 2021).

41   See Daniel Burdsey, 'Strangers on the shore? Racialized representation, identity and in/visibilities of whiteness at the English seaside', *Cultural*

Notes

Sociology 5(4) (2011): 537–552; on Margate and nationalism more specifically, see Ana Carolina Balthazar, *Ethics and Nationalist Populism at the British Seaside: Negotiating Character* (Abingdon: Routledge, 2021).

42 Owen Jones, 'Pessimism is toxic in Britain's coastal towns', *The Guardian*, 16 March 2017, https://www.theguardian.com/commentisfree/2017/mar/16/brexitland-britain-coastal-towns-decline (accessed 23 November 2021).

43 In one attempt to model the Brexit outcome taking account of age profile and overall voter turnout, Medway appears as an extreme outlier and was, along with Gravesham, more pro-Leave than Thanet. See David Manley, Kelvyn Jones and Ron Johnston, 'The geography of Brexit – what geography? Modelling and predicting the outcome across 380 local authorities', *Local Economy* 32(3) (2017): 183–203.

44 Arum Rawf, 'Councillor sends in shocking report of racism in Thanet', 7 July 2020, https://www.souththanetlabour.org.uk/councillor-sends-mp-shocking-report-of-racism-in-thanet/ (accessed 23 November 2021).

45 Lydia Chantier-Hicks, 'Thanet Conservative councillor Paul Messenger issues apology after being suspended over "Islamophobic" Facebook posts', *Kentonline*, 17 March 2019, https://www.kentonline.co.uk/thanet/news/suspended-councillor-apologises-for-historic-islamophobia-200877/ (accessed 23 November 2021).

46 Marijke Hall, 'Teenagers "shout coronavirus and fake sneeze" at Chinese student on a day-trip to Margate from London', 2 March 2020, https://www.kentonline.co.uk/thanet/news/teens-shout-coronavirus-and-fake-sneeze-at-chinese-student-222967/ (accessed 23 November 2021).

47 Marijke Hall, 'Community in Cliftonville and Margate call for action against racist and offensive graffiti', 10 July 2020, https://www.kentonline.co.uk/thanet/news/anger-at-white-lives-matter-graffiti-230187/ (accessed 23 November 2021).

48 Michael Balfour, 'Performing the promised land: the festivalizing of multi-cultures in the Margate Exodus Project', in Jodie Taylor and Andy Bennett (eds), *The Festivalization of Culture* (Farnham: Ashgate, 2014), 207–228.

49 Marijke Hall, 'Sculpture of British soldier pointing towards parliament to be installed on Margate seafront', *Kentonline*, 20 February 2020, https://www.kentonline.co.uk/thanet/news/sculpture-of-british-soldier-to-be-installed-on-seafront-222441/ (accessed 23 November 2021).

50 Rakowitz discovered in the process of preparing his artwork that Sassoon was one of his ancestors, hailing from the same Baghdadi-Jewish family as his mother. See Gareth Harris, 'Iraqi-US Michale Rakowitz's new anti-war monument in Margate points accusing finger at government', *The Art Newspaper*, 26 February 2020, https://www.theartnewspaper.com/news/michael-rakowitz-margate (accessed 23 November 2021).

Notes

Notes to Chapter 4

1   William Wordsworth, 'To the Men of Kent', in *Sonnets Dedicated to Liberty* (London: Claysmore, 1807), poem composed in 1803.

2   John Nurden, 'Director Ken Knowles irked as BBC sits on bomb-ship film *A Disaster Waiting to Happen*', 29 July 2017, https://www.kentonline.co.uk/sheerness/news/documentary-raises-ship-explosion-fears-129575/ (accessed 23 November 2021).

3   See David E. Alexander, 'The strange case of the *Richard Montgomery*: on the evolution of intractable risk', *Safety Science* 120 (2019): 575–582.

4   Published in English as Uwe Johnson, 'An unfathomable ship', *Granta* 6 (1982): 262–276.

5   Natalie Chalk, 'Memorial to infamous hero', *Daily Express*, 23 November 2008, https://www.express.co.uk/news/uk/72471/Memorial-to-infamous-hero (accessed 23 November 2021).

6   Marianna Torgovnick, *The War Complex: World War II in Our Time* (Chicago: University of Chicago Press, 2008).

7   Jacqueline Tivers, '"The home of the British Army": the iconic construction of military defence landscapes', *Landscape Research* 24(3) (1999): 303–319.

8   Eve Darian-Smith, *Bridging Divides: The Channel Tunnel and English Legal Identity in the New Europe* (Berkeley, CA: University of California Press, 1999).

9   David Herd, 'The view from Dover', *Los Angeles Review of Books*, 3 March 2005, https://lareviewofbooks.org/article/view-dover/ (accessed 23 November 2021).

10 HM Chief Inspector of Prisons, *Report on Unannounced Inspection of Dover Immigration Removal Centre*, 3–14 March 2014, p. 5, https://www.justiceinspectorates.gov.uk/hmiprisons/wp-content/uploads/sites/4/2014/07/Dover-2014-Web.pdf (accessed 23 November 2021).

11 '£4m dental suite built for illegals', *The Sun*, 9 February 2015, https://www.thesun.co.uk/archives/news/23857/4m-dental-suite-built-for-illegals/ (accessed 23 November 2021).

12 Patrick Cockburn, 'English exceptionalism is, in fact, unexceptional', *The Independent*, 1 January 2021, https://www.independent.co.uk/voices/brexit-english-nationalism-conservative-party-boris-johnson-b1781171.html (accessed 23 November 2021).

13 See, for example, Satnam Virdee and Brendan McGeever, 'Racism, crisis, Brexit', *Ethnic and Racial Studies* 41(10) (2018): 1802–1819; Ben Rogaly, 'Brexit writings and the war of position over migration, "race" and class', *Environment and Planning C: Politics and Space* 37(1) (2019): 28–40.

14 Joe Pettet-Smith and Charlotte Parkin, 'In defence of lost causes', *On Landscape*, 7 June 2019, https://www.onlandscape.co.uk/2019/06/in-defence-of-lost-causes/ (accessed 23 November 2021).

Notes

15 See Brian Dillon, 'Listening for the enemy', *Cabinet Magazine*, fall/winter 2003, http://www.cabinetmagazine.org/issues/12/dillon.php (accessed 23 November 2021).

16 See *LiveArtUK*, 17 October 2019, https://www.liveartuk.org/blog/selina-bonelli/ (accessed 23 November 2021).

17 See Kate Procter, 'Michael Gove appears to blame China over lack of UK coronavirus testing', *The Guardian*, 29 March 2020, https://www.theguardian.com/politics/2020/mar/29/michael-gove-appears-to-blame-china-over-lack-of-uk-coronavirus-testing (accessed 23 November 2021).

18 Amanuel Elias, Jehonathan Ben, Fethi Mansouri and Yin Paradies, 'Racism and nationalism during and beyond the COVID-19 pandemic', *Ethnic and Racial Studies* 44(5) (2021): 783–793.

19 Malcolm James and Sivamohan Valluvan, 'Coronavirus conjuncture: nationalism and pandemic states', *Sociology* 54(6) (2020): 1238–1250.

20 See David Miles, *The Land of the White Horse* (London: Thames and Hudson, 2019), on the disputed origins and meanings of the Uffington White Horse.

21 Pyrs Gruffudd, 'Reach for the sky: the air and English cultural nationalism', *Landscape Research* 16(2) (1991): 19–24. See also Tony Pratley, 'The Supermarine Spitfire: Palimpsest, Performance, and Myth', PhD thesis, University of Kent, 2017.

22 Cited in Will Butler, 'The arrival of Belgians at Folkestone', 18 August 2014, https://blogs.kent.ac.uk/gateways/2014/08/18/the-arrival-of-the-belgians-at-folkestone/ (accessed 23 November 2021).

23 Wilfred Owen, *The Collected Letters* (Oxford: Oxford University Press, 2008), 263.

24 Wilfred Owen, 'The Send-Off', in Jon Stallworthy (ed.), *The Complete Poems and Fragments of Wilfred Owen* (London: Chatto and Windus, 1983), https://www.poetryfoundation.org/poems/57369/the-send-off (accessed 10 February 2022).

25 Wilfred Owen, 'Anthem for Doomed Youth', in Stallworthy (ed.), *The Complete Poems and Fragments of Wilfred Owen*, https://www.poetryfoundation.org/poems/47393/anthem-for-doomed-youth (accessed 10 February 2022).

26 Aaron Winter, 'Race, multiculturalism and the "progressive" politics of London 2012: passing the "Boyle Test"', *Sociological Research Online* 18(2) (2013): 137–143.

27 Carol Ann Duffy, 'The Wound in Time', 2018, https://www.pagesofthesea.org.uk/the-wound-in-time/ (accessed 23 November 2021).

28 The Folkestone plaques feature two of the three verses of the poem, which was originally published alongside Owen's poem 'The Send-Off' in 2013. See https://www.theguardian.com/books/2013/oct/26/carol-ann-duffy-wilfred-owen-war-poem (accessed 23 November 2021).

Notes

29 Edward S. Casey, *Remembering: A Phenomenological Study* (Bloomington, IN: Indiana University Press, 2009).

30 Caitlin DeSilvey, 'Making sense of transience: an anticipatory history', *Cultural Geographies* 19(1) (2012): 31–54.

31 Alastair Sooke, 'Folkestone – a place where nothing ever happens', *The Telegraph*, 16 June 2008.

32 Richelle M. Bernazzoli and Colin Flint, 'Power, place, and militarism: toward a comparative geographic analysis of militarization', *Geography Compass* 3(1) (2009): 393–411.

33 Patrick Wright, 'The war goes on', *The Guardian*, 10 November 1994, 2.

34 Ministry of Information report on morale, 10 September 1940, http://www.moidigital.ac.uk/reports/home-intelligence-reports/morale-summaries-of-daily-reports-part-b-inf-1264/idm140465703531504/ (accessed 23 November 2021).

35 Owen Hatherley, *The Ministry of Nostalgia: Consuming Austerity* (London: Verso, 2016).

36 See https://www.nationaltrust.org.uk/south-foreland-lighthouse/features/mrs-knotts-tearoom (accessed 23 November 2021).

37 James Meek, *Dreams of Leaving and Remaining* (London: Verso, 2019).

Notes to Chapter 5

1 G. K. Chesterton, *The Ballad of the White Horse* (London: Methuen, 1911).

2 Edward Hasted, *History and Topographical Survey of the County of Kent* (Canterbury: W Bristow, 1797).

3 Anon., *The Handbook for Travellers in Kent and Sussex* (London: John Murray, 1858).

4 W. J. Jeaffreson, 'Castle Hill Folkestone', *Archaeologia Cantiana* 10 (1876): xliv–xlviii.

5 Mark Bowden, *Pitt Rivers: The Life and Archaeological Work of Lieutenant-General Augustus Henry Lane Fox Pitt Rivers* (Cambridge: Cambridge University Press, 1991).

6 Dan Hicks, 'Pitt Rivers in Kent' (2013), https://www.academia.edu/3071375/Pitt_Rivers_in_Kent (accessed 23 November 2021).

7 Augustus Pitt Rivers, 'Excavations at Caesar's Camp, near Folkestone, conducted in 1878', *Archaeologia* 4 (1883): 429–465.

8 Richard Preece and David Bridgland, 'Holywell Coombe, Folkestone: a 13,000 year history of an English chalkland valley', *Quaternary Science Reviews* 18(8–9) (1990): 1075–1125.

9 Roger W. Vickerman, 'The Channel Tunnel and regional development in Europe: an overview', *Applied Geography* 14(1) (1994): 9–25.

10 Robert Macfarlane, *The Old Ways* (London: Hamish Hamilton, 2012), 14.

Notes

11 Cited in Robert Macfarlane, 'Rites of way: behind the pilgrimage revival', *The Guardian*, 15 June 2012, 17, https://www.theguardian.com/books/2012/jun/15/rites-of-way-pilgrimage-walks (accessed 1 February 2022).

12 ElecLink is a joint venture of Groupe Eurotunnel and STAR Capital, adding capacity to the existing interconnection between the 400kv AC grids in France and England via a cable running through the Eurotunnel. The converter station was opposed by the Kent Downs Area of Outstanding Natural Beauty Unit because of its failure to 'sufficiently ameliorate its impact on the AONB'. See Folkestone and Hythe Council Minutes, Development Control Committee, 10 March 2015, DC/14/20 (Y14/1026/SH).

13 Tanya Brannigan, 'Butterflies stand in way of white horse', *The Guardian*, 20 April 2001, https://www.theguardian.com/uk/2001/apr/20/travelnews.travel (accessed 23 November 2021).

14 'White horse might be halted', BBC News, 8 May 2003, http://news.bbc.co.uk/1/hi/england/kent/3011715.stm (accessed 23 November 2021).

15 On the iconography of white horse carvings in the British landscape, see David Miles, *The Land of the White Horse* (London: Thames and Hudson, 2019).

16 Tellingly, as well as the chalk horse at Folkestone, a white horse was once planned for Ebbsfleet International Station at the other end of Kent. This 50-foot-high sculpture, designed by Mark Wallinger and dubbed the 'Angel of the South' by the press, remained ultimately unbuilt because of its prohibitive cost, but was intended to signal the renaissance of the Thames Gateway by marking its emergent role as a new borderzone with Europe. See Anthony Cooper and Chris Rumford, 'Monumentalising the border: bordering through connectivity', *Mobilities* 8(1) (2013): 107–124.

17 See, among others, Yasmin Ibrahim and Anita Howarth, 'Communicating the "migrant" other as risk: space, EU and expanding borders', *Journal of Risk Research* 21(12) (2018): 1465–1486; Jon E. Fox, Laura Moroşanu and Eszter Szilassy, 'The racialization of the new European migration to the UK', *Sociology* 46(4) (2012): 680–695; Bridget Anderson, 'Towards a new politics of migration?', *Ethnic and Racial Studies* 40(9) (2017): 1527–1537.

18 Chenchen Zhang, 'Mobile borders and turbulent mobilities: mapping the geopolitics of the Channel Tunnel', *Geopolitics* 24(3) (2019): 731.

19 Odile Heddebaut, 'The binational cities of Dover and Calais and their region', *GeoJournal* 54(1) (2001): 61–71.

20 Sandro Mezzadra and Brett Neilson, 'Between inclusion and exclusion: on the topology of global space and borders', *Theory, Culture & Society* 29(4–5) (2012): 58–75. On the biometrics of the border, see Louise Amoore, 'Biometric borders: governing mobilities in the war on terror', *Political Geography* 25(3): 336–351.

21 Adrian Favell, *Eurostars and Eurocities: Free Movement and Mobility in an Integrating Europe* (Oxford: Blackwell, 2008).

22 Nick Vaughan-Williams, 'Borderwork beyond inside/outside? Frontex, the citizen–detective and the war on terror', *Space and Polity* 12(1) (2008): 63–79; see also Thom Davies, Arshad Isakjee, Lucy Mayblin and Joe Turner, 'Channel crossings: offshoring asylum and the afterlife of empire in the Dover Strait', *Ethnic and Racial Studies* 44(13) (2021): 2307–2327.

23 Nira Yuval-Davis, Georgie Wemyss and Kathryn Cassidy, 'Everyday bordering, belonging and the reorientation of British immigration legislation', *Sociology* 52(2) (2018): 228–244.

24 Etienne Balibar, 'The borders of Europe', in Pheng Cheah and Bruce Robbins (eds), *Cosmopolitics: Thinking and Feeling beyond the Nation* (Minneapolis, MN: University of Minnesota Press, 1998), 217.

25 Andrew Church and Peter Reid, 'Cross-border co-operation, institutionalization and political space across the English Channel', *Regional Studies* 33(7) (1999): 643–655.

26 Four routes were proposed in 1988, with the 'New Kent mainline' confirmed in 1991 after considerable debate about the environmental and economic impacts of the route; see Richard A. Goodenough and Stephen J. Page, 'Evaluating the environmental impact of a major transport infrastructure project: the Channel Tunnel highspeed rail link', *Applied Geography* 14(1) (1994): 26–50.

27 On the use of the garden metaphor in opposition, see Eve Darian-Smith, 'Legal imagery in the "Garden of England"', *Indiana Journal of Global Legal Studies* 2(2) (1995): 395–411.

28 Christopher Rootes, Clare E. Saunders and Debbie Adams, *Local Environmental Politics in England: Environmental Activism in South East London and East Kent Compared* (2001), European Consortium for Political Research Joint Sessions, 6 April–11 July 2001, Grenoble.

29 Eve Darian-Smith, *Bridging Divides: The Channel Tunnel and English Legal Identity in the New Europe* (Berkeley, CA: University of California Press, 1999).

30 Daniel Pick, 'Pro Patria: blocking the tunnel', *Ecumene* 1(1) (1994): 88.

31 Eve Darian-Smith, 'Rabies rides the fast train: transnational interactions in post-colonial times', *Law and Critique* 6(1) (1995): 77. On rats as signifiers of deprivation and pollution, see also Susan Craddock, *City of Plagues: Disease, Poverty, and Deviance in San Francisco* (Minneapolis, MN: University of Minnesota Press, 2000).

32 Thirty years on, High Speed Two similarly tore villages apart in the Midlands; for example, see Graham Young, 'HS2 devastation makes our hearts sink into our boots', *Birmingham Mail*, 2 May 2021, https://www.birminghammail.co.uk/news/midlands-news/hs2-devastation-makes-hearts-sink-20207019 (accessed 23 November 2021).

Notes

33 Stuart Heritage, *Don't be a Dick, Pete* (London: Vintage, 2017), 17.

34 A discussion of the impact of the rail link on Ashford's economy can be found in Peter Thomas and Daniel O'Donoghue, 'The Channel Tunnel: transport patterns and regional impacts', *Journal of Transport Geography* 31 (2013): 104–112.

35 See especially Huw Marsh, 'Nicola Barker's *Darkmans* and the "vengeful tsunami of history"', *Literary London: Interdisciplinary Studies in the Representation of London*, 7 September 2009, http://www.literarylondon.org/london-journal/september2009/marsh.html (accessed 23 November 2021).

36 There is no apparent historical connection between Ashford and Skogin, whose apocryphal exploits were captured in the two-volume *Jestes of Skoygn*, first published at the end of the sixteenth century and popular for at least two hundred years.

37 Nicola Barker, *Darkmans* (London: Fourth Estate, 2007), 398–399, as cited by Alissa G. Karl, 'The zero hour of the neoliberal novel', *Textual Practice* 29(2) (2015): 335–355. On non-place in *Darkmans*, see also Hilary Black, 'Weren't all true Nomads at their happiest in Limbo?', in Dara Downey, Ian Kinane and Elizabeth Parker (eds), *Landscapes of Liminality: Between Space and Place* (Lanham, MD: Rowman and Littlefield, 2016), 111–133.

38 Barker, *Darkmans*, 399.

39 'Clarkson slams shared space "idiots"', *Kent Online*, 26 November 2008, https://www.kentonline.co.uk/ashford/news/clarkson-slams-shared-space-idi-a46890/ (accessed 23 November 2021).

40 Simon Moody and Steve Melia, 'Shared space – research, policy and problems', *Proceedings of the Institution of Civil Engineers-Transport* 167(6) (2015): 384–392.

41 Ole Brandt Jensen and Tim Richardson, *Making European Space: Mobility, Power and Territorial Identity* (Amsterdam: Psychology Press, 2004), p. 7.

42 John Morgan, 'A cultural geography of Brexit', *Geography* 102 (2017): 153–160.

43 Ben Wellings, 'Brexit, nationalism and disintegration in the European Union and the United Kingdom', *Journal of Contemporary European Studies* 29(3) (2020): 322–334.

44 See Gerard Delanty, 'What does it mean to be a "European"?', *Innovation: The European Journal of Social Science Research* 18(1) (2005): 11–22.

45 See https://www.statista.com/statistics/315456/channel-tunnel-and-short-sea-passengers-in-the-united-kingdom/ (accessed 23 November 2021).

46 Hansard, 7 Feb 2007, https://publications.parliament.uk/pa/cm200607/cmhansrd/cm070201/debtext/70201-0019.htm (accessed 1 February 2022).

47 One anti-Brexit group defaced the Welcome to Kent signs with this slogan; see Claire McWethy, 'Police investigate road signs describing Kent as the "Toilet of England" in anti-Brexit protest', *Kent Online*, 28 November 2020, https://www.kentonline.co.uk/maidstone/news/police-probe-toilet-of-england-sign-stunt-238277/ (accessed 23 November 2021).

Notes

48 Patrick Wright, 'The moral of Brenley Corner', *London Review of Books* 40(23), 6 December 2018, https://www.lrb.co.uk/the-paper/v40/n23/patrick-wright/short-cuts (accessed 23 November 2021).

49 See, for example, Rory Sullivan, 'I think it's going to be a nightmare', *The Independent*, 23 December 2020, https://www.independent.co.uk/news/uk/home-news/brexit-lorry-parks-community-fears-b1767505.html (accessed 23 November 2021).

50 See https://www.gov.uk/government/news/705-million-investment-for-gb-eu-border (accessed 23 November 2021).

51 Katie Boyden, 'Customs post at Ashford MOJO site will make M20 traffic like "Operation Stack" every day', *Kent Online*, 15 July 2020, https://www.kentlive.news/news/kent-news/customs-post-ashford-mojo-site-4330970 (accessed 23 November 2021).

52 Isabella Kaminski, 'Why did the EA refuse to release environmental information about a huge Brexit lorry park?', *Ends Report*, 12 May 2021, https://www.endsreport.com/article/1715700/why-ea-refuse-release-environmental-information-huge-brexit-lorry-park (accessed 23 November 2021).

53 Ed McConnell, 'Latest as France closes border after coronavirus strain out of control', *Kent Online*, 22 December 2020, https://www.kentonline.co.uk/kent/news/border-remains-shut-as-cases-of-new-strain-rise-239665/ (accessed 23 November 2021).

54 Antonia Paget, 'Christmas delivery! Villagers help stranded truck drivers', *The Daily Mail*, 25 December 2020, https://www.dailymail.co.uk/news/article-9086089/Villagers-help-truck-drivers-stuck-M20-Kent-lowering-food-parcels-motorway-bridge.html (accessed 23 November 2021).

55 Joe Evans, 'Downing Street incandescent after French closed border to British lorries', *The Week*, 22 December 2020, https://www.theweek.co.uk/brexit/951542/downing-street-incandescent-after-france-closed-border-to-british-lorries (accessed 23 November 2021).

56 Macer Hall, 'We don't need EU! 60m new jabs to be made in the UK', *The Express*, 30 March 2021, https://www.express.co.uk/news/politics/1416648/coronavirus-latest-60million-vaccines-made-uk-eu-jab-war (accessed 23 November 2021).

57 Fran Allfrey and Beth Whalley, 'Founders of England?', 5 September 2018, https://blogs.kcl.ac.uk/english/2018/09/05/founders-of-england/ (accessed 1 February 2022), refers to the White Horse stone as a site of pagan worship, noting its invocation as the 'true birthplace' of the English people. See also Ethan Doyle White, 'Old stones, new rites: contemporary pagan interactions with the Medway megaliths', *Material Religion* 12(3) (2016): 346–372.

58 James Lloyd, 'The Saxon steed and the White Horse of Kent', *Archaeologia Cantiana* 138 (2017): 1–36.

Notes

59 Helen Gordon, 'How chalk made England', *The Guardian*, 23 February 2021, https://www.theguardian.com/news/2021/feb/23/rock-of-ages-how-chalk-made-england-geology-white-cliffs (accessed 23 November 2021).

60 Robert Macfarlane, *The Old Ways* (London: Hamish Hamilton, 2012), 40. See also Richard Irvine, *An Anthropology of Deep Time: Geological Temporality and Social Life* (Cambridge: Cambridge University Press, 2020).

61 Catherine Parry, 'Pits, pylons and posts: writing under the English rural idyll', in Gary Bosworth and Peter Somerville (eds), *Interpreting Rurality* (Abingdon: Routledge, 2013), 109–121.

62 King himself was an outsider figure, a modern magus whose evident interest in deep history, folklore and the preservation of the English landscape presented Kent's landscape as a remarkable synthesis of nature, power and memory in need of preservation. Not that many paid attention: living his last years in a caravan in Norfolk, King expressed little desire ever to return to Kent, and died in 2018 at the age of 94. The dump where he used to play as a child, near Ash, is now a golf course.

63 See Melanie Küng, 'Guards of Brexit? Revisiting the cultural significance of the white cliffs of Dover', in Ina Habermann (ed.), *The Road to Brexit* (Manchester: Manchester University Press, 2020), 199–214.

64 See Philip Schwyzer, 'The scouring of the White Horse: archaeology, identity, and heritage', *Representations* 65 (1999): 42–62. Schwyzer argues that Chesterton, following Tennyson, invokes the white horse as a pre-historic figure, and suggests that it embodies a multicultural sense of Englishness, encompassing Celtic, Roman and Saxon identities.

65 Joseph R. McCleary, *The Historical Imagination of G. K. Chesterton: Locality, Patriotism, and Nationalism* (Abingdon: Routledge, 2009).

66 See Anssi Paasi, 'Border studies reanimated: going beyond the territorial/relational divide', *Environment and Planning A* 44(10) (2012): 2303–2309.

67 Sivamohan Valluvan and Virinder S. Kalra, 'Racial nationalisms: Brexit, borders and Little Englander contradictions', *Ethnic and Racial Studies* 42(14) (2019): 2393–2412.

Notes to Chapter 6

1 John Lanchester, *The Wall* (New York: W.W. Norton, 2019).

2 See https://you.38degrees.org.uk/petitions/no-development-on-prince-s-parade (accessed 23 November 2021).

3 Folkestone and Hythe Council, *Planning Application Reference 21/1209/FH* (2021), https://folkestonehythedc.force.com/pr/s/planning-application/a1n20000003JGYUAA4/211209fh (accessed 23 November 2021).

4 Ford Madox Ford, *The Cinque Ports: A Historical and Descriptive Record* (Edinburgh: Blackwood, 1900).

5   Here I am indebted to Anne Petrie's remarkable Hythe History blog for details of Moyle Tower and the connections between the Porter family and Hythe: https://hythehistoryblog.wordpress.com/2017/06/27/ (accessed 23 November 2021).

6   See Patrick Comerford, 'A colourful terrace in Dalkey tells a colourful family history', 3 January 2019, http://www.patrickcomerford.com/2019/01/a-colourful-terrace-in-dalkey-tells.html (accessed 23 November 2021).

7   'Seeking asylum, facing pirates, storms and gunfire to flee Vietnam', BBC News, 6 June 2019, https://www.bbc.co.uk/news/uk-wales-48501390 (accessed 23 November 2021).

8   See Becky Taylor, 'Refugees, ghost ships and Thatcher', 26 January 2015, https://www.historyworkshop.org.uk/ghostships/ (accessed 23 November 2021).

9   Cited in Jordanna Bailkin, *Unsettled: Refugee Camps and the Making of Multicultural Britain* (Oxford: Oxford University Press, 2018).

10 See Peter Walsh, 'Migrants crossing the Channel in small boats: what do we know?', 16 October 2020, https://migrationobservatory.ox.ac.uk/resources/commentaries/migrants-crossing-the-english-channel-in-small-boats-what-do-we-know/ (accessed 23 November 2021).

11 Details of the 290 estimated to have died crossing the English Channel between 1999 and 2020 are provided in the Institute of Race Relations, *Deadly Crossings and the Militarisation of Britain's Borders* (2020), https://irr.org.uk/wp-content/uploads/2020/11/Deadly-Crossings-Final.pdf (accessed 23 November 2021).

12 Kara E. Dempsey and Sara McDowell, 'Disaster depictions and geopolitical representations in Europe's migration "crisis"', *Geoforum* 98(2) (2019): 153–160. See also Lesley J. Pruitt, 'Closed due to "flooding"? UK media representations of refugees and migrants in 2015–2016 – creating a crisis of borders', *The British Journal of Politics and International Relations* 21(2) (2019): 383–402; Samuel Parker, Sophie Bennett, Chyna Mae Cobden and Deborah Earnshaw, '"It's time we invested in stronger borders": media representations of refugees crossing the English Channel by boat', *Critical Discourse Studies* (2021), https://doi.org/10.1080/17405904.2021.1920998.

13 See Kerry Moore, Mike Berry and Iñaki Garcia-Blanco, 'Saving refugees or policing the seas? How the national press of five EU member states framed news coverage of the migration crisis', *Justice, Power and Resistance* 2(1) (2018): 66–95.

14 Bastian A. Vollmer, 'Security or insecurity? Representations of the UK border in public and policy discourses', *Mobilities* 12(3) (2017): 295–310.

15 'Channel Tunnel, "2000 migrants" tried to enter', BBC News, 28 July 2015, https://www.bbc.co.uk/news/world-europe-33689473 (accessed 1 February 2022).

Notes

16 Chenchen Zhang, 'Mobile borders and turbulent mobilities: mapping the geopolitics of the Channel Tunnel', *Geopolitics* 24(3) (2019): 728–755.

17 'Calais migrant crisis', ITV News, 29 July 2015, https://www.itv.com/news/update/2015-07-29/pm-we-will-do-everything-we-can-to-improve-calais-situation/ (accessed 23 November 2021).

18 Luca Queirolo Palmas, '"Now is the real Jungle!" Institutional hunting and migrants' survival after the eviction of the Calais camp', *Environment and Planning D: Society and Space* 39(3) (2021): 496–513.

19 Thom Davies, Arshad Isakjee, Lucy Mayblin and Joe Turner, 'Channel crossings: offshoring asylum and the afterlife of empire in the Dover Strait', *Ethnic and Racial Studies* 44(13) (2021): 2307–2327.

20 Cited in Cole Moreton, 'I'm surprised more migrants haven't died in the Channel', 15 February 2020, https://www.theguardian.com/uk-news/2020/feb/15/migrants-cold-wet-frightened-crossing-channel-in-tiny-boats (accessed 23 November 2021).

21 Emma Jacobs, '"Colonising the future": migrant crossings on the English Channel and the discourse of risk', *Brief Encounters* 4(1) (2020): 37–47.

22 Nicholas De Genova, 'Spectacles of migrant "illegality": the scene of exclusion, the obscene of inclusion', *Ethnic and Racial Studies* 36(7) (2013): 1180–1198.

23 Joseph Maggs, 'The "Channel crossings" and the borders of Britain', *Race & Class* 61(3) (2020): 78–86.

24 'Channel migrants: 235 people in 17 vessels stopped in one day', BBC News, 7 August 2020, https://www.bbc.co.uk/news/uk-england-kent-53678928 (accessed 1 February 2022). See press release https://homeofficemedia.blog.gov.uk/2020/09/02/chris-philp-statement-crossing-english-channel-small-boats/ (accessed 23 November 2021).

25 'Migrant crossings: use of navy ships to stop boats "dangerous"', BBC News, 10 August 2020, https://www.bbc.co.uk/news/uk-england-53719575 (accessed 23 November 2021).

26 Cited in Aubrey Allegretti, 'This simply cannot go on: UK-France row intensifies as Channel migrant crossings top 4000', *Sky News*, 9 August 2020, https://news.sky.com/story/number-of-migrants-crossing-channel-in-small-boats-tops-4-000-this-year-12045832 (accessed 23 November 2021).

27 Jacob Sohlberg, Peter Esaiasson and Johan Martinsson, 'The changing political impact of compassion-evoking pictures: the case of the drowned toddler Alan Kurdi', *Journal of Ethnic and Migration Studies* 45(13) (2019): 2275–2288.

28 See, for example, Adam Sage, 'Gang "forced migrants onto death boat"', *The Times*, 29 October 2020, https://www.thetimes.co.uk/article/channel-migrant-boat-disaster-entire-family-and-two-others-feared-dead-zrj2br5rw? (accessed 23 November 2021).

29 Patrick Stephen Wright, 'Turning inward: Brexit, encroachment narratives and the English as a "secret people"', in Ash Amin and Philip Lewis (eds), *European Union and Disunion* (London: British Academy, 2017), 69.

30 Lisa Mckenzie, 'The class politics of prejudice: Brexit and the land of no-hope and glory', *The British Journal of Sociology* 68 (2017): s265–s280.

31 Satnam Virdee and Brendan McGeever, 'Racism, crisis, Brexit', *Ethnic and Racial Studies* 41(10) (2018): 1802–1819.

32 On the geography of Brexit voting, see David Manley, Kelvyn Jones and Ron Johnston, 'The geography of Brexit – what geography? Modelling and predicting the outcome across 380 local authorities', *Local Economy* 32(3) (2017): 183–203.

33 See https://www.britainfirst.org/migrant_invasion_britain_first_vessel_patrols_the_channel_to_deter_migrants (accessed 23 November 2021).

34 Duncan Weaver, 'Project Kraken: surveillance and liminality "on the edge" of land and water', *Geopolitics* (2020): 1–27, https://doi.org/10.1080/14650045.2020.1755267.

35 Ibid., 25.

36 The latter is discussed in Waqas Tufail, 'Media, state and "political correctness": the racialisation of the Rotherham child sexual abuse scandal', in Monish Bhatia, Scott Poynting and Waqas Tufail (eds), *Media, Crime and Racism* (Basingstoke: Palgrave Macmillan, 2018), 49–71.

37 Chris Britcher, 'Artist YZ unveils art in Folkestone and Coquelles to mark Eurotunnel 25th anniversary', *Kent Online*, 5 July 2019, https://www.kentonline.co.uk/kent-business/county-news/huge-artwork-unveiled-to-mark-anniversary-207931/ (accessed 23 November 2021).

38 Nicolas Whybrow, 'Folkestone perennial: the enduring work of art in the re-constitution of place', *Cultural Geographies* 23(4) (2016): 671–692.

39 See Jonathan Ward and Phil Hubbard, 'Urban regeneration through culture', in Tim Schwanen and Ronald van Kempen (eds), *Handbook of Urban Geography* (Cheltenham: Edward Elgar, 2019), 195–209.

40 Ellie Alexander, 'Why Folkestone is Kent's most underestimated seaside town', *Harpers's Bazaar*, 8 April 2021, https://www.harpersbazaar.com/uk/travel/a27583394/why-folkestone-is-kents-most-underestimated-seaside-town/ (accessed 23 November 2021); Helen Coffey, 'Why Folkestone isn't the new Margate – it's even cooler', *The Independent*, 5 April 2019, https://www.independent.co.uk/travel/uk/folkestone-visit-margate-creative-art-sculpture-triennial-regeneration-a8849361.html (accessed 23 November 2021).

41 Jonathan Ward, 'Down by the sea: visual arts, artists and coastal regeneration', *International Journal of Cultural Policy* 24(1) (2018): 121–138. See also David Batty, 'Coastal towns get trendy', *The Guardian*, 17 August 2016, https://www.theguardian.com/society/2016/aug/17/coastal-towns-trendy-arts-help-local-community (accessed 23 November 2021).

Notes

42   Stephen Pritchard, 'The artwashing of gentrification and social cleansing', in Loretta Lees and Martin Phillips (eds), *The Handbook of Displacement* (Basingstoke: Palgrave Macmillan, 2020), 179–198.

43   HM Chief Inspector of Prisons, 'Report on an unannounced inspection of the short-term holding facilities at Longport freight shed, Dover Seaport and Frontier House', 2016, https://www.justiceinspectorates.gov.uk/hmiprisons/inspections/longport-freight-shed-dover-seaport-and-frontier-house/ (accessed 23 November 2021).

44   Alex Jee, 'Napier Barracks in Folkestone to house people seeking asylum', *Kent Online*, 14 September 2020, https://www.kentonline.co.uk/folkestone/news/military-barracks-to-house-people-seeking-asylum-233772/ (accessed 23 November 2021).

45   Phil Hubbard, 'Accommodating otherness: anti-asylum centre protest and the maintenance of white privilege', *Transactions of the Institute of British Geographers* 30(1) (2005): 52–65.

46   John James, 'The disinformation and confusion around the Napier Barracks asylum seeker accommodation in Folkestone', *Kentlive News*, 22 September 2020, https://www.kentlive.news/news/kent-news/disinformation-confusion-around-napier-barracks-4538994 (accessed 23 November 2021).

47   See Richard Ford, 'Far right targets migrant camp', *The Times*, 17 September 2020, https://www.thetimes.co.uk/article/far-right-targets-migrant-camp-ww56z57zl (accessed 23 November 2021).

48   For perhaps obvious reasons, I am not citing the source of these tweets – some come from accounts that are, in any case, now suspended.

49   On fragile masculinity, racism and imaginations of nationhood, see Banu Gökarıksel, Christopher Neubert and Sar Smith, 'Demographic fever dreams: fragile masculinity and population politics in the rise of the global right', *Signs: Journal of Women in Culture and Society* 44(3) (2019): 561–587.

50   Jack Shenker, 'Locked in a barracks with COVID running rampant. Is this any way to treat asylum seekers?', *The Guardian*, 27 January 2021, https://www.theguardian.com/commentisfree/2021/jan/27/locked-covid-asylum-seekers-napier-barracks-kent (accessed 23 November 2021).

51   Cited at https://helprefugees.org/news/a-message-from-a-refugee-stuck-in-the-napier-barracks/ (accessed 23 November 2021).

52   See https://www.gov.uk/government/news/an-inspection-of-the-use-of-contingency-asylum-accommodation-key-findings-from-site-visits-to-penally-camp-and-napier-barracks (accessed 23 November 2021).

53   May Bulman, 'Army barracks deemed "not acceptable accommodation" seven years ago', *The Independent*, 15 February 2021, https://www.independent.co.uk/news/uk/home-news/napier-barracks-asylum-seekers-home-office-b1802355.html (accessed 23 November 2021).

54 Nigel Farage, 'Saving two migrants in the Channel has only confirmed to me the folly of the Government's approach', *The Daily Telegraph*, 1 December 2020, https://www.telegraph.co.uk/news/2020/12/01/saving-two-migrants-channel-has-confirmed-folly-governments/ (accessed 23 November 2021).

55 Sue Reid, 'Testing our goodwill', *Daily Mail*, 24 March 2021, https://www.dailymail.co.uk/news/article-9399621/Kent-locals-say-migration-not-fit-purpose-writes-SUE-REID.html (accessed 23 November 2021).

56 See https://www.inyourarea.co.uk/news/damian-collins-folkestone-column-for-week-ending-february-5/ (accessed 23 November 2021).

57 On hospitality and the asylum seeker, see Sarah Gibson, 'Accommodating strangers: British hospitality and the asylum hotel debate', *Journal for Cultural Research* 7(4) (2003): 367–386.

58 Whybrow, 'Folkestone perennial'.

59 Andrea Schlieker, *Folkestone Triennial: A Million Miles from Home* (Folkestone: Cultureshock, 2011).

60 Matthew Gandy and Sandra Jasper, 'The city as botanical field', in Matthew Gandy and Sandra Jasper (eds), *The Botanical City* (Berlin: Jovi, 2020), 6–15. See also Giovanni Aloi, 'Sorely visible: plants, roots, and national identity', *Plants, People, Planet* 1(3) (2019): 204–211; Marco Antonsich, 'Natives and aliens: who and what belongs in nature and in the nation?', *Area* 52(3) (2020): 303–310.

61 Tim Cresswell, 'Weeds, plagues, and bodily secretions: a geographical interpretation of metaphors of displacement', *Annals of the Association of American Geographers* 87(2) (1997): 330–345.

Notes to Chapter 7

1 John Keats, *To My Brother George* (London: James L. Weil, 1816).

2 Cited in Sarah Sturt, 'H. G. Wells "150th birthday"', *Kent Life*, 19 August 2016, https://www.greatbritishlife.co.uk/people/h-g-wells-150th-birthday-7192258 (accessed 23 November 2021).

3 Cited in Adam Roberts, *H. G. Wells: A Literary Life* (Berlin: Springer, 2019).

4 H. G. Wells, *The Sea Lady* (New York: Appleton, 1902), 202.

5 Emily Barritt, 'The myth of mermaids and stewardship of the seas', *Transnational Legal Theory* 11(1/2) (2020): 165–179.

6 Leah Gibbs, 'Shores: sharks, nets and more-than-human territory in eastern Australia', in Kimberley Peters, Philip Steinberg and Elaine Stratford (eds), *Territory beyond Terra* (Lanham, MD: Rowman and Littlefield, 2018), 203–219.

Notes

7 Philip Steinberg, 'The lighthouse as survival', in Veronica Strang, Tim Edensor and Joanna Puckering (eds), *From the Lighthouse: Interdisciplinary Reflections on Light* (Abingdon: Routledge, 2018), 179–183.

8 Tom Selwyn, 'Shifting borders and dangerous liminalities: the case of Rye Bay', in Hazel Andrews and Les Roberts (eds), *Liminal Landscapes: Travel, Experience and Spaces In-between* (Abingdon: Routledge, 2011), 169–184.

9 Charles Lyell, *Principles of Geology, Vol. 1* (London: John Murray, 1830), 271. See also Alexis Harley, 'Charles Lyell's *Principles of Geology*, the geological sublime, and the Romantic theatre', *Nineteenth Century Theatre and Film* 45(2) (2018): 254–269.

10 Lucas Pohl, 'Ruins as pieces of the real: images of a post-apocalyptic present', *Geoforum* 127 (2021): 198–208.

11 David Matless, 'The anthroposcenic', *Transactions of the Institute of British Geographers* 42(3) (2017): 363–376.

12 P. Hogarth, D. T. Pugh, C. W. Hughes and S. D. P. Williams, 'Changes in mean sea level around Great Britain over the past 200 years', *Progress in Oceanography* 192 (2021): 1–25.

13 Scott A. Kulp and Benjamin H. Strauss, 'New elevation data triple estimates of global vulnerability to sea-level rise and coastal flooding', *Nature Communications* 10(1) (2019): 1–12.

14 C. L. So, 'Some coastal changes between Whitstable and Reculver, Kent', *Proceedings of the Geologists' Association* 77(4) (1966): 475–490.

15 Barney Davis, 'Watch symbolic section of Dover cliffs crumble into sea', *Evening Standard*, 4 February 2021, https://www.standard.co.uk/news/uk/watch-huge-section-of-white-cliffs-of-dover-crumble-into-the-sea-b918559.html (accessed 23 November 2021). On the erosion of Kent's cliffs, see Frank A. Middlemiss, 'Instability of chalk cliffs between the South Foreland and Kingsdown, Kent, in relation to geological structure', *Proceedings of the Geologists' Association* 94(2) (1983): 115–122.

16 Rosa Rankin-Gee, *Dreamland* (London: Simon and Schuster, 2021).

17 Russell Hoban, *Riddley Walker* (London: Jonathan Cape, 1980). Mike Bintley and Sonia Overall explore the Kentish landscapes of *Riddley Walker* at https://blogs.canterbury.ac.uk/owhatwebcn/ (accessed 23 November 2021).

18 Anne-Marie Crowhurst, 'Interview with Rosa Rankin-Gee', *The Bookseller*, 8 March 2021, https://www.thebookseller.com/insight/springboard-rosa-rankin-gee-dreamland-1240240 (accessed 23 November 2021).

19 See https://sealevel.climatecentral.org/maps/ (accessed 23 November 2021).

20 John Betjeman, 'Fairfield Romney Marsh', in Stephen Games (ed.), *Betjeman's England* (London: John Murray, 2020), 81–82, originally written for Shell's Discover Britain motoring adverts 1956.

Notes

21 See Michele Sheldon's 2020 Heritage Lottery funded film 'The Beast of Romney Marsh', https://www.youtube.com/watch?v=CQLNkqOJWco (accessed 23 November 2021).

22 William Shaw, *Salt Lane* (London: Riverrun, 2018); William Shaw, *Grave's End* (London: Riverrun, 2020); William Shaw, *The Birdwatcher* (London: Mulholland Books, 2017).

23 Derek Jarman, *Modern Nature* (Minneapolis, MN: University of Minnesota Press, 2009), 113.

24 Roger Cardinal, *The Landscape Vision of Paul Nash* (London: Reaktion, 2013).

25 Andrew Causey, *Paul Nash: Landscape and the Life of Objects* (London: Lund Humphries, 2013), 29.

26 Paul Nash, *Outline – An Autobiography* (1949) (London: Lund Humphries, 1988), 143.

27 Cited at https://www.tate.org.uk/whats-on/tate-liverpool/exhibition/paul-nash/paul-nash-modern-artist-ancient-landscape-room-guide-1 (accessed 23 November 2021).

28 Nash, *Outline*, 47.

29 Pyrs Gruffudd, 'Reach for the sky: the air and English cultural nationalism', *Landscape Research* 16(2) (1991): 19–24.

30 See https://dymchurchworldnews.wordpress.com/2012/07/03/village-of-the-surreal-32/ (accessed 23 November 2021).

31 Paul Hendon, 'Paul Nash: Outline – the immortality of the "I"', *Art History* 20(4) (1997): 589–610.

32 See Denis Byrne, 'Remembering the Elizabeth Bay reclamation and the Holocene sunset in Sydney Harbour', *Environmental Humanities* 9(1) (2017): 40–59.

33 Nick Enoch, 'Four police officers are injured as hundreds attend illegal "cookout" rave on Kent beach organised by London jerk chicken shop before leaving mounds of litter', *Mail Online*, 10 August 2020, https://www.dailymail.co.uk/news/article-8610995/Illegal-rave-Kent-beach-sees-revellers-ignore-social-distancing-rules.html#comments (accessed 23 November 2021).

34 Tim Edensor, 'The deadly lighthouse beam', in Veronica Strang, Tim Edensor and Joanna Puckering (eds), *From the Lighthouse: Interdisciplinary Reflections on Light* (Abingdon: Routledge, 2018), pp. 189–191.

35 On plotlanders, see Denis Hardy and Colin Ward, *Arcadia for All: The Legacy of a Makeshift Landscape* (Nottingham: Five Leaves, 1984).

36 Mark Fisher, *The Weird and the Eerie* (London: Repeater Books, 2017), 61, as cited at https://xenogothic.com/2018/04/24/the-eerie-south-east/ (accessed 23 November 2021).

37 For example, Dungeness has featured in music videos for acts as diverse as The Wave Pictures and Nicky Minaj; was home to photographer Peter

Marlow, founder of the Magnum studio, until his death in 2018; and, for a short time in 2004, even boasted its own Banksy stencil on the side of rusted shipping container.

38 Nick Hunt, 'Why go to the Sahara when you can go to Kent?', *The Guardian*, 11 May 2011, https://amp.theguardian.com/travel/2021/may/11/why-go-to-the-sahara-when-you-can-visit-kent-desert-life-in-dungeness (accessed 23 November 2021).

39 Frank Collins, '*Doctor Who Claws of Axos* DVD review' (2012), https://www.cathoderaytube.co.uk/2012/10/classic-doctor-who-claws-of-axos.html (accessed 23 November 2021).

40 Jez Winship, 'The Garden of Axos' (2009), http://sparksin electricaljelly.blogspot.com/2009/11/garden-of-axos.html (accessed 23 November 2021).

41 Diane Rodgers, 'Why Wyrd? Why folklore? Why now?', conference paper, *Screening the Unreal*, University of Brighton, 4 July 2018, http://shura.shu.ac.uk/23227/.

42 Robert Macfarlane, 'The eeriness of the English countryside', *The Guardian*, 10 April 2015, https://www.theguardian.com/books/2015/apr/10/eeriness-english-countryside-robert-macfarlane (accessed 23 November 2021).

43 Mark Fisher, 'Hauntology in Dublin', 14 December 2006, http://k-punk.abstractdynamics.org/archives/008780.html (accessed 23 November 2021).

44 Brian Dillon, 'Listening for the enemy' (2003), http://www.cabinetmagazine.org/issues.12.Dillon.php (accessed 23 November 2021).

45 Adam Scovell, 'Wire and grass; landscape binaries in television and reality' (2016), https://celluloidwickerman.com/2016/08/01/wire-and-grass-landscape-binaries-in-television-and-reality/ (accessed 23 November 2021).

46 See Colin Sterling, 'Spectral anatomies: heritage, hauntology and the "ghosts" of Varosha', *Present Pasts* 6(1) (2014), https://presentpasts.info/articles/10.5334/pp. 57/ (accessed 23 November 2021).

47 Gareth E. Rees, 'Haunted by a nuclear power station' (2018), http://www.unofficialbritain.com/haunted-by-a-nuclear-power-station/ (accessed 23 November 2021).

48 Gareth E. Rees, *The Stone Tide* (London: Influx, 2018), 160.

49 'Flood safety fear shut nuclear reactors', BBC News, 19 March 2014, https://www.bbc.co.uk/news/uk-england-kent-26645490 (accessed 23 November 2021); 'Dungeness B: Kent's last nuclear power station closes early', BBC News, 8 June 2021, https://www.bbc.co.uk/news/uk-england-kent-57398732 (accessed 23 November 2021).

50 See Rees, 'Haunted by a nuclear power station'.

Notes

51 That is, until 1989, when national newspapers broke the story that Jarman had HIV and was planning to live out his last years 'in a shack'.

52 Luke Turner, 'Derek Jarman's garden' (2019), https://www.magnum photos.com/arts-culture/art/derek-jarman-garden/ (accessed 23 November 2021).

53 Jarman, *Modern Nature*, 78.

54 Ibid., 52.

55 Ibid., 31.

56 This idea of Jarman as martyr or saint is discussed in Brian Hoyle, 'Derek: portrait of a saint', *Studies in Documentary Film* 4(2) (2010: 137–147. See also Mark Hudson, 'A saint in the garden', *Gagosian Quarterly* (fall 2020), https://gagosian.com/quarterly/2020/10/01/essay-derek-jarman-saint-garden/ (accessed 23 November 2021).

57 Chris Steyaert, 'Queering space: heterotopic life in Derek Jarman's garden', *Gender, Work & Organization* 17(1) (2010): 45–68.

58 Christopher Lloyd, *Derek Jarman: A Portrait* (London: Thames and Hudson, 1996), 148.

59 Cited in Tim Ellis, *Derek Jarman's Angelic Conversations* (Minneapolis, MN: University of Minnesota Press, 2009), 67.

60 Jarman, *Modern Nature*, 74.

61 Melissa Zeiger, '"Modern Nature": Derek Jarman's garden', *Humanities* 6(2) (2017): 22.

62 Giovanni Aloi, 'Sorely visible: plants, roots, and national identity', *Plants, People, Planet* 1(3) (2019): p. 210.

63 Daniel O'Quinn, 'Gardening, history, and the escape from time: Derek Jarman's "Modern Nature"', *October* 89 (1999): 113–126.

64 See Daniel Burdsey, 'Strangers on the shore? Racialized representation, identity, and in/visibilities of whiteness at the English seaside', *Cultural Sociology* 5(4) (2014): 537–552.

65 Lisa Blackman, '"Loving the alien": a post–post-human manifesto', *Subjectivity* 10(1) (2017): 13–25.

66 Catriona Mortimer-Sandilands, 'Melancholy natures, queer ecologies', in Catriona Mortimer-Sandilands and Bruce Erickson (eds), *Queer Ecologies: Sex, Nature, Politics, Desire* (Bloomington, IN: Indiana University Press, 2010), 331–358.

67 Blackman, '"Loving the alien"', 21.

68 Joe Sweeney, cited at https://www.cobgallery.com/news/92/. The website associated with the installation provides a selection of the messages left by visitors: https://www.leaveamessage4europe.com; there is also a film '28 days in March' by Sweeney at https://vimeo.com/434352884 (accessed 23 November 2021).

69 Jarman, *Modern Nature*, 67.

Notes

Notes to Afterword

1 Ben Spencer, 'From the Garden of England to the slums of Calcutta', *The Sunday Times*, 25 April 2021, https://www.thetimes.co.uk/article/from-the-garden-of-england-to-the-slums-of-calcutta-our-kent-covid-variant-is-now-theirs-nszptr3sz (accessed 23 November 2021).

2 Mark Juergensmeyer, 'COVID nationalism', 6 September 2020, https://www.e-ir.info/2020/09/06/covid-nationalism/ (accessed 1 February 2022). See also Eric Taylor Woods, Robert Schertzer, Liah Greenfeld, Chris Hughes and Cynthia Miller-Idriss, 'COVID-19, nationalism, and the politics of crisis: a scholarly exchange', *Nations and Nationalism* 26(4) (2021): 807–825.

3 See Scott Lucas, *Brexit, Vaccine Nationalism, and the Future of the UK* (2021), http://www.open-access.bcu.ac.uk/10923/1/Brexit.pdf (accessed 23 November 2021).

4 Alok Sharma, Twitter post, 2 December 2020, as quoted in *The New European*, 9 December 2020, https://www.theneweuropean.co.uk/brexit-news/westminster-news/germany-responds-to-alok-sharma-covid19-claim-6639246 (accessed 23 November 2021).

5 See Ben A. Lohmeyer and Nik Taylor, 'War, heroes and sacrifice: masking neoliberal violence during the COVID-19 pandemic', *Critical Sociology* 47(4–5) (2021): 625–639.

6 Sarah Boseley, 'Has everyone in Kent gone to an illegal rave?', *The Guardian*, 3 April 2021, https://www.theguardian.com/world/2021/apr/03/has-everyone-in-kent-gone-to-illegal-rave-on-variant-trail-with-covid-detectives (accessed 23 November 2021).

7 Patrick Cockburn, 'In Kent', *London Review of Books* 43(5), 19 February 2021, https://www.lrb.co.uk/the-paper/v43/n05/patrick-cockburn/in-kent (accessed 23 November 2021).

8 See Helen V. S. Cole, Isabelle Anguelovski, Francesc Baró, Melissa García-Lamarca, Panagiota Kotsila, Carmen Pérez del Pulgar, Galia Shokry and Margarita Triguero-Mas, 'The COVID-19 pandemic: power and privilege, gentrification, and urban environmental justice in the global north', *Cities & Health* 1–5 (2020), https://doi.org/10.1080/23748834.2020.1785176.

9 Melanie Küng, 'Guards of Brexit? Revisiting the cultural significance of the white cliffs of Dover', in Ina Habermann (ed.), *The Road to Brexit* (Manchester: Manchester University Press, 2020), 199–214.

Index

Note: Novels, films, artworks and other media are listed by author/director/artist

Abbot's Cliff 89, 91
Abbott, David 73
Abercrombie, Patrick 84
AirBnB 187, 206
Akhtar, Adeel 90
Albion 5, 50, 72, 207
alcohol 28–29, 52
alienation 74, 122
aliens 170, 188–190, 195–196
Aloi, Giovanni 195
Anderson, Hans Christian 168
Anderson, Michael 79
  The Dam Busters (film) 79
animals 1, 45, 48, 72, 107, 119, 130, 167, 180, 184–185
  see also oysters
anthropocene 174
apples 12
aquaculture 34, 37, 42, 45
  see also fishing
archaeology 22, 100, 105–108
Arlington House (Margate) 14, 55–57, 176
Arnold, Matthew 5
  'On Dover Beach' (poem) 5

art 34, 38, 53, 66, 68–69, 74–75, 157
  see also creative and cultural industries
Artangel 74
  Exodus (art installation) 74
artwashing 157
Ashford (Kent) 8–9, 12, 113–128
  Ashford International (station) 9, 111, 116
Ashon, Will 17
asylum seekers 4–5, 55, 86, 137, 142–143, 148, 154, 158–164, 196, 213
  asylum detention centres 159
  see also refugees
Attlee, Clement 101
Auden, W. H. 187
authenticity 33–34

Back to Life (TV programme) 90
Bailey, Rachael Louise 42, 213
  The Black Stuff 42–43
Bailkin, Jordanna 142
Baker, Georgina 168
Baker, Tom 188

Index

Balibar, Etienne 113
Ball, Michael 202
Banksy 167
Barker, Nicola 121
    Darkmans (novel) 121–122
Barritt, Emily 171
Bates, H. E. 12
    The Darling Buds of May (novel) 12
Battle of Britain 91–93, 182
Beale, Benjamin 51
Becket, Thomas 108
Belgium 164, 207
Betjeman, John 177
Biggin Hill 92
Billig, Michael 10
Billingsgate 35
Birch, Eugenius 60
Birmingham 62
Black Lives Matter 202
Blackman, Lisa 196
Blackpool (Lancashire) 52, 58
Blake, William 71–72
Blitz (World War II) 101–102, 201
bohemians 14, 70, 72
Boltanski, Christian 99
    The Whispers (artwork) 99
Bolton, Henry 46
Bonelli, Selina 91
Booth, John and Sophia 62–63
border (national) 112–113
    'bordering' 10, 15, 19, 44, 91,
        112–113, 198, 207
    border controls 112, 128
    'border spectacle' 3–4, 7, 146
Boston (Lincolnshire) 201
Botany Bay 50
Bournemouth (Dorset) 58
Boyle, Danny 95
Braudy, Ben 97
Brenzett 93, 177
Brexit 7, 11–12, 14, 20–22, 48, 72–73,
    87, 100–101, 103, 112, 124,
    127–128, 130, 132–133, 136–137,

    147, 149, 160, 175, 197–198,
    200–203, 207–208
    Article 50 200
    referendum 4, 6, 46, 126–127, 129
Bridge (Canterbury) 127
Brighton (Sussex) 58
Britain First 47, 73, 150
Broadstairs 18, 50–51, 53, 71, 204
Brompton 81
Brooke, Rupert 95
    'The Soldier' (poem) 95
Brussels 9, 112, 132
buddleja 166–167
Burdsey, Daniel 14
Buren, Daniel 65
    Borrowing and Multiplying the
        Landscape (artwork) 65
Burns, Di 97
Burton, Decimus 155

Calais 3, 9, 20, 108–109, 112–114,
    126–128, 143–145, 155, 165
    'Calais Jungle' 3
    Calais-Frethun (station) 112
Callcott, Frederick 76
Camber (Sussex) 23, 184
Cameron, Angus 97
Cameron, David 144
Campaign for the Protection of
    Rural England (CPRE) 115
Canterbury 9, 20, 34, 40, 69, 81,
    84, 108, 118, 127, 179, 213
    Canterbury City Council 40, 213
    Treaty of Canterbury 108, 112
Capel-le-Ferne 91–92, 93
Casey, Edward 98
Causey, Andrew 182
Cazeneuve, Bernard 144
CCTV 81, 111, 145
chalk 1, 11, 25, 45, 50, 80, 90,
    92–93, 105, 109, 111, 134–135,
    175, 207
Channel Tunnel *see* Eurotunnel

Chas & Dave (musicians) 52, 71
Chatham 9, 71, 80–81
Cheltenham 201
Cheriton 8, 96, 108–109, 111, 113
Chesterton, G. K. 105, 135
   The Balled of the White Horse
    (poem) 105, 135
China 166
Chipperfield, David 63
Christianity 105–106
Churchill, Winston 101, 202
Cinque Ports 7, 138–139
   see also Dover, Hythe, New
    Romney, Sandwich
Clarkson, Jeremy 122
Cliftonville 53, 58, 60, 67, 74, 206
climate change 15–17, 22, 171, 176,
   191
   sea level change 171–174, 176–177,
    180, 185
Cockburn, Patrick 87, 205
Cold War 81, 83–84, 189
Collins, Damian (MP) 99, 159
colonialism 18, 116–117, 145
Colquhoun, Mark 186
commemoration 20, 98–99, 101
   see also memorialisation
Congo 55, 75
Conrad, Joseph 169
Considine, Paddy 56
Conyer (Kent) 25
Corbyn, Jeremy 101
coronavirus (COVID-19) 3, 14, 25,
   39, 74, 87, 91, 100, 130–132,
   146–147, 149, 152, 156, 158–159,
   161, 163, 184, 200–208
COVID nationalism 202
Cox, Jo (MP) 47
Cozette, Philippe 112
creative and cultural industries 64,
   67, 157
Cresswell, Tim 167
Crofts, John 63

Cuarón, Alfonso 160
   Children of Men (film) 160
Cushing, Peter 39

Darian-Smith, Eve 82, 115
Dartford (Kent) 23, 127, 135
Davies, Jonathan 45
Davis, Russell T. 160–161
   Years and Years (TV programme)
    160–161
Davis, Sophia 16
De Genova, Nicolas 146, 164
De Haan, Roger 96, 156
Deal (Kent) 18, 81, 145, 172, 175
deCaires Taylor, Jason 6
   Pride of Brexit (sculpture) 6
deep topography 14, 18–19
deindustrialisation 5, 28, 88
Dempsey, Kara 143
dereliction 13, 25, 59, 90, 155–156,
   166
Derrida, Jacques 190
Detling (Kent) 92
Dickens, Charles 9, 53
Digan, Yseult 155
Dillon, Brian 26, 90, 190
displacement *see* migration
Doctor Who (TV programme)
   188–189, 195
Doherty, Pete 171
   see also The Libertines (band)
Donaldson, Carol 24
Dover (Kent) 1, 3–8, 13, 20, 38, 56,
   81, 83–90, 93–94, 100, 102, 112,
   124–125, 127, 130–131, 145, 148,
   150, 152–153, 158, 167, 175, 207
Dover Castle 83, 85–86, 112
'Down from Londons' (DFL) 14,
   31–32, 38, 40, 69, 156, 176,
   206
Dreamland (Margate) 51, 55, 57, 60,
   70, 75, 176
   see also Rankin-Gee, Rosa

Index

Duffy, Carol Ann 96
  'The Wound in Time' (poem) 96
  'An Unseen' (poem) 96
Dungeness (Kent) 14, 20, 109, 184, 187, 207
  Dungeness lighthouse 184–185, 187, 196–197
Dunkirk (France) 3, 83, 87
Dymchurch (Kent) 14, 107, 178–183

East Anglia 28, 174
Eastchurch (Kent) 175
Ebbsfleet (Thanet, Kent) 105
Ebbsfleet International Station (Gravesend, Kent) 8, 111, 113
ecology 1, 25, 37, 44–45, 49, 195
  biodiversity 1, 25
  'eco-nationalism' 44–45, 49
  ecosystem 37, 44–45
  invasion biology 44
  queer ecology 195
edgelands 16
  see also liminality
eerie 29, 186–187
Egypt 75
Eliot, T. S. 72, 76
  The Waste Land (poem) 76
Elphicke, Natalie (MP) 20, 131
Emin, Tracey 66, 156
encroachment myths 148–149
  see also invasion
English Channel 3–4, 7, 63, 82, 126, 143, 145–149, 152, 169
  crossings (refugees) 4, 126, 143, 145–149
English Coastal Path 20, 50, 152
English Heritage 86
English Nature 15, 110
Englishness 7, 13, 71, 90, 134, 136, 149, 192, 207
Environment Agency 130, 180
Environmentally Sensitive Area 24
Essex 26, 35, 106

Essex, David 32
European Union (EU) 4–7, 21, 49, 74, 87, 110–112, 127, 113, 142, 197, 202
Eurotunnel 8, 23, 81, 88, 109, 111, 114, 121, 131, 145, 155
  Eurostar 8, 108, 112–114, 116–117, 143–144
  Le Shuttle 8, 108–109
exclusionary nationalism 10, 19, 44, 49, 88, 91, 198, 202, 207
  see also nationalism, racism

Fagg, Graham 112
Fall, Juliet 44
Falmouth (Cornwall) 35
Faraday, Michael 185
Farage, Nigel 45–46, 73, 162, 202
Farthingloe Valley 88
Favell, Adrian 112
Faversham (Kent) 25–30, 32, 47, 80, 118–119, 131
femininity 170, 183
Festival of Britain 102
Firmin, Emily 65
Fisher, Mark 102, 186, 190
fishing 9, 19, 34, 41, 45–49, 51, 138, 152, 185, 193
  Fishing for Leave 45–46
Floyd, George 74
folk horror 188, 190
Folkestone (Kent) 8, 14, 20, 46, 76 78, 81, 88, 93, 96–101, 98, 100, 105–106, 109–110, 113–114, 125, 133, 136, 138, 145–146, 155–159, 162, 164–171, 175, 187, 193, 207
  Castle Hill 105–108
  Folkestone Fringe 94
  Folkestone Triennial 156
  Folkestone Warren 78
foodism 34, 37
Ford, Ford Madox 139, 169

Index

France 3, 8, 26, 77, 83, 86–87, 99, 112–114, 131, 133, 145–147, 155
Friends of the Earth 110
Fukushima 191

Gandy, Matthew 13
'Garden of England' mythology 11, 25, 82, 93, 115, 126–127, 200
Gardner, James 68
    Jellyfish (film) 68
Geldof, Bob 46
gentrification 28, 31–32, 34, 38, 49, 67–68, 72, 138–139, 158, 187, 206
Germany 24, 78–80, 83, 92, 95, 105, 121, 165, 169, 182
Gibbs, Leah 171
Gladstone, Herbert 183
Glancey, Jonathan 64
Goodall, Stephen 21
Gordon, Helen 134
Gormley, Antony 75, 156
    Waste Man (artwork) 75
Gorrel (stream) 35
Graveney (Kent) 32
Gravesend (Kent) 57, 76, 131
Gray, Harry 92
Grayling, Chris 48
Great Yarmouth (Norfolk) 58
Greatstone (Kent) 183–184
Green, Barrie 36
Green, Damian (MP) 125, 129
Greenhithe 26
Grey, Chris 4
Griffin, Nick 73
Grissoni, Tony 29
    Southcliffe (TV series) 29
gunpowder 26, 28, 80
Guston (Dover) 130

Haggard, Daisy 90
Hall, Peter 117
Hampton (Kent) 175

Harbledown (Canterbury) 127
Harper, Charles 23, 52
Hartlepool 201
Harvey, Ellen 65
    Arcade/Arcadia (artwork) 65
Hasted, Edward 106
Hatherley, Owen 102
hauntology 17, 59, 103, 188–191
Hawkinge (Kent) 91, 92
Headcorn (Kent) 93
heavy goods vehicle (HGV) 28, 125, 127–128, 130, 133
Hemingway, Wayne 70
Hendon, Paul 183
Hengist 73, 105, 134, 207
Herd, David 86, 212
Heritage, Stuart 118
Herne Bay (Kent) 50, 79
High Speed One 23, 32, 113, 116, 118, 124
High Street (retail) 31, 40, 59, 61, 74, 138, 156, 197
Hill, Harry 32
Hill, Joe 72
hipsters 67–68, 72, 103, 157
Hoban, Russell 176
    Riddley Walker (novel) 176
Hong Kong 49
Hoo (Kent) 26
Hook, Anthony 20–21
Hopper, Justin 17
hops 28
Horsa 73, 105, 134, 207
hospitality 57, 94, 137, 160, 163
hostile environment (policy) 7, 113, 137, 167
houses in multiple occupation (HMOs) 53, 58, 205
housing 12–13, 38, 40, 53–54, 58, 81, 85, 101, 119–121, 129, 138–139, 141, 159, 176, 178, 200, 206
Howard, Michael (MP) 110

Index

Hunt, Nick 187
Hythe (Kent) 7, 19–20, 106–107, 138–142, 160–163, 175, 177–180

Inland Border Facility 129–130, 133
invasion myths 81–83, 105–106, 115, 148–150
Iraq 3, 74–76, 142
Islamophobia 151
'island-nation' myth 5, 11, 13, 22, 123, 135, 137, 207
Isle of Sheppey (Kent) *see* Sheppey, Isle of

James, Malcolm 91
Jarman, Derek 178, 192, 194–195, 207
  Modern Nature (book) 193–194
Jarrold, Walter 5
Jeaffreson, W. J. 106
Jensen, Ole 123
Johnson, Alan (MP) 47
Johnson, Boris (MP) 46, 100–101, 126, 130, 197, 201–202
Johnson, Uwe 24, 78
Jones, Hannah 47
Juergensmeyer, Mark 202

Keats, John 168
  'To My Brother George' (poem) 168
Keiller, Patrick 17
Kent County Council 63–64
Kent County Cricket Club 93, 133
Kent Refugee Action Network 160
Kent Trust for Nature Conservation 115
Kent Wildlife Trust 25
Khan, Sadiq 73
King, Clive 135
  Stig of the Dump (book) 135
King's College London 12, 47, 74, 183
King's Lynn 201

Kingsdown (Kent) 152, 154
Kingsnorth (Kent) 120
Kit's Coty (Kent) 134–135
Kurdi, Alan 148

Labour Party 101
Lambarde, William 134
Lanchester, John 138, 151
  The Wall (novel) 138, 151
landscape 7–8, 10–11, 13–19, 22–28, 30–34, 45, 65, 75, 82, 88, 90–92, 98, 103, 105, 109, 111, 124, 133–135, 137, 174, 177–178, 181–185, 187–190, 192–194, 197, 207
Latour, Bruno 174
Leadsom, Andrea 101
Led By Donkeys (protest group) 21
Lefebvre, Henri 122
legal geography 40–41
Leigh, Mike 62
  Mr Turner (film) 62
Lettsom, John 51
The Libertines (band) 50, 70–71
Lichtenstein, Rachel 23
lighthouses 83, 86, 102, 184–185, 150, 187, 191, 196–197
Lilley, Hannah 16
liminality 15, 24, 49, 171, 178, 188
Littlestone-on-Sea (Kent) 183
Lloyd, Christopher 193
Loach, Ken 101
  Spirit of 45 (film) 101
London 12, 20, 30, 53–54, 184
  London Air Defence 90
Lower Halstow (Kent) 25
Lumley, Joanna 110
Lydden (Kent) 86
Lyell, Charles 172
Lynn, Vera 100, 103, 201

Mabey, Richard 15
Macfarlane, Robert 108, 134, 189

Index

Mackinder, Halford 23
Macron, Emmanuel 6
Maggs, Joseph 146
Maidstone (Kent) 12, 113–114, 117, 125, 128, 135
Mair, Thomas 47
Maldon (Essex) 35
La Manche see English Channel
Manston (airport) 8, 86, 91–92, 131
Margate 50–76
 see also Dreamland (Margate)
Marples, Ernest 108
marshland 14, 178
Martello Towers 7, 81, 94, 139, 180
masculinity 160, 183, 195
Matless, David 16, 174
May, Theresa 46, 113, 144, 197
McCloud, Kevin 187
McDowell, Sarah 143
media (news) 148–149
Medway (Kent) 23–24, 134
 River Medway 23
Meek, James 103
memorialisation 22, 39, 75–76, 91–93, 98, 100, 103, 108, 196
Merkel, Angela 6
Mersham (Kent) 113, 117, 128–129, 131–132
Messenger, Paul 74
migration 4, 44–49, 54, 73–74, 86, 111–113, 137, 141–143, 145, 147, 149, 154, 161, 164, 171, 207
 displacement 3, 14, 22, 143, 164, 195
 'migrant crisis' 14, 150, 163, 203, 207–208
military (landscape) 7, 80
Milligan, Spike 110
Mitchell, Don 10
Mitterrand, François 108
mobilities 4, 45, 49, 109, 122–125, 127, 132, 137, 144, 164
modernism 91

Monderman, Hans 122
Moore, Tom (Captain) 100, 202
Mosley, Oswald 73
motorways 23, 108, 113, 116, 127, 131, 133, 203
 see also Operation Brock, Operation Stack
Moyle, Frederick and Sarah 141
multiculturalism 11, 73, 149, 164
munitions 77–78, 80, 96, 103

Napier Barracks (Folkestone) 158–163
Nash, Paul 180–183
 Nostalgic Landscape (painting) 183
nation-state 4, 19, 136, 195
 nationalism 4, 19, 44–45, 49, 74, 88, 91, 95, 100–101, 104, 137, 198, 202, 207
 national identity 5, 9–10, 16, 19, 45–46, 208
 see also Englishness
National Health Service (NHS) 100–102, 202
National Trust 2, 95, 103
Natural England 25, 43
nature writing 15–17, 19, 24, 189
Nazism 103, 149, 165
Neal, Sarah 11
Nejed, Artin Iran 148
Nesbit, May 170
Newington, Charles 109
NIMBY 115–116
Niven, Alex 11
Nord pays De Calais (region) 112
 see also Calais
Normington, David (Sir) 147
North Downs 1, 11, 88, 90, 108, 118, 135, 177
North Kent Marshes 24–25
North Sea 50, 60, 63
Northfleet 26
nuclear power 185, 187–188, 190, 193–195

Index

O'Grady, Sean 12
Oare (Kent) 26
Only Fools and Horses 52
Ono, Yoko 156
Operation Brock 128, 131
Operation Stack 125–129, 133
Orient Express 155, 165
Osborne, George (MP) 126
Othering 137, 208
Overall, Sonia 17
Owen, Wilfred 94–96
  'Anthem for Doomed Youth'
    (poem) 95
  'The Send Off' (poem) 95
Oxfordshire 106
oysters 14, 38, 42–49, 72, 166
  Oyster Festival (Whitstable)
    36–37, 42

Palmer, Samuel 89
Paris 8–9, 48, 112, 118
Parker, Cornelia 168–169, 171
  The Folkestone Mermaid (artwork)
    168–171, 207
Passport to Pimlico (film) 128
Patel, Priti (MP) 147, 159, 162
Pawlikowski, Pawel 55
  Last Resort (film) 55, 57–58
Pegwell Bay 8, 73, 105
Pennines 17
Perks, Robert (MP) 183
Pertwee, Jon 188
Pettet Smith, Joe 90
  In Defence of Lost Causes 90
Philp, Chris 147
Pilgrim's Way 20, 108
Pitcher, Ben 15, 45
Pitt Rivers, Augustus 106–107, 139
plants 1, 24, 110, 165, 193–195
  see also buddleja
Platt, Len 19
plotlanders 185, 187, 192
Plymouth 53, 84

Pohl, Lucas 173
prisons 26, 86–87, 160–161
Project Kraken 150–151
psychogeography 17–19, 24

queer theory 192, 195

racism 5–6, 14, 49, 73–74, 91, 150,
  161, 206–207
Racowitz, Michael 75–76
  April is the Cruellest Month (artwork)
    75–76
Rahman, Muzna 45
Rahman Haroun, Abdul 143
railways 26, 31, 35, 51, 55, 57, 65,
  75, 88, 94, 118, 124, 155,
  164–166, 179, 185, 193
  see also Ashford International,
    Ebbsfleet International,
    Eurotunnel, High Speed One,
    Stratford International
Ramsgate 8, 46, 52, 73, 90, 125, 204
Ramutsindela, Maano 15
Rankin-Gee, Rosa 176
  Dreamland (novel) 176
Ravilious, Eric 89, 181
  Bombing the Channel Ports (painting)
    89
Rawf, Aram 74
Rayner, Jay 30
Readman, Paul 5, 13
Reculver 50, 79, 81, 172–174
Red Sands Maunsell Forts 25
Rees, Gareth E. 191
  The Stone Tide (novel) 191
Rees-Mogg, Jacob 101
refugees 3–4, 7–8, 14, 55, 57, 75, 94,
  137, 141–142, 146, 148, 151, 154,
  158–159, 165, 203–204,
  206–207
  see also asylum seekers
remembrance 91, 95, 97–100, 103,
  189

Index

Reynolds, Simon 103
Rhyl (Denbighshire) 58
Richard Montgomery (ship) 78, 104
Richardson, Tim 123
Ringwould (Kent) 153
Ripley, Faye 32
Rochdale 154
Rogers, Richard 119
Roman (occupation) 34, 50, 81, 83,
    105–107
Romney Marsh 19–20, 72, 106, 109,
    176–180, 185
Romney, Hythe and Dymchurch
    railway 179
Rother (River) 177
Rotherham 154
Royal Military Canal 19–20, 81,
    139–140
Royal Society for Protection of
    Birds (RSPB) 24–25, 185
ruins 16, 72, 90, 164, 173–174, 189
rurality 10–11
Rye (Sussex) 177
Rye Bay 172

St Mary's Bay (Kent) 178
Samphire Hoe (Kent) 150
Sandgate (Folkestone) 81
Sandwich (Kent) 7, 9, 78, 84, 197
Sangatte 3
    Sangatte Protocol 111
Sassoon, Siegfried 76
Saxon Shore Way 50
Schengen agreement 111
Scogin, John 121
Scovell, Adam 190
sea bathing/swimming 19, 49, 51,
    60, 140, 184, 196
Seabrook (Kent) 81
Seabrook, David 17–18, 73
Seasalter (Kent) 32, 175
seaside resorts 51–52
Sebald, W. G. 27

second homes 33, 38, 206
Self, Will 18
Sellindge (Kent) 8, 114
Selwyn, Tom 172
Sethi, Anita 17
Sevington (Ashford) 129–130
    see also Inland Border Facility
Shakespeare, William 97
shared space 122–124
Shaw, George Bernard 169
Shaw, Kate 189
Shaw, William 178
    The Birdwatcher (novel) 178
    Grave's End (novel) 178
    Salt Lane (novel) 178
Sheerness (Kent) 78, 81, 206
Shepherd Neame 28–29
Sheppey, Isle of 23–26, 78, 172, 175,
    204
    see also Sheerness, Eastchurch
Shoard, Marion 13, 59
Shorncliffe Barracks (Folkestone) 81,
    96–97, 99, 107, 111, 158
Sidaway, James 19
Sinclair, Iain 18
Site of Special Scientific Interest 25,
    93, 110
Situationist Internationale 17
Somerset Maugham, William 31
    Cakes and Ale (novel) 31
sound mirrors 90–91, 185, 190
soundscape 116
Southend (Essex) 52
space of flows 109, 112, 122, 133,
    136, 206
Spellar, John 116
Spencer, Stanley 181
Spitfire (aeroplane) 91–93
Stoke-on-Trent 21
Stone. C. J. 31, 44
Stour (River) 119
Stratford International (station) 113
Streeter, Cathy 119

Suggs (musician) 32
surveillance 17, 81, 145–147, 150, 189
   see also CCTV
Sussex 11, 84, 106, 109, 139, 145,
   172, 182, 184
Swale 25, 35, 204–206
   River Swale 23, 35
   Swale (local authority) 204–206
Swanscombe (Kent) 25
Sweeney, Joe 197
   Leave a Message for Europe (artwork)
   197

Tankerton (Kent) 30
TARDIS (*Doctor Who*) 198
Taylor, Peter 10
temporality 10, 99, 103, 122, 135
Tennyson, Alfred 97
   'Ode on the Death of the Duke
   of Wellington' (poem) 97
Texaco Caribbean (ship) 168
Thames, River 23–24, 28–29, 35,
   46
   Lower Thames Crossing 23–24
   Thames Barges 28–29
   Thames Gateway 117
Thanet (Isle of) 7, 17–18, 43, 50–51,
   54, 59, 62, 73–74, 93, 107, 131,
   174–176, 204–206
   Thanet District Council 54,
   63–65, 206
   see also Broadstairs, Margate,
   Ramsgate
Thatcher, Margaret 108, 141
   Thatcherism 100, 124
Thorndyke, Russell 178
   Dr Syn (novel) 178
Thornes, John 62
Tolia Kelly, Divya 11, 18
Torovnick, Mariana 80
Tour de France 9
tourism 36, 52, 57, 112, 155, 179,
   191

Trafalgar Square 6
Trans European Transport Network
   (TEN-T) 124–127
Transmanche (EU region) 8,
   112
Trower, Shelley 16
Tubbs, Henry 183
Turner, J. M. W. 9, 61–67, 69–70,
   76, 89, 173
   *The Eruption of the Souffrier
   Mountains in the Island of St
   Vincent* (painting) 65
Turner, Luke 17, 192
Turner Contemporary (gallery) 61,
   64–66, 69–70
Tweedy, Dan 78
   The Sheerness Mermaid 78–79

UK Border Agency 109
UKIP (party) 46, 73–74
University of Kent 9, 212–213
Uplees (Kent) 26
urban sprawl 12, 120–121

Valluvan, Sivamohan 91
Vaz, Keith (MP) 73
Vietnamese (refugees) 141–142, 160,
   163, 207
Vortigen 134
Voysey, C. F. A. 169

Wakefield (West Yorkshire) 63
Walker, Duncan 150
walking 18–19, 50, 52, 59, 96, 103,
   107–108, 163, 196
Wallace, Gregg 32
Wallinger, Mark 99, 156
   Folk Stones (artwork) 99
Wallis, Barnes 79
Walmer (Kent) 81, 105, 145, 152
Wantsum Channel 50, 176
Ward, Jon 157
wartime consciousness 80

Index

Watkin, Peter 86
   The War Game (TV programme)
     86
Watling Street 114, 135
Weald 11–12, 118
Weisz, Varga 164–165
   Rug People (artwork) 164–165
Wells, H. G. 169–170
   The Invisible Man (novel) 169
   The Sea Lady (novel) 170
   The War of the Worlds (novel) 169
Wentworth, Richard 165–167
   Racinated (artwork) 165–166
Westwood Cross 59
White, Elizabeth 62
white cliffs (of Dover) 1–2, 5, 13, 20,
   84–85, 87, 103, 124, 158, 175
   White Cliffs Visitor Centre 1
whiteness 6, 11, 17, 47
   White Lives Matter 73–74
Whitstable (Kent) 7, 20, 30–49, 69,
   72, 77, 140, 187, 197, 207

Whitstable Oyster Fishery
   Company 35–37, 42
Williams, Rowan 108
wind farm 32–33, 43, 109, 177
Wooldridge, S. W. 11
Wordsworth, William 77
World War I 5, 26, 81, 94, 96–97,
   99, 158, 164, 181–182, 181, 207
World War II 7, 21, 25, 77–78, 81,
   83, 86, 90, 93, 100–101, 103,
   138, 150, 201
   see also Battle of Britain, Blitz
Wright, Patrick 24, 100, 127, 148,
   213

Zborowski, Louis 179
Zeigler, Melissa 195
Zeta-Jones, Catherine 12
Zhang, Chenchen 111, 144
Žižek, Slavoj 90